Managing Performance Improvement

From TQM to six sigma and the balanced scorecard, there appears to be no end to the "revolutionary" approaches proposed to improve business performance. However, on closer inspection, most new performance improvement approaches offer few differences from their predecessors.

This thought-provoking book provides a critical perspective on the management of performance improvement initiatives by relating major theories to practical examples from a wide range of organizations. Baxter and MacLeod analyze ideas on performance improvement and discuss how these concepts may not make any impact on organizations, using cases as diverse as telecommunications, cement manufacturing, a major airport, and an economic development organization. In their critique of popular performance improvement "innovations," the authors highlight the possible damage to organizations they can cause. In response to prevailing performance improvement practices, the authors put forth the concept of repair as a way to rescue these efforts. Working from their extensive research, the authors present alternative perspectives on improvement that shifts forward the stagnant debates on these processes.

Offering a needed alternative perspective and real insights into the process of implementing performance improvements, this book will prove invaluable to advanced students and MBAs studying quality, performance improvement, operations management and HRM.

Lynne F. Baxter is Senior Lecturer in Management Systems at The York Management School.

Alasdair M. MacLeod is an Honorary Research Fellow at Heriot-Watt University.

Managing Performance Improvement

Lynne F. Baxter and
Alasdair M. MacLeod

Routledge
Taylor & Francis Group

NEW YORK AND LONDON

First published 2008
by Routledge
270 Madison Ave, New York, NY 10016

Simultaneously published in the UK
by Routledge
2 Park Square, Milton Park, Abingdon, Oxon OX14 4RN

Routledge is an imprint of the Taylor & Francis Group, an informa business

© 2008 Lynne F. Baxter and Alasdair M. MacLeod

Typeset in Sabon by
HWA Text and Data Management, Tunbridge Wells
Printed by Edwards Brothers

Library of Congress Cataloging-in-Publication Data
Baxter, Lynne F., 1961–
    Managing performance improvement / by Lynne F. Baxter and Alasdair M.
    MacLeod.
        p.   cm.
        Includes bibliographical references.
    1. Total quality management.   2. Reengineering (Management)
    3. Performance—Management.   4. Organizational effectiveness.
    I. MacLeod, Alasdair M.   II. Title.
    HD62.15.B39 2008
    658.4´013–dc22   2007023656

ISBN10: 0–415–36680–1 (hbk)
ISBN10: 0–415–36681–X (pbk)
ISBN10: 0–203–01943–1 (ebk)

ISBN13: 978–0–415–36680–9 (hbk)
ISBN13: 978–0–415–36681–6 (pbk)
ISBN13: 978–0–203–01943–6 (ebk)

For
Nicola, Mhari and David M. Baxter
and
Pearl MacLeod

Contents

SECTION 3
Repair   **133**

  9 Repair at the level of the organization: the
     contribution of external frameworks   151

10 Conclusions   167

     Discussion question hints   175
     References   181
     Index   190

Illustrations

Acknowledgments

We would like to thank the people in the companies we visited for giving us so much of their time. By far the best part of this work has been the many trips we made to organizations and the helpfulness of many people, especially Harvey MacMillan now retired from Quality Scotland Foundation, who funded us against the judgement of his boss, and the Institute of Management Services who awarded us their R. M. Currie fund money to support our travel.

We are extremely grateful for the patience of our publishers – both of us have had major operations delaying our progress – and although we have worn out one editor (Jacqueline Curthoys) we hope Nancy Hales has not found us too arduous. We would like to thank Emma Joyes and Felisa Salvago-Keyes too for their forbearance.

The support of family, friends and colleagues at Heriot-Watt University and the University of York has been invaluable. Sadly, we have just the memory of Marilyn Stone's warm encouragement, but like the woman herself it is an extremely bright, dynamic memory that has continuing impact.

Earlier versions of Chapters 5, 6 and 9 appeared in the following journals, and we thank the publishers for giving us permission to build upon them here.

Baxter, L.F. and Hirschhauser, C. (2004) Reification and Representation in the Implementation of Quality Improvement Programmes. *International Journal of Operations and Production Management* 24 (2):207–24.

Baxter, L.F., and MacLeod, A.M. (2005) Shifting forms of Masculinity in Changing Organizations: The Role Of Testicularity, *Journal of Organizational Change Management*, 18 (6): 627–41.

MacLeod, A.M. and Baxter, L.F. (2001) The contribution of business excellence models in restoring failed improvement initiatives, *European Management Journal*, 19 (4): 392–403.

1 Introduction

Innovation and rapid change are normal features of organizational life and usually associated with the goal of improving performance. There are many parties interested in developing specific initiatives, models, and sets of ideas designed to assist in realizing objectives: academics, consultants, government agencies, and industry and professional associations to list but a few. It would be pointless to speculate when people became interested in improving performance, but interest has accelerated since the "industrial revolution," and a popular perception is that the speed of development is now at its height. Victorian pioneers of new technology, Taylor, the Gilbreths, Shewhart, the "quality gurus" popularized in the 1950s, the Japanese Manufacturing debate of the 1970s and 1980s, TQM, BPR, "Lean" "Six Sigma," the list is endless, but the intention is the same—improving competitiveness through improving performance. Many of the approaches share similar characteristics and are implemented in similar ways. They all involve close examination of processes, suggest involving the people closest in devising better ways of working, and infer that any improvement is likely not to impact performance if not linked to what the end recipient values, namely what the customer wants. The approach itself is heralded as "new," a flurry of activity ensues while the range of techniques is learned and implemented—and typically fizzles out after about a year.

For their part, in organizations, people put considerable effort into engaging with these initiatives, addressing shortcomings with existing ways of doing things and "second guessing" future needs, especially when this is associated with personal career advancement. The intention is to progress something but, in our experience initiatives, which can be labeled "improvements" with any long-term confidence, are all too rare and any link to a particular model or set of ideas frequently very hazy. "Improvements" can generate additional problems, fail, or even make the situation worse.

The aim of the book is to provide a critical perspective on the management of performance improvement initiatives through relating theory in the area to practical examples from industry. We position our work between existing texts that, we think, adopt a stance that is not constructive for people working in organizations, tending to be either overly positive or unduly negative. Some texts trumpet "innovations" designed to be implemented in organizations to accelerate improvement without stopping to consider any downside to their suggestions; others criticize changes without putting forward any practical ideas as to how jobs are to be maintained and organizations to be developed. Our book presents a critique of these innovations, questioning the so-called theory in itself but also using the knowledge we have gained through different writers and researching organizations to derive alternative angles to shift a stagnant debate forward.

In this introductory chapter, we discuss our reasons for writing the book and continue by pinpointing our specific concerns with the existing literature before outlining our methodology and the rationale behind what we have included and why. We are well aware that there are many texts in the area; when we accessed www.amazon.com in October 2006, we found that there were 23,300 books connected to "performance improvement" when we typed it into the search engine. The number actually increased by four during our session! A look down the findings backs up our impression that they are for the most part highly repetitive: Similar topics crop up; for example, new tools, project management aids, how to manage employees. We are working in a heavily populated area, but we hope we are doing so from a fresh perspective, using ideas that have not been aired in this way before.

The initial impetus for the book stemmed from our unhappiness with the materials others had developed and which we used in our teaching, which encompasses undergraduate, postgraduate, and post-experience courses with classes of students already familiar with introductory operations management. We perceived a need paradoxically for both a more global and a more local perspective! We began to contact and research organizations. We think that our work is of use in specialist modules. Other academics should also find it of interest; from our experience in carrying out the research and presenting our findings to a range of people, we would extend our readership to those who are working in organizations that are also keen to learn about how others have gone about improving their performance and want to build their understanding from the broadest possible base. Perhaps this differs from the many books that focus on one specific tool or on one specific organization.

We hope the book contributes to understanding at a number of levels, which we will now outline and then describe more fully in the rest of the chapter. First, we want to engage with other writers; we have reviewed key literature in the area and believe we have useful points to make on existing work. Our perspective, developed from engaging with several areas of the literature and the cases, produces insights that we believe to be different—for example, we have not come across any work that discusses the damage that improvement can cause. Second, we hope our ideas on improvement shift the debate from what we perceive to be a recursive loop—what we mean by this is that for a long time, "what has to be done" has remained relatively stable, it is the implementation that has not been straightforward; however, most writers have chosen to rehash the list of what has to be done rather than to investigate in any grounded way why the implementation has stalled. Third, we have carried out research in a wide variety of organizations, manufacturing, service, and a public sector example, and the descriptions of our findings should be of general interest, and shed more light than the arid distant survey techniques beloved by some academics.

We are very different people in ourselves, and our discussions have sparked alternative interpretations. Last, we hope the whole package is constructive in a practical way, enabling a wide range of people to consider problems with improvement from a different perspective. The next sections of the chapter explore these points further.

The existing literature

The texts we have read, curiously for what we consider to be such a holistic subject, can be divided into many subcategories, none of which seem to engage fully with one another. There are "guru" prognostications, company war stories, repetitive text books, and a cache of "critical" literature, which carries an assumption that all management attempts to improve performance will undermine the position of the employee.

If we were to describe existing work in the area, we would conclude that most of the "uncritical" texts are based on a modernist perspective, of the kind that has been undermined in other branches of social sciences for more than thirty years. Improvements can be achieved if lists of areas are attended to. There is an assumption of progression of ideas and "causal" relations that can be manipulated. This is seen most strongly in the journal articles wherein the relationships among "variables" are investigated in a survey population (see, for example, Samsom and Terziovski, 1999), but it is also evident in the textbooks (e.g., Evans and Lindsay, 1999 and Beckford, 2000), those putting forward "new" sets of ideas, such as Hammer and Champy (1993) and the reconstructions of activities portrayed in books about individual organizations (Welch, 2003 and Semler, 2003). We have included discussion of these books in ours because we want to engage with the ideas, but our view of organizations is subtly different. We think that it is difficult to base social science ideas on a model of natural science that does not even apply. There has been a vast body of work detailing how scientists do not use scientific method (e.g., it is not the logical exploration of variables but often hunch and "happenstance" that lead to breakthroughs). However, most improvement cycles boil down to the use of scientific method (see, for example, "DMIAC" in Six Sigma). We subscribe to the view that individuals, time and space vary (Giddens, 1976). What occurred for one person in one organization at one point in time might well not apply to the same person the following week; social life is so much more complex than is often portrayed in the improvement literature. We agree with Feigenbaum (1991) in his irritation with the "instant pudding" approach to change.

This means we would rule out making sweeping generalizations. Our conclusions are designed to provide instances to promote understanding and spark further ideas. This type of system has worked very well in the legal profession.

We will now go on to develop our argument that the literature is very similar and recursive: For example, text books follow remarkably consistent formats (i.e., introducing the "gurus" and following up with subcategories that cover the areas of people involvement, process improvement, and implementation processes). "Leadership" is discussed, but the performance improvement writers rarely include organization behavior writers who have carried out extensive research in the area, meaning the discussion concludes with ideas that have in some instances been superseded long ago.

Similar topics are managed in similar ways. For example, the same set of exhortations has been repeated in only slightly different guises for fifty years. Given the stability of these ideas, it is odd that there is also widespread agreement on the high failure rate for performance improvement!

Two authors whom we admire are Juran, the famous guru, and Heller, a UK management commentator. Despite a difference of more than fifty years in their idea development, they seem to cover remarkably similar ground (Table 1.1).

From this table, the reader can pick up on the consistency of the themes. Prepare people, set stretch objectives, divide up the tasks, set up an organization structure to manage the improvement process, think through the wider implications of individual projects, reward effort, and be persistent. Heller (1997) includes a possible "hurdle" of negative past cultures; however, he fails to raise the issue that negative past cultures may well be the result of previous attempts to address his other points! At least he acknowledges that the organization might have a "past"—few authors do, far less admit that individuals' previous experiences with improvement initiatives might affect their approach to the current one.

These ideas remain at the level of recommendations; the specific methods to achieve them are not often developed. If we were being unkind, there seems to be a stream of exhortations that seldom go beyond the rhetorical for the employees trying to improve actual processes in organizations.

Table 1.1 A comparison of established and current ideas on performance improvement

Juran's ten steps (Juran and Gryna, 1988, but 1950s origin)	Heller's Points (1997)
Create awareness of the need and opportunity for quality improvement	Change the process; if necessary tackle the whole system
Set goals for continuous improvement	Focus on business processes: Don't have separate task forces for each function
Build an organization to achieve goals by establishing a quality council, identifying problems, selecting a project, appointing teams, and choosing facilitators	Recognize that successful reform of business processes will trigger radical changes elsewhere in the system
Give everyone training	Involve people, their values and beliefs, rewards and recognition in the process.
Carry out projects to solve problems	Go for big prizes
Report progress	Keep right on to the end of the road
Show recognition	Don't admit constraints on problem definition and on the scope of the study required
Communicate results	Remove existing corporate cultures and management cultures should they be in the way
Keep a record of successes	
Incorporate annual improvements into the company's regular systems and processes and thereby maintain momentum	

Given that one of our objectives is to teach people who do or intend to manage organizations, this is far from helpful.

Underlying the approach we have adopted for our text has been the strong conviction that introducing a fresh perspective into how the basic issues associated with improving performance in the organization were reviewed was opportune.

Methodological considerations

Alasdair spent the major part of his industrial career in the ICI group deeply involved in studying how operations might be conducted more effectively—he managed other people and utilized work study in implementing the improved methods that emerged from his work and that of his colleagues. As we discuss in chapter 4, work study may be regarded now as being somewhat past its "sell by" date; but its ethos—the analytical, questioning approach that lies at its heart—is as relevant now as it ever was. Alasdair has carried this over into his academic work. Lynne's career is the converse of this: predominantly academic with periods of consultancy. She worked with colleagues in improving supply-chain management in a wide variety of organizations but decided that she enjoyed researching more and has been involved in a series of research projects using her skills in qualitative methods to generate practical findings and theoretical insights. Both of us have been trained in the past as assessors for the European Foundation for Quality Management (EFQM) excellence model.

The book is an outcome of a research process that has lasted just past a decade. As we indicated earlier in this chapter, we were keen to seek out and present cases to illustrate how organizations on this side of the water have gone about improving their performance to help to illustrate our points while teaching. With this aim in mind, we approached a daughter organization of the EFQM, Quality Scotland Foundation (QSF), who gave us a list of possible contacts that we added to our own. We were told later that we were extremely lucky to obtain a small grant from QSF to cover our travel expenses in exchange for some short cases for the organization to use in its introductory literature on the EFQM model for members.

The first phase of the research involved visits to a wide range of local organizations. We asked each contact if they had a significant "improvement project" that we could learn about by visiting their company and interviewing those involved. It was made clear that the cost to the organization would be limited to the time their people spent with us describing the project. We visited more than a dozen companies and interviewed people whom our contact person thought relevant, usually the contact person, supplemented with one or two colleagues.

It became clear that despite considerable effort being put in at a general level, few of the organizations had any initiatives for us to study in depth. At that time, it was suggested by a publisher visiting the university that we travel further to include mainland European organizations, and we contacted the EFQM in Brussels, where a facilitator kindly forwarded a list of contacts. We also obtained a further small grant from the UK Institute of Management Services. The response was again mixed, with this time, most of the organizations not following up on our enquiries. We are eternally grateful for the warm reception we received from the organizations kind enough to take part in our more in-depth studies, and our period of more intensive research took place between 1998 and 2004.

In total, we studied eight organizations in greater depth, visiting them and interviewing a wide range of stakeholders, in some instances several times. We found it insightful to see how our contacts formed our list of people to interview—we asked them to include a broad range of people who had been involved. The numbers we spoke to varied from organization to organization, ranging from about fourteen in one to six in another. We usually talked to the managers steering the initiative and those managers involved in the associated changes. In the majority of organizations, we interviewed "front-line" employees. It was intriguing to us when the managers who chose our interviewees did not include such employees. Both of us interviewed together, one taking notes while the other attended to asking the questions. We saw around each facility, although it has to be admitted this was not very extensive in office-type organizations. We had a discussion after interviews and adjusted our questioning accordingly. In many instances, we were given documents and other materials to help our understanding of the initiatives.

We wrote up our interviews and constructed draft case studies that were submitted to the company for review, amendment as necessary, and comment. Each company would have right of veto over the content of their particular case. In practice, we found that the process of securing approval to undertake the studies took much longer than we had expected, although a benefit of this was sometimes further visits and interviews to obtain more information. The companies whose cases we document cover a wide spectrum of activities—from airline ground services to cement manufacture—and include telecommunications equipment manufacture, health diagnostics, and agro-chemicals. From their association with EFQM, we might have presumed that their approach to improvement might be expected to have been guided by its model. However, we found that even though they had all recently gone through a major process of change with the expectation that their performance would improve significantly as a consequence, the evidence from our studies suggests that this was not always the case.

The foregoing applies to all but one chapter, which features a discussion of the work of Constanze Hirshhauser, Lynne's PhD student. Constanze, because she was a full-time student, was able to spend much more time in her chosen organization (six weeks of participant observation at each site) and she thus interviewed a very wide range of people.

We construct the book in the way we have constructed each chapter. We want to demonstrate that we are familiar with the conventional thinking in the area; we have some points to make on it, and our concern is practical, so we then describe our findings from organizations—often at variance with the existing texts—before trying to reconcile the two. This is very explicit because our final section is about repair. It is important to engage with existing texts with which our readers are familiar before making our points and suggesting alternatives. The final part of this chapter explains the contents of each succeeding chapter and introduces the organizations that we studied.

Section 1: The management role in performance improvement

The first section explores familiar topics in the area. Samsom and Terziovski (1999) note that the "soft" aspects of management have the greatest effect on performance improvement and ask for more work on how these can be changed. We hope that our chapters make such a contribution. We discuss leadership and strategy in separate chapters. Performance measurement is not considered a soft topic; however, how systems are designed includes soft aspects, something we view as key to their success or failure.

The nature or quality of leadership has been a feature suggested by Deming and Juran in the 1950s as a way of differentiating their initiatives from simple assurance and process control. The term recurs in excellence models and is intended to signal to senior managers that they should be active in the process: Improvement is not solely about getting other people to change their behavior; it is also about joining in and generating enthusiasm. Our chapter discusses some of the theories in the area, and we highlight some of the practical issues with two different examples wherein the improvements were in one case capable of being sustained when the leader who gave the process impetus left and the other wherein they were not; the improvements fizzled out when the leader left the business unit. The leaders themselves shared many characteristics, although the organizations in which they worked were in very different industrial sectors—one senior manager was the head of an aircraft engine maintenance and repair facility, owned by a global organization; the other was a site manager of a cement plant, Blue Circle, also owned by a global organization. The initiatives they instigated differed markedly and so did the outcomes. The aircraft company achieved a measure of success that was restricted by their management's ambition; the cement site achieved success that reached beyond the limits of their own ideas. We conclude with some points that we hope are of use; paradoxically, good leaders are one of the team!

A similar message emerges from our discussion of strategy. Again, this is a highly familiar concept in improvement, without much agreement on what precisely it stands for! Many writers are wary of isolated attempts to improve aspects of organizations, fearing that they might trigger problems elsewhere. Consideration of strategy is intended to encourage a holistic approach, with priority setting in a long-term, wider context seen as useful. Implementing strategies is seen as a major difficulty, and our two cases show completely different organizations sharing a sharpness of process at the planning and direction stage carrying forward to implementation. The management skills they had at one level applied equally well to the enactment, something that perhaps Juran (Juran and Gryna, 1988) might think odd! Our cases are drawn from an electronics multinational,

Nortel, and a local government economic development organization, Govan Initiative. A key feature in their success in meeting their strategic objectives and improving their organizations in a clear, material way was the range of stakeholders they included in the development of strategy, which promoted innovation and accountability.

The last chapter in this section explores performance measurement, which can often be highly contentious at a personal level. We want to make the point that daily moments of contention are systematized in grander "systems" wherein financial and nonfinancial criteria are open to debate. Our cases for this chapter are drawn from two similar organizations, one that was making agro-chemical products and merged with a pharmaceutical organization to become Astra-Zeneca, whereas the other, Akzo Nobel, makes pharmaceutical and chemical products. The managers at both companies decided to devise their own systems: In one case, there was no corporate support; in the other, the site was embracing a highly comprehensive corporate system and tailoring it for their needs. One might think that the simpler, restricted system would be more long lasting; however, our cases show the value of having a detailed, multilayered system in conveying to every employee the seriousness of the approach and the possibility they have to contribute to it.

Section 2: Improvement as damage

The second section of the book considers negative or damaging impacts brought about as a consequence of performance improvement initiatives that have not gone according to plan. We use a variety of "critical" perspectives to discuss more cases, again with the intention of being constructive.

Chapter 5 is the only one we did not create together; it is a revised version of a paper Lynne wrote with Constanze (Baxter and Hirschhauser, 2004). Constanze carried out her fieldwork and coined the term *pink factory* to describe the façade that organizations can construct to convey the impression of being engaged in improvements, rather than actually making a material difference. We discuss this concept in relation to Lave and Wenger's "community of practice" ideas (Lave and Wenger 1991, Wenger 1998). The complex construction that is the impression of improvement draws in customers, consultants, managers, and even academics. Appearing to know the latest trend in improvement is often more important than having participated in actually making changes. As we mentioned, the case in this chapter concerns two sites of an automotive company, a sector that features extensively in "best practice" tomes. The excess capacity in the sector is well known; however, the various companies continue to churn out the cars and the like, but this chapter demonstrates an organization less skilled at actual improvements than it might appear to be at first glance.

The next chapter continues the discussion of superficiality with a case of a major airport. The airport had to cope with a self-generated excess of customers, as it had a strategy of being a "hub." It chose to restructure its operations using business process reengineering (BPR), with a "big bang" approach. The approach was rejected by the staff, and a modified alternative was introduced much more slowly. It brought to mind the analogy of diet and fitness, and we draw the analogy between BPR and cosmetic surgery, especially liposuction, contrasting this with the more incremental approach of continuous improvement. BPR was appealing as a quick fix; however, it did not really address the underlying problem. We hope the use of the metaphor encourages people to think about the long-term implications of initiatives and the role of consultants in creating visions of what might be, which prove impossible to realize with the material at hand.

The last chapter in this section explores the day-to-day dynamic of improvement from a gender perspective. We are convinced nobody has looked at the issue from this angle; we do so because a key area of improvement is employee involvement. The "employee" is ill defined in performance improvement and usually thought of as "male." In our cases, we found that several women progressed up the organization thanks to their participation in improvement initiatives showcasing their skills. We also found that some men lost out in the process but were used as "totems" of the old regime. We argue that there is a shift in the acceptable form of masculinity associated with successful improvement initiatives in our two cases, a move from autocratic to more facilitative, encouraging male leaders. There is not a "feminizing" of the workforce. Managers hoping to improve processes and engage employees in the process may well need to have a more subtle conception of the employee as an individual.

Section 3: Repair

The last part of the book explores performance improvement using a word that is not normally associated with the area: repair. We would argue that unintended or not, improvement activities can lead to damage that in turn may require repair.

Almost every book we have read in the area adopts a forward-looking, modernist perspective on improvement. A set of ideas is presented, not in relation to deficiencies in previous attempts but rather as *ab initio* methods to deliver objectives. There is a consumerist culture with management ideas. Initiatives are adopted, used for a while, and dispensed with in shorter and shorter cycle times. This ignores in the organization elements of continuity that existed before any initiative and will continue afterward. As the manager at the airport we studied argues, change can cause "scar" tissue, and maybe there is a case for extending the body metaphor to suggest that repeated interventions to improve something can indeed weaken it further. We are not new in pointing out either the layering or the damage caused by the bombardment of initiatives, but our contribution is to suggest that it might be worthwhile considering the concept of repair and how repair as a process might have a useful role in achieving the desired objectives ultimately. Just as maintenance and repair operations are often the Cinderella of organizations, almost never being considered key business processes, we think the processes of organization improvement involve an element of repair and consider the facets of this in the next two chapters, where we make our case at two levels. The first explores some of the individuals we met and interviewed and how their relationship with their work was in a sense repaired; the second looks at the role frameworks have in repairing and restoring faith in improvement activities.

We especially wanted to finish on a constructive note and would argue that, rather than managers losing face from admitting that they might have been wrong in the past, they effect some kind of apology. Making "reparations" or repairs can create a better platform for fresh initiatives. Employees are not without memory and are more resentful of supposedly innovative practices being trailed as having all-encompassing powers!

We finish the book with a short chapter collecting together our main conclusions, drawing out our own "truisms" as a complement to the table we constructed for this chapter. The book is not intended to be a stiff academic tome—but by the same token is not intended either to lack academic rigor! We firmly believe that it will indicate how theory and practice inform each other—as the cases should make clear.

Section 1

The management role in performance improvement

This first section explores conventional topics in the area: leadership, strategy, and performance improvement. These topics are concerned with the managers' role in the improvement process, which many authors have thought of as key. When we were teaching classes to postgraduate students studying part-time, we were struck by the stories they told us of initiatives that fizzled out because they were tied to an individual's career or heralded with great fanfares and then under-resourced when the strategic priority of the organization changed. We have lost count of the number of instances in which we have heard of performance measurement schemes that hamper improvement through being redundant, having low "torque" with the main processes that need to be improved, or driving activities that are actually counterproductive to improvement.

Our opening substantive chapters examine topics concerned with purpose. Leadership as a topic is an antidote to the issue of "senior management commitment," which turns up as a suggested main cause of initiative failure on a regular basis. We discuss many theories on the topic, none of which fully captures our sense of who the managers we could call "leaders" were. Some theorists even think the topic is a silly one. However, when we analyzed our cases, it was absent in the unsuccessful initiatives and clear in the successful. Someone took responsibility, and people seemed to want to be "led." A key differentiator was whether the "leader" created a lasting effect. As our research involved more than one contact with each of our organizations, in some cases over many years of knowing them and whether for casual updates, unrelated seminars, or at formal interviews, we were able to see that in some instances an initiative fizzled out after a person was promoted out of a position. In a few cases, this did not happen, because the leadership activities still took place and "leadership" was vested in the organization, not in an individual. The leaders in our cases themselves shared many characteristics, though the organizations in which they worked were in very different industrial sectors: one in a globally owned aircraft engine maintenance and repair facility, another a site manager of a cement quarry and processing plant,

Blue Circle, now also owned by a global organization. The initiatives they instigated differed markedly—as did the outcomes—with the cement factory continuing and developing the ideas and the aircraft factory stalling in its pursuit of reduced cycle times. The initiative stopped because of a rational decision, but we doubt whether this would have happened if its founder had not left.

Strategy is even more obviously linked to planning and purpose. Please forgive Lynne for this one point: that strategy does seem a predominantly masculine interest in the literature, if not in organizations. It is a highly familiar concept in improvement, in that it is included in many models, and theorists argue it is essential, but there is not much agreement on what precisely it is about! Writers fear that isolated improvements might well lead to problems elsewhere; however, many strategic plans might frame in the first year initiatives that might then be ditched in the second. Organizations we perceive to be successful stick with a plan longer, having based it on better information, and check their progress on it regularly. Our two cases, the economic development company, "Govan Initiative," and the Northern Irish unit of Nortel, though both very different, showed that the management skills they had at one level applied equally well to the development and implementation of their strategies. A key feature of their improvement processes was the clear, material way of involving the range of stakeholders in the development of strategy, which promoted innovation and accountability. Some might view this as time consuming and irrelevant, but we think it yielded huge dividends to both organizations.

The last chapter in this section explores performance measurement, again viewed as essential but by no means straightforward to implement. Systems have a long history; people have been wrestling with how to do this for a long time. Many so-called new approaches have great similarities with earlier systems, though often this is not acknowledged! Creating a shorthand for measuring performance when most people would have a different view of what is involved is problematic. Aggregate systems are built on daily moments of contention, where financial and nonfinancial criteria are open to debate—although they are very much in vogue today. Deming argues powerfully that they might be a distraction. Our cases for this chapter are drawn from two similar organizations: one that was making agro-chemical products and merged with a pharmaceutical organization to become Astra-Zeneca, the other, Akzo Nobel, making pharmaceutical and chemical products. The managers built their own systems; in one case, there was no outside support; on the other site, a support unit of the business had resources that the subunit could tailor to meet its needs. One might think that the simpler, restricted system would be more long-lasting; however, our cases show how the complexity helped to convey the seriousness of the approach and opened up multiple opportunities for people to contribute to it.

2   Leadership

Summary introduction

This chapter discusses:

- The concept of leadership
- Who can be a leader
- How leaders emerge
- A case of leadership that had no lasting impact on improvement
- A case of leadership that had continuing effect on improvement
- The damaging effects of leadership
- The relationship between leadership and improvement.

Introduction

Our research backs such authors as Rahman and Bullock (2005) and Soltani, van der Meer, and Williams (2005), who argue that the so-called soft aspects of management have a greater impact on whether an improvement activity realizes its objectives. Our specific contribution lies in adding detail to how this can or cannot be achieved. Leadership is valued in performance improvement as it is seen as the answer to the problem of lack of management commitment, which has for a long time been highlighted as the reason why most forms of organization activity fail, especially performance improvement.

In this chapter, we investigate some of the extensive literature on leadership and relate this to two of our case organizations. The literature is broadly concerned with questions of identifying modes of leadership and whether leadership can be learned or is inborn. Some authors, such as Alvesson and Sveningsson (2003), argue that leadership should not be subject to so much attention, a view perhaps shared by many of the "led." Many of the writers we have consulted have given the impression that there is either leadership or no leadership, and its absence creates problems for improvement activities. We then move on to describe and analyze two cases from our research. Both the leaders we discuss exemplify aspects of good leadership; however, the first leader failed to encourage others to take on these aspects, and his initiative ground to a halt after he left the organization. In the second case, the person's approach was infectious, and sustained change was achieved, despite his leaving. We analyze how this occurred. A different perspective from the normal is conveyed by Lipman-Blumen (2005), who points out that some leaders enact the leadership role with "toxic" effect. We discuss this argument and draw a link from her "relational" theory of leadership to Max Weber's discussion of political leaders and "charisma."

What is leadership?

Leadership is a much misunderstood term; it is not a synonym for management. Stogdill (1950, p. 3) defined leadership as "the process of influencing the activities of an organized group in its efforts toward goal setting and goal achievement." However, Field Marshal Slim of Burma, speaking to the Australian Institute of Management, may have got even closer to the heart of the matter when he stated that "Leadership is of the spirit, compounded of personality and vision. Its practice is an art. Management is of the mind, more a matter of accurate calculation, of statistics, of methods, timetables and routines. Its practice is a science. Managers are necessary—leaders are essential!" (Adair, 1990, p. 61)

Drawing a distinction between leadership and management is a common theme in the literature; differences lie in where the boundary is drawn. There is disagreement as to whether leadership is one and the same thing as management, a completely different skill, or whether management is a subset of leadership, as the authors we discuss below reveal; indeed, there is even the view held that leadership is a subset of management!

Drucker contended that the role of the manager is to provide leadership: "The manager is the dynamic, life-giving element in every business.... In a competitive economy, above all the quality and performance of the managers determine the success of a business, and indeed they determine its survival. For the quality and performance of its managers is the only effective advantage an enterprise in a competitive economy can have" (1955, p. 13).

Kotter (1990) used his text, *Leadership Differs from Management*, to distinguish one from the other. He differentiated between the managerial, organizational, and control roles and the dynamic, future-thinking, creative, and connective roles of the leader. A slightly different emphasis has been given by Christenson (1987), who attributes some of the tasks Kotter (1990) would ascribe to management to a specific form of leadership. They argue that there are three prime roles of the CEO as organization leader, personal leader, and chief architect of organizational purpose. These are:

- As *organizational leader* the key responsibility is to achieve the outcomes based on previously prepared plans—the critical taskmaster role. The second principal function is to maintain and develop the organized capability that makes achievement possible. The third is to integrate the necessary specialist functions-marketing, research and development, finance, manufacturing, HRM, logistics, etc., that enable the organization to work.
- As *personal leader* the prime function is to communicate both purpose and policy. Personal energy, style, character and integrity will determine the extent to which the leader becomes the focal point for the respect or admiration of subordinates.
- As *chief architect of organizational purpose* the leader's most testing role is as 'custodian of corporate objectives'- the functions involve include establishing goal-setting and resource allocation processes, choosing between strategic alternatives as well as elucidating and defending these goals. A vital skill is identifying alternative strategies in the first place, which can arise from many sources, inside and outside the organization (Christenson, 1987). Perhaps the unique talent required is "the intellectual capacity to conceptualise corporate purpose and the dramatic skill to invest it with some degree of magnetism."

Farkas and de Backer (1995), following a two-year-long series of interviews with 161 executives worldwide, identified five distinct styles or approaches that their interviewees had adopted. The two researchers then amplified and personified these styles; however, their contention that these cover the whole gamut of the topic may be too sweeping a generalization!

The first of these is the "strategic" approach epitomized in a "futures" person whose prime interest lies in establishing where the organization needs to go and how it should get there. The second is the "human assets" approach embodied in a "people" person who believes and acts on the principle that from effective management of human resources flows success. Number three is a style based on expertise expressed by the individual who develops and applies the most up-to-date technology as the key route for the organization to take to succeed. The "box" approach (number four) is best reflected by the "organization" person who sets up rules, systems, boundaries, and values and is primarily concerned with ensuring that the system and rules initiated will yield the most effective control. Finally, there is the "change promoter" exemplified by the individual who embraces change and who chooses enterprise and originality rather than formal control mechanisms as the way forward.

In summary, leadership is seen as a creative, future-oriented force for change requiring attention to resourcing to back up any goal attainment activities and the coordination and chemistry of the workforce.

The next section delves more deeply into the performance of leadership within organizations. We begin by examining the work that tries to identify specific characteristics of people perceived to be good leaders. For example, as long ago as 1914, Weber discussed the role of charisma in leadership, a rare attribute we might safely assert (Runciman, 1978). Management educators have tried to move the debate away from innate attributes to consider the context and relationships in which leaders have to carry out their jobs. However, first we describe the long list of desirable attributes once thought essential for a leader to possess and deploy.

Who can be a leader?

Early work in the area focused on researching common elements of leaders with the implication that people had if possible to acquire these characteristics if they were to become leaders. For example, Stogdill (1948, pp 35–71) compiled a list of the traits believed to be most relevant from a literature review. This encompassed a strong drive for responsibility; focus on completing the task; vigor and persistence in pursuit of goals; venturesomeness and originality in problem solving; drive to exercise initiative in social settings; self-confidence; sense of personal identity; willingness to accept consequences of decisions and actions; readiness to absorb interpersonal stress; willingness to tolerate frustration and delay; ability to influence the behavior of others; and capacity to structure social systems to the purpose in hand.

Though this list is long, trait theory has been criticized because possessing or trying to acquire certain characteristics can only ever be part of leadership. For example Peter Drucker (1990, p. 14) is adamant that "there are no such things as 'leadership traits' or 'leadership characteristics.'" He goes on to argue that leadership skills can be learned by most people, albeit conceding that there are some who find that they would rather be followers than leaders, as they genuinely find that they cannot learn the necessary skills.

Contingency approaches

Most writers have acknowledged that irrespective of personal characteristics, the context and task at hand might affect appropriate leader behavior. Tannenbaum and Schmidt (1973) suggested representing these as a continuum that had at the one end a "boss"-centered, or autocratic, leader extending at the other end to a subordinate-centered, or democratic, individual. They believed this was the best way to reflect the range of styles from which a leader might select those judged most appropriate to the people and the culture of the organization. Perhaps the best illustration of the autocratic leader is the "command and control" approach characteristic of the armed services. At the other end of the spectrum might be found the research institute where scientists are encouraged to exercise a considerable degree of autonomy in furthering their work.

Oppenheimer's leadership of the development of the atomic bomb in the later stages of World War II, known as the Manhattan project, is an interesting contradiction of such a continuum. His leadership was seen as decisive and perhaps autocratic but, at the same time, he did not limit the perceived autonomy of each of the illustrious scientists working on the project. One of them, Teller, who had an acrimonious split with Oppenheimer, later made it clear that the "amazing success grew out of the brilliance, enthusiasm and charisma with which Oppenheimer led" (Bennis and Biederman, 1997, p. 187).

Hersey and Blanchard's contingency-based Situational Leadership Theory (1993) is a further attempt to develop a relational theory of leadership. The leadership role changes with the increasing ability of the employees to perform their work independently as they become more experienced. "High task" behavior and "low relationship" is presented as the approach that may initially be required, moving through high task and "high relationship," then high relationship and "low task" until finally some kind of nirvana is reached where low task behavior and a low relationship (i.e., minimal intervention from the leader) is all that is needed. Though the terms that the two researchers use to explain their theory might have been more felicitously chosen, the key message that should be drawn is best demonstrated by the approach to training that the Honda plant in Ohio took in 1993. The company at that time took advantage of a downturn in production to increase the amount of technical training substantially. The way in which this was done enabled Honda to increase markedly the ability of their employees to function without constant direction from the formal leader to the long term benefit of the company (Mair, 1998).

Barbara Cassani is one of the few female leaders whose attributes we have found discussed. Her case is interesting in that she demonstrated many of the attributes of leadership when she initiated and "grew" the budget airline "Go," which was the British Airways venture into the cut-price air travel market. The British Airways board gave her £25 million to start up the organization. It was finally sold to Easyjet for £374 million five years later (Wolff Olins, 2007), and she left the company. Her leadership was key in growing the business and creating a different product offering to the market; she was very publicly tied to the organization and the image it portrayed: "My job is to transfer vision. I can feel, taste, and smell what this service is going to be like. A fresh smell, something new and clean and fresh" (Park and Cassani, 1997, p. 27). She was instrumental in creating what amounted to a fashion retail appearance and process for air travel, in contrast to the militaristic esthetics of other providers.

The reason we quote Cassani in this section is that she did not remain with the organization after it was taken over and, after a short break, was made the leader of the London 2012 Olympic bid. It was widely reported that she did not fit as the leader of this initiative and that when Lord Sebastian Coe took over, momentum was much greater. This may or may not be the case, as it has also been reported that the successful outcome of the bid was in fact put down to an error in the voting process!

Kiefer's advocacy of executive team leadership (1994) further extends the relational aspect to leadership. His suggestion was to include the senior management in the leadership role, as they probably had valuable experience and skills. The members of the senior team would share responsibilities but have clear accountabilities. Moreover, the team would initiate and develop strategy. Decision taking would be by consensus, whereas the roles normally undertaken by the chief operating officer would also become a collective responsibility. These ideas are appropriate when considering day-to-day activities; however, one of the key leadership roles has been about effecting change, and more recent theories have particularly addressed this point.

The concepts of "transactional" and "transforming" leadership

Leadership can be exercised in a seemingly infinite number of ways. Peters and Waterman, in their much criticized text, *In Search of Excellence* (1982), suggest that it can be patient coalition building. The development of like-minded groupings in the organization is seen as necessary to inject the necessary stimuli for change; thus, the manipulation of meetings so that agendas can be changed so that issues that have been on the "back burner" are brought forward and are given the necessary prioritization.

Burns (1978) terms "transactional leadership" the necessary activities of the leader that take up most of the day, such as listening carefully, stimulating and encouraging people, and carrying out actions and delivering words: "a hundred things done a little better," as Henry Kissinger once put it.

The foregoing seems to imply some exchange of value to get things done, a position arrived at through some sort of bargaining process—not unlike the "mafia" way of generating reciprocal obligation if one were to be skeptical about it!

In addition, Burns also put forward the view that "transforming leadership," though it is less frequently encountered, is a much more profound concept. This is concerned with effecting material change, making one's mark, managing performance improvement! Burns defined transforming leadership as occurring when one or more persons engage with others in such a way that leaders and followers raise one another to higher levels of motivation and morality. Transforming leadership is dynamic leadership in the sense that the leaders throw themselves into a relationship with followers who will feel" elevated" by it and often become more active themselves, thereby creating new cadres of leaders.

Micklethwait and Wooldridge (1996) present a way of linking some of the debates on leadership. They agree that vision is critical, as was noted earlier. They suggest that, to secure organizational change, the adoption of a particular set of ideas or values is important. An example of this point of view might be Richard Branson of Virgin who seems to epitomize a set of values that characterize his company. Second, they assert that the gulf between transactional and transformational leadership has widened. (Their view of transactional is again quite cynical; it implies dealing with followers on a "tit-for-tat" basis: You support me and I will find you a job!) However, their transformational leader is one who has identified some profound need, unrecognized by the follower until that moment, and has taken steps to meet it. Their third observation on today's business leadership is that being a maverick has distinct advantages! Ricardo Semler entitled his first book this way (1995). With Semler, there does not appear to be a gulf between transactional and transformational leadership. In the same vein, the maverick Ricardo Semler's Brazilian company, Semco, has become famous by standing the accepted corporate rule book on its head. Semler's book, *The Seven Day Weekend* (2003), describes what by normal standards appears to be a recipe for disaster. Semco has no written set of policies, no human resources department and, now, not even a headquarters! The organization does not even plan which businesses to enter. Its current portfolio is an odd mixture of machinery, property, professional services, and high-tech spin-offs. Nevertheless, it turns more than $160 million, up from $4 million two decades ago. The underlying message of the book is, paradoxically, the rigor of the system. It is claimed that this is what happens when an organization puts into practice "trust" and "delegation." Semler (2003, p. 175) argues that the reason he does not have to perform as a textbook leader is that "people bring their talents and we rely on their self-interest to use the company to develop themselves in any way they see fit. In return they must have the self-discipline to perform." Over the years, the nature of the business has changed, and Semler has continued to be a maverick (e.g., going on a sabbatical to gain fresh ideas to contribute to the mix). Through his approach to transactions with other employees, he has managed to effect a huge transformation, and he embodies the authentic leader discussed below, because although in politics the ethics and motives of a leader have long been scrutinized, it is a little-discussed topic in management, and such recent events as the collapse of Enron might direct us to consider whether leaders always have the best of intentions.

In a paper entitled "The ethics of authentic transformational leadership," Price (2003) has developed the transformational concept further, identifying four distinct leadership types (see Figure 2.1).

Price (2003) raises the important point that leaders do not always effect the changes they plan, and he puts forward a reason as being the relationship between their individual values and their behavior. Authentic transformational leadership is about successful achievement of performance improvement in an ethical way. Incontinent pseudo-transformational leadership is characterized by good intentions that the person cannot live up to personally. Base pseudo-transformational leadership is typified by the adoption of wrong values throughout the organization; the selfish pursuit of antisocial goals is the end result (Enron). Opportunistic pseudo-transformational leadership is distinguished by shifting behavior dependent on when what is right conflicts with selfish interests.

In our experience, employees are extremely perceptive in sniffing out incongruent behavior and also whether a leader is egotistical. For example, one of the organizations we visited appeared to have a leader who seemed authentic. At least when we interviewed senior management, they told us of practices that seemed authentic, both congruent and altruistic. However, when some other managers attended a course we conducted, they separately recounted to their syndicate groups that the leader of their organization did hold regular meetings with a wide variety of staff but did not actually remember any of them and had his staff allocate seating

		Behavior	
		Congruent	Incongruent
Values	Altruistic	Authentic transformational leadership (1)	Incontinent pseudo transformational leadership (2)
	Egoistic	Base pseudo transformational leadership (3)	Opportunistic pseudo transformational leadership (4)

Figure 2.1 Authentic and pseudo-transformational leadership   (Source: Price, 2003, p. 71)

around the table so that he could appear to remember employee's names. The employees had fun sitting in different seats and playing along with the boss, who then failed to match the details to the individuals. There was nothing authentic about these meetings!

Critical views of leadership

Mahen Tampoe (1998) considers leadership from another angle, namely those who are at the receiving end. This innovative study found that leaders who are able to liberate the latent leadership qualities in others defend their followers from attack; furthermore, they develop, through a careful teaching and support process, both self-esteem and an ability in protégés to learn.

They manage by employing a blend of direction, delegation, and well-tuned listening skills; they enable their followers to become more valuable people by making certain that their output, taken in its widest context, is really worthwhile. Critically, good leaders are supposed to have "antennae" so tuned that they can develop the most appropriate solution to fit both people and circumstance.

The behavioral characteristics associated with this and with which people can readily associate are enthusiasm, support for individual effort, and personal integrity. Intimidation and "my way or the highway" are seen by the "consumers" as seriously negative. This research highlights that leadership has to have diffuse impact, not a simple matter at all. Leaders need to impact the organization as a whole, the suppliers and customers, too.

Some researchers perhaps become somewhat overly introspective in researching leadership, even questioning whether it really exists! In this vein, Alvesson and Sveningsson from Lund University report their experiences when studying the topic in a research and development company (2003). They point out that claims about leadership values and styles become somewhat diffused when managers in this rather specialized environment are asked how they understand and practice their role as leaders. These researchers were sufficiently doubtful about leadership as a "construct" to raise seriously the possibility of its nonexistence! "Leadership from within is more valuable than leadership from above?"

Though personal qualities in a leader are of key importance, Pedler and Aspinwall (2004) suggest that a better way of considering leadership is as a response to challenge, a performance art, devolved to every person within the organization, so that they can act on what they see. This is yet another reason why devolution of leadership and continuous improvement in performance are seen as being closely linked.

The unique nature of most organizations makes it rather unlikely that there will be a specific leadership model that can be taken down from the shelf and applied in any given set of circumstances. However, there are pointers that can be valuable in helping to assess whether the leadership system an organization has adopted is likely to be appropriate and will enable it to achieve the objectives to which it aspires. For example, a good summary is provided by the European Foundation for Quality Management (EFQM), which has developed a model for business excellence that includes a self-assessment process for reviewing an organization's activities and results referenced against a model of business excellence (http://www. efqm.org/). This procedure enables the organization to determine its strengths and areas in which improvements can be made. The leadership subcriteria set by the EFQM include developing the corporate vision, demonstrating personal commitment, supporting improvement activities, engaging with external stakeholders, and motivating and recognizing employee efforts. In the United States, a parallel approach is represented by the Baldrige Award, widely portrayed (http://www.nist.gov/) there as the standard for performance and business excellence. Again, leadership is a key criterion in the assessment process—how it is exercised, formally and informally, throughout the organization—the basis for, and the way in which, key decisions are made, communicated, and carried out. The award criteria specify that "[S]enior leaders set directions and build and sustain a leadership system conducive to high performance, individual development, initiative, organizational learning and innovation" (NIST, 2005, p. 1). The approach again emphasizes that an effective leadership system creates clear values respecting the capabilities and requirements of employees and other stakeholders. To be effective, a critical feature in such a system includes mechanisms for the leaders' self-examination, receipt of feedback, and improvement.

The two cases that follow describe organizations that have won regional competitions based on the EFQM model. One organization behaved as if the winning of the prize were the climax of its effort in the area; the other thought merely that it signaled the beginning of the process of organizational change. The leader of the first organization left, and the effort petered out, whereas this was not what happened in the second case. Clearly, for real performance improvement, leaders have to create momentum that lasts.

Airco

The first case concerns a senior manager in an aerospace service company, whom we will call Martin Simpson. The company is subject to this sector's fluctuations in demand and in addition has had four owners in the ten years, during which we have been familiar with it. Martin, like almost every other senior manager of the business units we visited, was sensitive to the quite precarious position of the operation vis-à-vis global competition and tried to protect it from closure by adopting a proactive approach to quality improvement. The organization invested considerable resources in setting this procedure in motion.

The company employs some 900 people on the overhaul of jet engines. This operation, which may cost as much as £1.2 million or as little as £0.2 million, is carried out on a four-shift basis 361 days in the year. Some three years before we studied the company, Martin, then production director, championed the introduction of a total quality (TQ) initiative that he termed Air Care. The TQ initiative began with a four-month diagnostic study carried out along with consultants, aimed at building a profile of the company's culture. Air Care focused on delivery of jet engine overhaul based on partnerships with customers, employees, and suppliers using as a framework the identification and measurement of the cost of quality.

Martin realized that he would need to secure commitment from his senior people. He felt he signaled this in a small way by using economy class when traveling long-distance by air. The initiative demanded consistency and constancy of purpose, which led in turn to the need for dynamic leadership that had been insufficiently demonstrated up until then. Commitment on the necessity for change had to be secured from senior staff; without this, it would have been pointless to proceed. Continuous "people involvement" inevitably meant that learning, and thus training, had to be ongoing. Training, especially in developing understanding of total quality management (TQM), was deemed to be crucial if the company was to develop a consistent TQ culture. Accordingly, a cascade training process was initiated, and some of the facilitators were drawn from the shop floor to help gain a wider "buy-in."

Though the initial phase of Air Care saw 90 percent of managers developing problem-solving teams, most employees felt uninvolved. By halfway through the following year, however, some successes had been reported. Some straightforward projects had been completed and their favorable outcome publicized. However, management's review at this stage judged Air Care only moderately successful. Expectations generated during training had not been fulfilled; some cross-functional applications from which much had been looked for had failed because inadequate support, financial and otherwise, had been given. As a consequence, Martin decided to retrain everyone in TQM—some 800 people in twenty-one days!

The outcome of this latest initiative was a decision to set up "improvement teams." These would meet weekly: Each would have a facilitator and would be free to choose their own projects. Again, the end results were patchy. The success of individual projects depended significantly on management support, but employees had specifically asked for no management participation! Effectively, therefore, management buy in was insufficient and thus restricted scope or empowerment for idea or improvement implementation. This phase ran for a year and produced many useful but limited improvements.

Martin then re-energized the quality process at the company in a different way. He decided to introduce, running alongside the existing activities, a business process re-engineering initiative aimed at shortening the cycle time of the process from its then current 70 days to 35, calling this "Project 35." With the further aid of consultants, teams were formed to address this.

Four Project 35 teams were set up. Their composition and structure were decided by the nature of the assignment (usually three external consultants and seven employees). A "portakabin" was placed on the factory floor, and this served as the office for the consultants and had space to hold meetings. One of the first things a team investigated was the process of transferring an engine from an aircraft to the factory. Information was gathered and retained about each individual engine, and planned maintenance cycles triggered the ordering of relevant parts that were scheduled to arrive at the same time as the engine. Engines were removed from aircraft at different airfields and transported as cargo to the factory. The timing of this was crucial to reducing the overall cycle time. Another team identified a bottleneck process, another machine that had far higher capacity was installed, and the cycle time was improved again. Something it was difficult to publicize was the comment that one manager made to us as we were leaving the site. A reduction of days in the cycle time had been achieved, and nobody could find a cause: it just happened in the middle of the process. Perhaps it was a delayed form of the "Hawthorne effect," so-called from the Roethlesberger and Dixon studies in the 1930s, wherein performance improved merely because a project to investigate it had been set up! In any case, it was common knowledge in the organization but not remarked on in a similar way to the customer management and process improvement projects where causes were clear.

Over the period of a year, the teams brought the cycle time down to forty-two days, but after another takeover of the organization, Martin left. When he went, the project stayed in place until it was disbanded after two years, but the cycle time remained at forty-two, and the decision was taken that it was not "economically viable" to make further progress.

Although the initiative had fizzled out, we found out later that the cycle time had given the site "leadership" within the industry. When researching the airport case that we discuss in chapter 7, we toured the facility for maintaining engines. We found that a huge improvement effort had taken place because the site had a cycle time much poorer than Air Care. Controversially for the sector, the airport had gone for a total empowerment approach very different from the management-initiated change at Air Care, but the way that they had done it had created chaos, unlike our second example of leadership discussed next.

Blue Circle

Blue Circle at Dunbar, Scotland consists of a quarry and a cement-processing facility. In the quarry, they dislodge by using explosives 5 million tons of rock a year, the equivalent of an Egyptian pyramid, transport it to the factory, and combine it with 2 million tons of limestone ground as fine as talcum powder. It is then roasted until the rock almost melts; is cooled, and ground into cement; and is bagged and transported to the customer. It is a hot, dirty, potentially dangerous process.

The manager, Ross Dunn, was aware that the site was marginal, in terms both of geography and viability. He decided to give TQM another try. They had had two previous attempts that were unsuccessful; one employee had characterized the management as being "like headless chickens." One of the differences in the third attempt was that Ross included everyone in the process at an early stage and invited everyone to attend to hear what was proposed. People were asked, not told to participate. Although at first the words seemed very similar, the employees decided to give it a try and "go for the hat-trick."

Ross was attempting to set in train a complete reversal of thirty years of autocratic management. Everybody without exception was trained in improvement techniques and what TQM entailed.

1. **Communication.** The organization communicates detailed business information, so that the workforce is aware of current productivity rates, costs, and the like. This helps them to create relevant initiatives and take sensible decisions. There is a wide variety of mechanisms used, and the process is two-way.
2. **Stability.** To aid worker security, the company has introduced new long-term shift patterns that enable people to plan their lives more effectively. They pay their workers on a salaried, not hourly, basis.
3. **Respect.** The management has come to respect the workforce and to appreciate their expertise, experience, and knowledge, in the same way as the workforce has come to respect the management.

An organization was designed to support the initiative; it was suggested that a total quality steering group (TQSG) be formed, and that group was cross-functional, consisting of management, crafts, technical people, and representatives from the whole workforce. It was headed up by the accounting controller (not Ross), and he was charged with overseeing the process. It viewed presentations from teams, produced a vision statement, and was tasked with actually making the vision happen (none of the previous initiatives had had this stipulation).

The vision they came up with was "with honesty, commitment, trust, and pride, a'body workin' side by side":

- Safety first—environment too
- Customer satisfaction
- Operate profitably
- Teamworking through consensus
- Look for continuous improvement
- All for one and one for all
- Natural choice
- Determined

"Tae be the best"
(source, Blue Circle company document)

(For non-Scottish readers "a'body" is Lowlands Scots for everybody and "tae" is to.)

The support infrastructure for the improvements stressed support rather than hierarchy (see Figure 2.2).

The TQSG wanted to support ideas and enable people to carry them out. Too often in the past good ideas had been lost. In some cases, people knew what to do, but others let them down. The process allowed people to get things done if they could; there was no excuse. If they needed help, the sources for that were accessible and accountable. To this end, they developed a flow chart of the process people were intended to follow (see Figure 2.3).

This diagram was thought to be very useful. It meant that people could air ideas and build up consensus. Anybody who wanted to do something could contribute; indeed, the flow diagram was the product of a team activity.

From a management perspective, key business processes were identified, benchmarking was carried out; and more facilitators were trained to develop ownership. Families were encouraged to become involved; indeed, the whole community was invited to open days. Different things were tried to keep things interesting (e.g., team meetings were once held at a zoo some thirty miles away to spur creativity). In the early days of change, it was thought that trust was fundamental; however, you cannot trust people you do not know! Ross advocated stability in the management team, and he required managers to be there for long enough to develop their skills and, most important, to work in step with trust so that people progressed together. He considered his highest achievement was then possible: everybody working together. His objective was to develop a culture resistant to reverting to how things had been before.

Improvements led to a doubling of the profits in a difficult market. The subtler aspects of the environment and culture were more difficult to bring about. It was all very well to say "We trust you!" and train people, but some of the steps were thought to be verging on foolish (e.g., passing

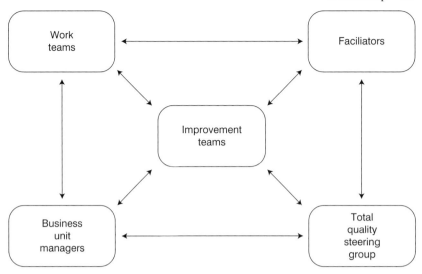

Figure 2.2 Blue Circle organization structure (Source: Blue Circle company document)

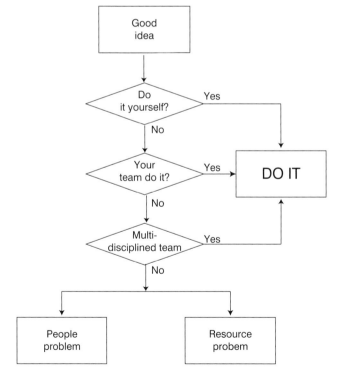

Figure 2.3 Empowerment process flow diagram

on financial information), but when the transparency led to improved decision making and cost control, people were soon reassured.

Ross behaved in such a way at meetings as to let other people have their say. When the company was invited to tell others of their success, he insisted that a spread of workers give the presentation, as they best knew the detail of the improvement activities. He tried to make things fun. Workers decided on what improvements were to be made, and Ross sorted out the resources and training.

Just as in our first case, Ross moved on after promotion within the group. However, the momentum for quality improvement remains as strong as ever. Some ten years after the third attempt at TQM, the organization still operates in this way; improvements are still being made at the site through the empowerment process while the site continues to be used as a model for others in the group. Blue Circle was taken over by Lafarge recently; however, the Dunbar site thrives.

Discussion

It is clear from the case information that both Martin and Ross displayed many of the leadership attributes and were well versed in what they were striving to achieve. Martin established direction, made clear his vision of the future, and set in place a strategy to enable the company to realize this. Through the ways in which he developed his people, he tried to communicate this vision, specifically by training in TQ as a necessary step to the creation of problem-solving teams. These had a proportion of shop floor employees in their membership though they operated under consultancy guidance. Though they produced some useful productivity gains, overall the benefits were not what had been expected. Specifically, the cross-functional approach that Martin looked for had just not materialized. Moreover, employees at many levels felt uninvolved. Resource, both financial and managerial, appeared to be restricted, and the critical urge to succeed appeared to be absent at many levels.

In contrast, although if anything the financial constraints were even stricter, Ross managed to create the vision and resource the initiatives, and the involvement was far wider, with leadership qualities being displayed in many parts of the organization.

The repeated training at Airco, though ambitious, seems almost punitive, especially in comparison to the more supportive relations at Blue Circle, and it is interesting that Martin thought that involvement would be brought about by restricting management input at meetings, whereas Ross's approach was to promote cross-status and cross-functional teams. The subsequent handing over to consultants to manage a business process–reengineering project seems to us to be an admission of failure and an abrogation of responsibility.

Martin seemed to need quick, controlled action, to get "others" to do things, resembling an autocratic leader (Tannenbaum and Schmidt, 1973), whereas Ross was at another point along any given continuum. Martin's approach was more like the behaviors and traits of a "manager" in Kotter's terminology (1990), with small symbolic acts to show he was a "man of the people" (e.g., the economy-flight tickets). Though the business circumstances were healthier for Airco, the circumstances were not sufficiently demanding for a leader to emerge, for employees to feel that they had to galvanize behind some improvement activity. It should be pointed out, though, that the air industry is reassuringly heavily regulated, and the procedures and conformance culture of the federal aviation requirements lead to a bureaucratic approach to management that must affect any change process. So Martin's behavior was consistent with Hersey and Blanchard's views (1993) on the appropriateness of forms of leadership styles being dependent on the state of affairs of the organization. It follows that for improvement purposes, it was not good leadership.

Both men, to our knowledge, were good transactional leaders (Micklethwait and Wooldridge, 1996) but, given the previous sentences, it will come as no surprise that we believe Ross to be the authentic transformational leader and that, ultimately, Martin's activities might place him in the fourth of Price's boxes (2003) in that we have said his behavior was not entirely consistent with leadership theory, nor did his leadership sustain improvement beyond his tenure.

Whereas it would be true to say that Martin's former employees remembered him fondly, for Ross's it was even more so, though his leadership was about enabling others to fulfill themselves in participating but not dominating initiatives, similar to Tampoe's ideas (1998). Consistent with Pedler and Aspinwall's view (2004) of leadership being a performance art, Ross was on the stage but knew when not to "hog" it, whereas Martin put in an appearance at the start of each Act and then departed. The conundrum from Alvesson and Sveningsson's research (2003) is that yes, it is good to engender leadership from within but, to do this, you need examples close by from which to learn, examples who are sufficiently comfortable "in their own skins" to let you gain your performance skills.

What was little covered in the case material above was that both men were keen to lead their organizations within their wider business area and promoted their sites' interests. They also led their organizations within the community, and their use of the EFQM model encouraged this further. It is disappointing that one of the activities that dropped off at Air Care with Martin's departure is their engagement with the improvement organizations in their locale.

With the benefit of hindsight, it is possible to argue that Martin rated highly on leadership skills and activities when he was in office but that, because his approach did not spread the activities (cf. Kiefer, 1994), their "post hoc" ratings might be different. Conversely, Ross in the cement plant created the momentum by being almost absent from what is often regarded as the traditional idea of the leader. Burns's definition of transforming leadership mentioned earlier in this chapter almost exactly encapsulates how Ross discharged what he saw as his role as leader. Perhaps a further test of whether there is effective leadership is when autonomous work groups are in evidence (Semler, 2003)?

Leadership as a subject

Lipman-Blumen's work (2005) on "toxic" leaders has echoes of Weber's original discussion of charisma. Weber was keen to differentiate between traditional familial forms of domination, rational-legal domination, and another form that arose from a mix of "social circumstances and individual psychology" (Runciman, 1978, p. 210). Charisma has no formal backing as such; it depends on whether the followers subscribe to a person's legitimacy to lead. This is not a very secure basis. The leaders have to continue to give proofs of their skills. Weber argues that this form can occur in any society at any time—it is not a "primitive" arrangement but a human one (Runciman, 1978). "The power of charisma, by contrast, depends on beliefs in revelation and heroism, on emotional convictions about the importance and value of ...manifestation, or heroism, ...or judicial wisdom or magical or other favours. Such belief revolutionizes men 'from within' and seeks to shape things and organizations with its revolutionary will" (Runciman, 1978, p. 231). The words of the text seem curiously familiar to the management gurus seeking wholesale change (Oakland, 1995). Ross was charismatic in this sense, Martin was not. It appears that Martin used his position in the organization to get others in the shape of consultants and lower level staff to realize improvements.

A far more recent text that carries these ideas is Lipman-Blumen (2005). She concurs with the "relational" concept of leadership, that leaders cannot be discussed in isolation from those whom they "lead." She says that leaders "come to power by addressing their followers' needs, from their existential angst to various strands of their psychological motives and the cultural expectations that shape their behaviour" (Lipman-Blumen, 2005, p. 127). She disagrees with situational theorists, such as Hersey and Blanchard (1993), in that she thinks that leaders and their skills do not so much come to the fore given the right situation but, at the right point in their identity, as a person, a point she attributes to James March. Her most interesting contribution lies in her discussion of why toxic leaders gain positions of power. Some people are always toxic; others acquire toxicity in office (another concept that would not be unfamiliar to the readers of Weber and other political sociologists, such as Roberto Michels).

Her book focuses on how followers allow leaders to carry on with toxic activities—by *toxic* here we mean self-aggrandizing, nefarious, or even merely incompetent activities that result in the organization's being less well off on a variety of criteria than before this person occupied a position of power. Leaders frequently emerge at a point of crisis, which can be defined in many ways. They rise to prominence and, once they are there, it is hard to challenge them. The main thrust of her argument is that the followers are routinized into supporting the person and do not think they can act to provide alternatives. There is a complex brew of individual experiences with early leader figures in our lives and social acculturation that make it seem silly to challenge the boss. The whistleblower always comes off worst.

Relating these arguments to performance improvement, people such as Ross were in the minority of the cases we researched. Ross himself was not toxic; much the reverse. He had been in this organization for a while, had seen elements of toxicity, and wanted to act on them. Martin was driven by the wider cultural norm of improvement as a response to perceived competitive pressures.

Conclusions

In this chapter, we have explored the concept of leadership, thought by many to be critical in improving performance. We have reviewed some of the extensive literature on the subject and described two of the leaders from our research. Just as there are many ways to perceive leadership, there are many ways to interpret individuals' behavior. We think Ross's leadership was more effective because it was devolved widely. In short, there was continuity in the improvement effort. Ross managed to "personalize" the improvement process in an authentic way, a feature that emerges with other, successful leaders we describe in later chapters.

Summary conclusions

This chapter has discussed:

- Various concepts of leadership
- The case of the temporarily good leader of an air sector company
- The case of the cement factory leader whose main work was to set up an initiative that continued after he left
- That the negative effect of leaders and leadership should be considered
- The importance of creating authentic "personalized" work relations
- That many good leader appear "egoless"—they recognize that others might not share their views and that this might be a good thing for performance improvement.

Discussion questions

- How can the people in an organization tell whether a good leader will last?
- How can an egoless leader still maintain momentum?
- Is enabling everyone to be a leader creating chaos?

Further reading

Lipman-Blumen, J. 2005. *The Allure of Toxic Leaders*. Oxford: Oxford University Press.

Price, T. L. 2003. The Ethics of Authentic Transformational Leadership. *Leadership Quarterly* 14 (1):67–81.

Rosener, J. 1990. Ways Women Lead. *Harvard Business Review*:119–25.

3 The relationship between strategy and performance improvement

Summary introduction

This chapter will discuss:

- Definitions of and approaches to implementing strategy
- The relationship between strategy and improvement
- Whether strategy is necessary
- Two cases of very different organizations that used similar approaches to strategy
- The importance of setting up external relationships for monitoring progress
- The need to consider the intricate network of relations and activities necessary to implement a strategy within the organization.

Introduction

Strategy is an attractive concept that seems integral to any improvement activity. In this chapter, we explore the relationship between improvement and strategy, briefly discussing why an organization might require a strategy, what it is theorized to be, and how strategies are developed and implemented. We then describe two of our case organizations, Govan Initiative (GI) and Nortel. GI operates at the fringes of the public sector and has been set up as a catalyst to develop the local economy. It enacts a systematic strategy development process that one might assume would stifle creativity and performance but instead provides a framework and justification to operate in a highly innovative way to meet stakeholder expectations. The Nortel case is more typical of a successful implementation of a strategy of performance improvement. We analyze both cases in relation to the strategy literature and conclude the chapter with a discussion of how the organizations managed to integrate and align strategy with improvement.

We think it helpful to begin by examining what the term *strategy* really means in the context of performance improvement. It is used in so many different contexts in warfare, in politics, in sport, and in business that not only its origin but frequently its essential meaning and significance have become less than clear. The *Oxford Dictionary* defines strategy as "the art of war; art of planning and directing larger movements and operations of campaign or war" (OUP, 1974, p. 549). There are several elements to this definition; it implies an author, a hierarchy of plans, and a long-term perspective, but the use of the word *art* suggests that implementing any strategy might be far from straightforward. Even Napoleon had some poor campaigns!

Harvard Business School (1991, p. 9) describes

> Corporate strategy as the pattern of decisions in a company that (1) determines, shapes and reveals its objectives, purposes or goals; (2) produces the principal policies and plans for achieving these goals; and (3) defines the business the company intends to be in, the kind of economic and human organization it intends to be, and the nature of the economic and non-economic contribution it intends to make to its shareholders, employees, customers and communities.

In their colorfully titled *Strategy Safari* (1998, Mintzberg et al. (1998, pp. 9–17) develop an even more exhaustive consideration of the many-sidedness of strategy. They provide a comprehensive definition of strategy, noting many dimensions that have both positive and negative aspects. They review "strategy" from ten distinctly different perspectives, each of which the authors designates as a "school," and agree that strategy can be seen as a plan or a direction, guide, or course of action for the future; it charts the way forward for the organization but in addition points out that, followed blindly, it may lead into uncharted dangerous water. Strategy is a pattern, demonstrating consistency in behavior over time. It reduces ambiguities and provides a sense of order, but again there is a potentially restrictive side to this. Strategy is about positioning, locating particular products in particular markets. Strategy focuses effort through promoting the coordination of activities, but again, this might be overly narrow. Strategy is about defining an organization, but changing circumstances might render this obsolete. They argue that strategy is a ploy or a specific maneuver, a subterfuge, to outwit an opponent or a competitor. Many writers share some of the definitions of Mintzberg et al. (1998), some disagree on points, and this is elaborated below.

Strategy in action

Early management writers on the topic, such as Ansoff (1965) and Chandler (1962), considered the relationship between organization structure and strategy: The idea was that if the structure were correct, the strategy could be realized. Questions of "fit" and "alignment" have dominated since, for example, Peters and Waterman (1982, p. 4) suggested that Chandler's dictum "had the makings of universal truth". However, they argued "a strategy of broad diversification dictates a structure marked by decentralization," but they concluded "that strategy rarely seemed to dictate unique structural solutions"; furthermore, "the crucial problems in strategy were most often those of execution and continuous adaptation."

Discussion has also focused on questions of scope—diversity or focus—with perhaps contrasting views presented by the Boston Consulting Group, which made its name developing an approach to manage a "portfolio" of businesses, with strategic decisions taken at the center determining how to allocate scarce resources, particularly financial, between each of the separate businesses, which have been given their own strategic mission vis-à-vis the others in the organization to grow, contract, or act as a cash "cow" (Hedley, 1977). Hamel and Prahalad (1994) presented an opposing view that focus was important and that organizations should concentrate on their "core competences" and spend time deciding which these were; the answers to these questions then determined the allocation of resources.

The most popular strategists in the improvement literature are Miles and Snow (1978), famous for their specification of four types of strategies that an organization can pursue. The first is the innovative "prospector" type, the second is the consolidating "defender," the third is the unfortunate "reactor" type that waits for other organizations to take a lead. Less well known is the "analyzer" type that surveys the circumstances and then decides on a course of action. These types are accompanied by forms of action that lie in the area of market, services, revenues, the external organization, and the internal organization. Croteau and Bergeron (2001) note that individual organizations can appear to display every type of strategy simultaneously, indeed, can wheel through each cyclically over time. However Andrews et al. (2006, p. 52) have concluded that "organizational performance is positively associated with a prospector stance and negatively with a reactor stance."

Porter (1980, 1985) is famous for encouraging companies to consider external relations as part of the strategic decision process, borrowing heavily from industrial economics. He was much concerned with the long-term profitability of organizations and thought that could be supported by developing strategies that helped to determine where the organization could best compete. Improvement initiatives take place to support competitive performance. Above-average performance derives from choosing one of three defensible positions open to strategists, which they term *generic strategies, cost leadership,* and *differentiation* or *focus*. Porter maintains that these are the only feasible options through which a sustainable competitive advantage can be realized. Cost leadership is achieved through having tight cost controls applied in stable product areas. Differentiation involves offering unique products or services associated with minimizing sensitivity to price. Improvements could be geared to creativity and customer awareness. However, an organization may also opt to concentrate on particular customer groups, product lines, or specific markets wherein it can differentiate itself either because of its low-cost operation or the special nature or other characteristics of the products it offers. Porter emphasized that "a firm that engages in each generic strategy but fails to achieve in any of them becomes 'stuck in the middle'" (1985, p. 16), because it possesses no distinctive competitive advantage and is thus more likely to turn in a below-par performance. Miller (1992) among others has questioned Porter's assertion that an organization has to follow one strategy or else become stuck in the middle. He suggests that such strategic specialization might "cause inflexibility and narrow an organization's vision" (Miller, 1992, p. 37). Toyota might be used to support Miller's argument, having all three strategies in operation in a way that beats other automotive companies

Mintzberg et al. (1998) broaden the concept of strategy further when they suggest that it is best portrayed as a recognizable pattern in a stream of decisions. Mintzberg himself is famous for his earlier distinction between the sources of strategies, namely "deliberate" and "emergent" strategies (1978). The former reflects where an organization, having determined its goals, implements its planned strategy to attain these; in contrast, emergent strategies are those that have been developed either as a logical and realistic outcome of the implementation process or arise naturally from the constructive thinking of lower management.

Kay (1993) argues that strategy should be constructed round identifying an organization's strength in four fields: its reputation, its ability to innovate, its strategic assets (e.g., patents), and its network of relationships. He contends that each firm's situation is different and that there are no generic indicators to strategic success.

Building on this, Hamel and Prahalad (1994) argue that companies need to be considered as collections of skills. Though traditional strategists do their best to position their organization as astutely as possible in existing markets, they contend that a company should endeavor to reinvent its whole industry. It should strive to envisage what the future might hold for it—and strategy is about developing an imaginative approach to enable it to formulate and realize its vision of the future. Kao (1996) asserts that the chief strategic aim of a company should be to encourage creativity. He points out that under the old planning scenario, planners used to hand out sheets with precise descriptions of what each individual was required to do. No longer, he argues; the strategist should set the overall direction, but the employees should improvise in the manner of jazz groups. Kim and Mauborgne (2004) reviewed the last century or so of corporate history and found that most of the well-known industries of today did not exist in 1900, and this even applied looking back just thirty years! They therefore concluded that there is a hugely underestimated capacity to create new industries. The entire discipline of strategy has been focused on beating the competition in already existing markets, which has led companies to fight over existing terrain instead of creating fresh opportunities. They believe that the crux of the problem lies in discovering how to move into a "blue ocean" of uncontested market space. Management has to sit back and say, "How can we create a whole new industry?" A company that they cite as an example of "blue-ocean strategy" and which has managed to create new markets with the minimum of resources is Starbucks, which reinvented coffee drinking without spending a fortune on advertising. Blue-ocean strategy creates a leap in value for the company and for buyers and breaks the trade-off between differentiation and low costs.

Performance improvement and strategy

It is difficult to distinguish strategy from performance improvement. Forms of performance improvement have been seen as strategies in themselves (Oakland, 1995), and the European Foundation for Quality Management (EFQM) and Baldrige models of business excellence used by organizations to guide improvement include strategy as a key criterion. The Baldrige Award has strategy mentioned twice in its model (NIST, 2005), as an individual planning criterion and as an overarching concept that is intended to guide performance improvement. The EFQM (1998) has strategy as a criterion and encourages an organization to gather information from a wide range of sources to include in the formulation process, ranging from wider economic conditions to employee views and capabilities. How the policies are formulated should be similarly all-encompassing. Once formulated, it should be communicated and deployed but thoughtfully and periodically revised on the basis of careful measurement of the effects. It is clearly thought that having a strategic perspective facilitates long-term performance improvement. The link has to be drawn between the overall strategy, and its operations strategy and improvement activities. Operations strategists, such as Skinner (1969) and Hill (1995), have long pointed out the ways to link the two. Smith and Reece (1999) note from Skinner (1969) that any performance gains from improving productivity on the "shop floor" might be fleeting if these are not linked with the overall strategy of both operations and the organization. They also draw attention to a major contribution of Deming and Edwards (1982) in including the customer in any thoughts about improvement or strategy.

Performance-improvement writers also contribute to how strategies can be developed and implemented; for example, "hoshin kanri," or catchball (Akao, 1991), is more discussed in this literature as compared with strategy, though it is a means by which ideas can be communicated through, and modified by, a wide number of employees.

Pascale (1990) has pointed out that performance improvement approaches such as total quality management create practices that "define a process that encompasses R & D, extends to the customer, entails competitive analysis, resource allocation, and implementation and operations" (1990, p. 248). As a consequence, this may confidently be expected to generate competitive advantage in areas in which the company has sought to differentiate itself, which is, as Pascale points out, synonymous with strategy. He goes on to ask, "What then is the difference between quality and strategy?" (ibid, p. 248).

Most of the traditional quality gurus would assert that performance improvement is the main way in which managers can realize the competitive advantage of the business strategically (Juran and Gryna, 1988; Crosby, 1980). Peters and Waterman (1982, p. 4) have argued that "[T]he crucial problems in strategy were most often those of execution and continuous adaptation."

Improvement without a strategy?

Given that the model for performance improvement in action tends to be Toyota (Ohno, 1988), it seems odd for Porter and Tanner to conclude that Japanese companies "rarely have strategies" (1996, p. 63). In the opinion of Mintzberg et al. (1998, p. 119), this perception is not true at all. They suggest that the Japanese might have something useful to say to Porter about strategy—clearly this might be so!

According to Inkpen and Choudhury (1995, pp. 313–4),

> [T]he absence of a strategy need not be associated with organizational failure. Organizations with tight controls, high reliance on formalized procedures and a passion for consistency may lose the ability to experiment and innovate. Nucor (the American steel maker) has no written plan, no written objectives and no mission statement. For Nucor, an absence of many of the supposed elements of strategy is symbolic of the no-frills, non-bureaucratic organization Nucor has worked hard to become.

It should be pointed out that some organizations spend much time formulating a strategy only to leave it on the shelf or as empty rhetoric

(Collins and Porras, 1998). As discussed in chapter 6 in this book, managers think they should have one but either appear not to understand the implications or fail to engage properly with the underlying ethos, meaning the strategy has no dynamic for improvement.

The next part of the chapter introduces our case organization that has adopted a very systematic approach in developing a strategy that is highly innovative and moreover has clearly been successful in achieving the objectives that it has set for itself and which the community recognizes as of key importance. Their holistic strategy, which is not overly prescriptive, has enabled their stakeholders to feel that they can contribute in ways that are satisfying not only to themselves but also to furthering the achievement of their corporate goals.

Govan Initiative Ltd

For much of the last century, the economy of the area south of the River Clyde in Glasgow, Scotland was dominated by the boom-and-bust cycles of heavy engineering and particularly shipbuilding. Between 1965 and 1985, the area fell into sharp decline, shipyards closed, and their subcontractors found alternative work impossible to obtain. The skills that had been in such high demand in the past were no longer required. There was a huge increase in unemployment, and a rise of social problems blighted an already depressed business community.

However, in 1987, a partnership was formed between several economic development agencies, local government, and representatives of the private sector to establish a new organization, Govan Initiative Ltd (GI), to address these issues. Its board comprises a wide range of local stakeholders.

GI is charged with regenerating Greater Govan by working with other agencies and with local residential and business communities. It has set itself five key goals: (1) the regeneration of the local Govan economy; (2) the provision of opportunities to Govan people through the achievement of social and economic prosperity; (3) the creation of a lifelong learning community, both business and residential; (4) the development of an environment that meets the current and predicted needs of its communities; and (5) the achievement of recognition of the company by its customers and the community as an excellent company, a leader in economic and social development.

The company in 2004 managed thirty-two separate projects with an annual turnover of £4.9 million. It delivers its services from five office bases, three nursery units, and fifteen community outlets located throughout the area. Everyone sees it as their responsibility continuously to review the work they undertake to ensure that the needs of their customers are identified and serviced in the most effective way.

The senior management team is responsible for the strategic direction and operational management of the company. The core workforce has grown from four to ninety-one. The company has supported the generation by staff of a system of values that outline a code of practice underpinning how it operates. These are:

- Pursuit of excellence: The objective is to strive always to improve its performance.
- Caring for people: Relationships should always be based on integrity, trust, and understanding of the changing needs of its customers.
- Partnerships: The company will constantly seek to identify and develop partnerships to help in achieving its goals.
- Prodigious effort: Individually and collectively the organization will strive to meet its goals in a stimulating and productive environment.
- No fear of failure: Staff will be encouraged and supported in the creation, development, and implementation of new ideas.

Like many of our other case organizations, GI has adopted the EFQM model to shape improvement. The company has sought external recognition for its efforts, has been accredited by the Scottish Quality Management Systems and Investors in People Award since 1995, and has been reaccredited in 1998, 2001, and 2004. In 1997, the company was awarded the Quality Scotland Foundation's Award for Business Excellence in the Small to Medium-sized Enterprise category and was a finalist for the European Quality Award in 1999. There was a lull in the early part of this century, but fresh efforts have been made in pursuing the EFQM award again.

Formulating a strategy

As a necessary background in helping to determine its strategic priorities, the company uses both primary and secondary research, much of which is conducted by the company's Community Knowledge Centre (CKC). The center is directed by the senior economic research officer to identify opportunities, particularly for employment, to ensure that the services provided to the community are appropriate to their needs. The CKC commissions any necessary primary research, especially in relation to the future demand for labor in the wider Glasgow South West area but also including work, for example, on literacy and innumeracy, child care provision, and health and education. This process also incorporates the preparation of a SWOT analysis. Annually it also provides information to update the Greater Glasgow Baseline study, which itself contributed the case for founding GI.

Govan has a particularly large number of people on incapacity benefit and many in "earner-less" homes but, where people are eager to work, a massive challenge for the company to address.

In planning how their future strategy might be developed, the company has adopted a benchmarking approach. Thus it has sent staff to a number of European and American cities that have been troubled in ways similar to those of Glasgow. Their experience and the nature of the actions they have taken have been reflected in many of the Govan initiatives (e.g., see below with the Hills Trust Academy).

When different priorities are identified, the company pinpoints "best practice" in other organizations, in particular those who might be interested in working to address the issues jointly with GI (e.g., Careers Scotland to support youth initiatives). The company has also participated in an evaluation of local socioeconomic strategies (ELSES) in disadvantaged urban areas along with cities in Holland, Sweden, France, Italy, and Germany. This study has examined how the economic and social fabric of distressed areas in these cities is being regenerated and is an important source of information and a stimulus.

The company's strategic priorities that have emerged from its review processes are:

- To empower residents by supporting and encouraging individual growth.
- Through helping to build the capacity of community and voluntary organizations, to incorporate the active contributions of local people.
- To improve the competitiveness and performance of the local economy and to increase its size, scale, and diversity.
- Through partnerships to develop and improve the comprehensive learning opportunities in the Greater Govan area.
- To enhance the learning, vocational, and social skills of the local community.
- To develop and secure employment opportunities that offer choice and encourage career progression.
- To stimulate, develop, and implement a comprehensive approach to resolving economic, environmental, and social concerns in the Greater Govan area .

Some indicators of the organization's success are shown in Table 3.1.

This kind of social change is very difficult and slow to bring about, but unemployment is diminishing and other indicators are all improving. At a time when the relative position of Glasgow as a whole has not benefited from the wider economic stability, the development has mainly taken place at the periphery, making the Govan figures all the more impressive.

Table 3.1 Govan Initiative performance

	1986	2003
Unemployment	32.6 percent	8.5 percent
Population	29,500	29,928
Housing stock	13,000	13,781
Owner occupied	3641	5065
Crime	Worst of 32	20th of 32
Business base	385	810
Business survival to 1 year	37.5 percent	90 percent
School leavers into further education	5 percent	17 percent
Physical investment	Negligible	More than £600 million

Internal review

Annually, senior management carries out an "evaluation review" of all projects. This examines how each of their projects has performed overall, notably including the extent of customer satisfaction. It assesses how far the goals and strategic priorities set have been attained and how effectively the financial resources deployed have been used. It also registers the key achievements and determines the areas for improvement.

Employees are encouraged to feel part of decision making in the widest sense (e.g., twelve improvement action teams provide an opportunity for staff to become involved in domains not specifically in their own area of expertise). Annually an employee satisfaction survey is carried out, from which *inter alia* areas for improvement are identified. A quarterly news sheet, Initiative ID, was introduced in 2002; a key feature highlights staff commendations. In each issue, the continuing need for effective communications is emphasized through an article written by the chief executive.

Initiatives

A valuable example of these is in the work that the company undertakes with the European Social Fund; 106 companies have been created through their enterprise, the sixth best outcome in Scotland. The company has particular skills in preparing funding applications and also in identifying opportunities that might otherwise have been missed because these may appear at first sight to lie outside their strict remit. Regeneration of the local economy has to lie at the heart of their efforts. Clearly crime and area dereliction influence how they go about this. Thus, emphases on education and on securing understanding and publicity from the media about their objectives are critical as is gaining positive support from the police authorities. They try to develop small to medium-sized enterprises, improve the physical infrastructure, reduce unemployment, and create inward investment in many innovative ways. Thus, when the celebrated Harry Ramsden restaurant chain began operations in Govan, the company contacted Ramsden's by phone, offering to train their people. Not only was the offer accepted but the approach was so warmly welcomed that it resulted in a number of Govan people securing employment.

Not all the jobs are low level; a seam of increasing significance derives from the imminent relocation of TV companies to the south bank of the Clyde, with consequential opportunities for learning, and employing, media skills. Indeed, the company launched its Creative Media project in 2002 .This works closely with the BBC, Channel 4, and Scottish Enterprise Glasgow. The workshops that it provides are aimed at training individuals in script writing, editing, video production, and the like.

An interesting example is the relationship developed with Cisco systems, which Cisco began by providing GI with access to its "on-line" curriculum. The partnership flourished so successfully that in 2002 it was awarded the Cisco Europe, Middle East, & Africa Project of the Year. Cisco has invested a further $500,000 in the Hills Trust Learning Foundation and has committed itself to the investment of a further $1 million to extend the Govan partnership model to three other areas in Glasgow.

Recent research has indicated that up to one-third of local children have no positive destination when they leave school. Govan Initiative is now working closely with Careers Scotland to secure access to these children at a sufficiently early stage to make a real difference to their lives (e.g., with Modern Apprenticeship and Get Ready for Work schemes aimed specifically at 16- to 18-year-olds). It is noteworthy that, whereas in the past "learners" used to come to one of the GI centers, this is no longer the case. It is now necessary for GI actively to seek out those people who require help; intriguingly, this is done through libraries or community centers. In April 2002, the company opened its Community Learning Academy that focuses on industry-led training and brings the latest developments in information communication technology (ICT) to the wider Govan community. The Academy combines the most up-to-date e-learning delivery with group work and lab-based practical experience. To ensure its long-term future, the company has set up the Hills Trust Foundation; funding of £5 million secured for this project is being used to build a business center locally, the annual rental income from which will provide a long-term sustainable resource stream for lifelong learning in the area.

GI has also been involved in three significant schemes involving total capital of £6.6 million; two of these are owned by the company, are fully occupied, and yield annual rental of some £0.5 million. Four further projects are planned. In assessing their viability, GI always adopts a prudent approach to ensure not only that funds are in place before the contract is let and work commences but that the project shows and is seen to achieve an appropriate return on capital employed.

Partnerships

As a key feature of its development work with the community, GI is closely involved in partnerships; no fewer than eighty have been identified in a recent study. A notable example lies in crime prevention, wherein their partnership with Strathclyde Police is now positively influencing levels of crime. It also fully participates in the Greater Govan Social Inclusion Partnership and, in particular, in the work of its implementation groups, such as those on combating poverty, tackling drug misuse, and community potential.

A further initiative seeks to address the significant and hitherto largely excluded ethnic minority resident in Govan. Here a partnership developed with the Ethnic Minority Enterprise Centre (EMEC) supported, in 2004, some thirty-seven learners in the city center and a further forty-nine in the Ibrox Library. Another barrier to learning and thus to employment has been the lack of child care provision in the area. As far back as 1990 and 1991, the company had identified this as another hurdle to overcome; in response to this need, it opened three nurseries in the Greater Govan area to provide seventy-five full-time places, thus enabling local people who wished to return to full-time education or employment to do so.

Govan Initiative's strategy

Llewellyn and Tappin (2003) discuss the role of strategy in public sector organizations and note that it is a comparatively recent addition to the managerial trend. They argue that public sector organizations differ from private ones in that they do not usually compete with one another; there is an element of stability. The problems public sector organizations are set up to address are intractable. This may well apply to the type of organization these authors were concerned with in their paper, but it seems far from the mark when describing Govan Initiative. Although there might not be an organization entrusted with discharging precisely the same role as GI, there are some fulfilling almost the same role, and there are other economic agencies that could be seen as competitors for some elements of the task. It depends on which level of analysis is followed. The nearby agencies will be keen to attract inward investment and grants and develop the kind of relationship Govan has with Cisco.

It well may be reasonable to suggest that, while the nature of the task is stable, elements of it change (e.g., the switch from heavy industry to service sector jobs) and thus it requires a different labor force that takes time to emerge. Though we would argue that the rate of change might not appear to be so quick, tracking and anticipating seem to be key features of GI's strategy.

Last, there may well be an insoluble element to economic problems, but major gains can be made. We think GI's use of strategy has enabled them to innovate and generate opportunities and resources for the area. The strategy is far from being "dormant documents" (Llewellyn and Tappin, 2003) written purely to obtain funding and then never consulted again; the strategy development process is systematic and involves all key stakeholders. The timing and methods include stakeholders' results, and there are many opportunities to develop new initiatives that address the task at hand in a supportive way. Whereas it is normal for economic development agencies to invest in infrastructure and training to support inward investment, it is unusual to hear of them liaising with the police—as they do in Govan—to improve the locale. The repeated attempts at making training available to everyone and anyone in a way that suits them demonstrates creativity in thinking beyond the norm.

Llewellyn and Tappin (2003) quote Mintzberg (1994), who argues that strategy in the public sector is formed, not formulated, and we would assert that the reverse seems true for Govan. The organization has established challenging goals; it has formulated a coherent strategy to enable it to attain them and thoroughly assesses how effectively it is progressing toward meeting them, recently reinvigorating its efforts at self-assessment through the EFQM. After their huge success at the European level, there had been a change of leader, and the new person thought the organization needed a rest from the intense process of applying. Though the rewards they achieved from their entries were encouraging for their people, the work involved in the preparation of their submissions, and particularly the "feedback" from the judges, have been even more critical elements in enabling the organization to map the way forward and to measure their progress in their challenging task, which is why after a short hiatus they have been engaging in the process again.

The organization appears to us to be a "prospector" in Miles and Snow's terminology (1978); however, the case does illustrate how difficult it is to apply these labels, especially in a public service organization. In no way is GI a differentiator in the strict sense of Porter's definition (1980); however, it differentiates itself in the way it provides some of its education and training. The particular strengths of the GI approach are in its breadth of input. The environmental scanning, stakeholder awareness, partnership development, and benchmarking with global experts in the area are consistent with a competitive strategy for a leading private organization.

Some of their individual strategies no doubt "emerged" as part of a learning process. Mintzberg et al. (1998) suggest that strategies cannot necessarily be cut and dried, particularly in the circumstances that confronted the Govan team when they began their journey. In this case, they had to be developed incrementally as the team developed the appropriate approaches.

Kay's ideas (1993) fit very well here too; GI develops its reputation through participation in external assessments and interacting with stakeholders in such a way as to meet their objectives. Nobody questions its ability to innovate, and it pays close attention to developing its strategic assets, particularly its people. The exchange of staff with other organizations, such as the police, and global benchmarking highlight how it pays close attention to its network of relationships

Nortel

Nortel is the current owner of a site at Monkstown, Ulster that has been manufacturing and exporting telecommunications transmission access and switching systems for some thirty-six years. They acquired the factory from STC in 1991, since when it has become the company's manufacturing base for European Standard (ETSI) transmission products for world markets. Located on a thirty-four-acre site on the northern shore of Belfast Lough, the plant exports to sixty-three countries, though not to the United States. Of the company's worldwide 63,000 employees, about 1,000 work at Monkstown; of these, some 850 are permanent, 150 temporary. There are also around twenty-five specialist technical personnel supplied by another organization on site.

To the onlooker, Northern Ireland may seem a somewhat peripheral location for a manufacturing site, requiring complex transport links for access to major markets. Nortel has closed down some of the plants it took over from STC, but Monkstown has developed its position steadily over recent years. There are two main reasons for this. The first is the local infrastructure: Government is keen to develop the area, and there are excellent universities nearby. The second reason Monkstown has flourished in the face of strong competition from elsewhere is the commitment to improving processes within the organization to make the plant as competitive as possible.

Growing levels of customer satisfaction can be demonstrated by the increasing proportion of the process customers expect Nortel to carry out for them. Instead of merely providing equipment for the inside of exchanges, customers now expect Nortel to run networks of exchanges for them. For example, Nortel is responsible for the networks in the Moscow Underground, Ariane Space Centre in French Guyana, Bulgaria Telecom, and applications in Colombia and Brazil. Their success is further demonstrated by the winning of business from customers who would be expected to source with the telecoms company on their doorstep (e.g., in France against Alcatel). Ways of improving the whole process is an integral part of the business. Speed to market, total identification with and satisfaction of customer requirements, and proven process control are pinpointed as the key elements in the company's success in the market place.

Previous attempts at improvements had been made, but it was not until they became integral to the company's strategy that they became real and relevant. This was achieved in part through the use of the EFQM model. Initially, management at Monkstown did not actually use the model; they evaluated it as a tool. They shaped their own strategy using the model, along with alterations required through legislation in the human resources (HR) area, to forge their own framework for changing things. It is recognized that the EFQM model does provide helpful information for organizations on how to incorporate employees into the strategic planning process.

Strategic plans are considered three times a year: at Easter, in September, and in November-December. The senior management team is gathered off-site where information is shared. One or two alternative scenarios are developed on a flip chart then considered. At each meeting, another plan is examined, either relating to operations or to budget.

The strategic plan covers a three- to five-year span with implications for year one in detail. The core elements are the corporate server and the rest of the product family. The focus is on the supply chain. Much effort is devoted to identifying the chain and on benchmarking to facilitate improvements. The supply chain is geographically dispersed with customers distant from the plant. Monkstown's organization has control over part of order management, the make or buy decisions, building the equipment, shipping, and post-implementation service. They have plotted out their supply chain to include orders from actual customers. Monkstown's part of the operations takes up two weeks in an average forty-week lead time, which is quite small. Improving performance on that is difficult, so the thinking is that Monkstown need to expand visibility and influence from two weeks to minimize the forty weeks for Nortel as a whole, so perhaps Monkstown take up three weeks of a possible total of thirty.

The chief manager has encouraged 30 percent of the organization to include an element in their jobs related to strategy. The overall objective is to achieve "culture change," but this is viewed as a bit of a holy grail; it exists somewhere maybe but is not tangible. Thus, it has been translated into the idea of "common processes." Fifty of these have been identified and, with a fair amount of effort, twenty have been labeled as major. Project teams to address issues are staffed with people borrowed from the business. Frustrated people are encouraged to become involved with a change group so that they can contribute ideas on what should be changed to improve performance. Membership of the groups themselves changes, and responsibility for customer satisfaction rotates between two on the senior management team. Monkstown people believe this approach enables step changes in performance—not merely incremental ones—to be achieved.

Every month there is a business review wherein performance targets are realigned to the business model. Each area (e.g., finance, manufacturing, inventory, and delivery) has to show how it has performed against the model. Using these, Monkstown people are either second or leading the rest of Nortel and are naturally keen to retain that position.

There is also a series of meetings between the levels at which more basic business information is cascaded down. Line managers, who can add their own comments if they wish, also carry out monthly briefings. Whether they do so is verified. This may be viewed as an old-style tool, but it was thought that it had the advantage of being predictable, consistent, and succinct. The thought process behind "gain-sharing" is that a link can be drawn for people and the business aims by conveying the information explaining the method of determining the pay-out; this, in turn, energizes the workforce into working toward their accomplishment.

There have been both external and internal attempts at benchmarking. The telecommunications group in the EFQM network used "PRTM" consultants to carry out a review, based on a thirty-seven-point questionnaire, of the supply chain to develop worthwhile benchmarks. This was considered informative but insufficiently comprehensive. In the questionnaire, measures on delivery time were standardized against intercompany revenue. Monkstown people are trying to secure relevant data so that the benchmarks are closer to their "lines of business," their chief performance measure.

The PRTM study showed that Nortel was not first in any category and indeed lagged in a number of areas. There is a core benchmarking team pulled from finance and customer satisfaction that began by working on pilot studies in the communications process and business planning.

Strategic change

There are two main areas of change: customer scheduling and twenty-four-hour cycle time. Both require major effort to break barriers between functions. Previously, the number of staff aware and involved in specific customer orders was small (estimated at 5 percent), mainly in distribution. There has been a drive to move back within the plant the "decoupling point" wherein a product becomes specifically for one customer. The organization has been changed to support this approach with some 25 percent of employees now having customer orders as their focus.

Customer focus is built into the strategic and operations planning process. To Monkstown, customers are represented by four lines of business and account teams. At the top level, allocation of resources such as research and development, performance measurement, enforcement of legislation, and so on are handled through this framework. The line of business covers the task of getting information to senior managers in functional areas (e.g., duties, tasks, any requirement for R&D). The direct interface with the customer is the account team, which is assigned on a regional basis. Information indicating what the market wants also influences R&D spent on building new products. (There is an R&D facility on site.)

Customer satisfaction surveys are carried out recurrently by independent agencies covering basic quality issues related to the product and service. These are primarily (1) delivery-hardware quality, (2) post-installation support, and (3) warranty and repair time, though others such as retention and loyalty are also covered. Monkstown people measure these three main indicators and identify common trends, which are fed into customer satisfaction action plans that frequently involve workshops (e.g., they held a "dependability forum" during which twenty-four elements that were identified could provide a customer with a better delivery service). As a consequence, 90 percent of all orders now reach distribution on the planned date, whereas in the past just 25 percent did so. The measure of "on time" delivery has changed from "reaching distribution," as was the case three or four years ago, to the time the customer actually required the product. Performance indicators are analyzed together with "nuggets" of verbatim comments.

In the past, manufacture and delivery of a product used to be planned to the month. Now there is a thirty-day plan with specific dates to the week or day, and the actual customer requirement date is stipulated. As customers are using the product in telephone exchanges, the infrastructure has to be in place, so Monkstown's product arriving early is as big a problem as it would be if it were late!

Analysis

Just how strategy can relate to performance improvement is illustrated in the Nortel case study. Only when the concept of "continuous improvement" was enshrined as a key differentiating element (Porter, 1985) of the company's overall strategy did the organization really begin to drive forward—using the mechanism of the EFQM model to do so. We do not have the access to their customers to assess whether this differentiation was clear to them; however, it was very clear to the people we spoke to at Monkstown—a slightly different spin on the usual sense of differentiation. The belief demonstrated by the Nortel management in the EFQM model, when they could have followed the North American alternatives of the company's home location, was a key feature of their approach. Understandably the strategy that emerged from the work of the team of senior executives involved much careful thought, in particular "learning" from the inadequacies of their past procedures.

Do the development and implementation of a strategy in, and for, the organization have any impact on performance improvement? In the case of Nortel, the importance and the alignment were communicated widely and were seen to be authentic. Put another way, if an organization introduces some improvement initiative merely as an element in their change mechanism without presenting or arguing the case for doing so—other than that it was bound to be beneficial—the effort might not merely be wasted; it might even be counterproductive (a topic we explore in chapter 5).

After some early failures, Nortel adopted an even more thoughtful and perceptive approach that also echoes some of the issues aired in a paper on "Understanding and managing cynicism about organizational change' (Reichers et al., 1997). Of these, three are particularly relevant: credibility, need to see change from the employees' perspective, and provision of opportunities to "air" feelings. The amount of effort displayed by senior management, the radical restructuring, the inclusion of employees in strategy development and customer management, and the support for developing employees were all in place to support performance improvement.

These authors claim that it is possible to distinguish between mere organizational change and transformation. Change, they argue, is constantly occurring; transformation, however, happens only when the logic underpinning the thinking and consequent actions of each of the organizational subgroups becomes realigned (i.e., when the interests of each subgroup are perceived to be consistent with the action that each has taken), a not unreasonable point to which we will return later in chapters 9 and 10.

We selected GI and Nortel because, despite their obvious differences, we feel that they share many features. We think they both succeed at their performance improvement initiatives because they are so strongly aligned to their strategies, which are so carefully socially constructed they could not ever seriously be considered dormant documents.

The input to the strategy formulation was, as the excellence models encourage, comprehensive. It would be wrong to say that the organizations had one particular competitive strategy, as Miles and Snow (1978) or Porter (1985) would promote; rather, they had a set of strategies more in keeping with the Croteau and Bergeron (2001) assessment of organizations. We are not really in a position to say whether they focused on their "core competences" (Hamel and Prahalad, 1994). There is no doubt that both efforts were consonant with Kay's ideas (1993) that a strategy should be consistent with the organization's capabilities, its reputation, ability to innovate, strategic assets, and network of relationships; certainly both senior managements take the organization's reputation extremely seriously and attempt to build it at every opportunity, not in a hollow way but through performance gains. Although there was the possibility for strategies to emerge, by far the most striking feature was the "deliberate" approach to improvement as a strategy (Mintzberg, 1998).

Conclusions

One of the underlying questions in this chapter has been whether, because no one really agrees on what strategy is or how one should go about devising it, devoting time to strategy is worthwhile. As has been pointed out, Nucor manages without what most people would regard as a formal strategy—and performs well. Porter may have thought in 1985 that Japanese companies did not have strategies as he would understand them; few would argue that they have lacked the ability to compete internationally. Perhaps the discussion should not be centered on whether a formal strategy does or does not exist in the organization but rather on the benefits that follow from the processes that the development and implementation of strategies, such as performance improvement, bring about. Our cases illustrate that to affect performance improvement materially any strategy has to be intricately aligned and integrated.

Summary conclusions

This chapter has discussed:

- Approaches in the literature to strategy
- The similarities of two different organizations, including:
  - the holistic approach to developing strategy
  - the thoroughness of implementing
  - the need to set up good sets of external relations to sustain momentum.

Discussion questions

- Think of an organization with which you are familiar. Who would be the external stakeholders who would keep tabs on progress?
- What would you do to manage contradictions in the way strategy is implemented?
- Does the strategy formulation process need to be inclusive?

Further reading

Andrews, R., Boyne, G.A., Walker, R.M. 2006. Strategy Content and Organizational Performance: An Empirical Analysis. *Public Administration Review* 66 (1):52–63.

Inkpen, A., Choudhury, N. 1995. The Seeking of Strategy where it is not—Towards a Theory of Strategy Absence. *Strategic Management Journal* 16 (4):313–23.

Kay, J. 1993. *Foundations of Corporate Success: How Corporate Strategies Add Value*. Oxford: Oxford University Press.

4 Performance measurement

Summary introduction

This chapter discusses:

- The roots of current performance measures
- Self-generated performance measures
- A comparison of external frameworks for performance measurement
- A locally devised performance measurement system at Astra Zeneca
- A corporate-wide system customized for a unit of Organon Teknika
- The vexed relationship between measurement systems and improvement.

Introduction

The study of what constitutes work and how it should be assessed must surely be as old and as venerable as the human race. In one way or other, people must have had to work out how best to hunt, to sow seed, to cultivate, and to harvest. Inevitably this would have involved determining how effectively the processes associated with these operations were being carried out. Effectiveness is a core concept of modern management and depends on an understanding of the process and an ability to measure it. In this chapter, we explore the development of various attempts to measure performance that have the objective of improving processes and entire organizations. Abdel-Maksoud et al. (2005) conducted a literature survey and found that improvement initiatives, such as total quality management (TQM) had a better chance of success if coupled with performance measurement systems and that these initiatives required systems that went beyond solely financial measurement. The literature on performance measurement is so diverse that many areas of management consider it their "patch," including most notably accountancy; however, Ittner and Larker (1998) surveyed the literature and subdivided its approaches into three categories: value-based, nonfinancial, and public sector. Waggoner et al. (1999) construct six: engineering, systems, management accounting, statistical, consumer marketing, and conformance to specification approaches.

Ittner and Larker's review concludes with asserting that performance measurement has shifted from process control to customer satisfaction. This chapter details this shift. We begin by focusing on how individual performance has been measured in the carrying out of basic processes, as we believe there are important parallels between this and the development of every system. The pattern nowadays is to recognize that measurement systems have to include the context more and possess criteria devoted to stakeholder requirements.

We begin by exploring how early work on measuring the labor process developed and go on to discuss how these approaches have expanded to encapsulate the entire organization. The most popular performance measurement system in the organization (Pun and White, 2005) is the "balanced scorecard" (Kaplan and Norton, 1992), so we discuss it in the context of our understanding that many organizations use some form of internal scorecard at the early stages of their attempts to improve the organization as a whole and then move on to achieving external confirmation and accreditation. There are many examples of outside sources of criteria sets, such as the Baldrige process in the United States or the Deming and Shingo prizes from Japan. Our access was mainly through European Foundation for Quality Management (EFQM) contacts, so it is perhaps not surprising that it crops up in our research more than most. We use this chapter as an opportunity to identify how alike or different the EFQM model is from other options.

Over the years, performance measurement appears to have grown exponentially, its scope of coverage, the detail and analysis; however, this view stems from an overly narrow focus on well-known people and practices; much of what is considered "new" has been about for decades if not centuries! Unlike, for example, such measures as temperature, there are no "variables" as such but activities open to interpretation. Our cases illustrate the options available to managers thinking about their performance measurement system. The first, Astra Zeneca, is where one site's attempt to initiate "in-house" performance measures derived much benefit for the subunit but did not appear to be enough to sustain the effort. The second is Organon Teknika, where a wider system of "evidence of success" statements seemed to us to be more "embedded" for the long term. We discuss the implications of these cases, particularly that keeping performance measures relevant is key to sustaining effort. The setup and running costs even for a year-long project are not sensible. All forms of system begin from a basic understanding of the tasks carried out; the next section of the chapter discusses well-known approaches and how they were developed.

Pioneers

We begin with an overview of the work of some famous pioneers in the area and comment on their wider significance. Though there is some evidence that one Walter of Henley (Currie, 1977, p. 4) as far back as the thirteenth century measured how to plow to best advantage and, later, that no less a genius than Leonardo Da Vinci was keenly interested in establishing the best way for a man to shovel earth (Currie, 1977, pp. 4–5), the distinguished mathematician Charles Babbage, working in the early part of the nineteenth century, seems to provide the first example of the measurement of work being applied in management. Babbage may be recognized uniquely as the inventor of the first mechanical computer, but he—more than any other author of the time—initiated and developed a scientific approach to the study of management. To do this, it appears that he first divided the task into its constituent elements, emphasizing the importance of balancing the individual operations in a process and the principle of optimum size for the manufacturing unit for each product group. This is a common feature of every performance measurement approach or system we have encountered. (Though F. W. Taylor is universally recognized as the "father of scientific management," Babbage's contribution to the topic might well earn him grandfather status!) As Hopper et al. (1998) note, performance measurement is the application of scientific method to organization processes, and criticisms about scientific method and its applicability particularly to the social life apply equally well to performance measurement systems.

As early as 1800, the Soho Engineering Foundry of Boulton, Watt and Company provided one of the earliest examples of scientific management in operation. Even in those far-off days, many modern practices seem to have been in use, even including techniques such as market research, production planning, and cost accounting (George, 1972). Moreover, much attention was paid to working conditions and even to the provision of housing for employees. About the same time in New Lanark on the banks of the River Clyde in Scotland, Robert Owen was also demonstrating that the exploitation of labor need not be a necessary concomitant to the process of industrialization. Owen was decades ahead of his time in paying at least as much attention to the welfare of his employees as to their output; in particular, he established better working conditions for his employees, even extending to the provision of housing and schooling facilities for their children (George, 1972, pp. 62–3). Over-reliance on financial criteria (Kaplan and Norton, 1992) may well be a comparatively recent phenomenon.

Many books discuss the input of F. W. Taylor to work measurement (see, for example, Buchanan and Huczynski, 1985), and the labor process debate was started when Braverman (1974) critiqued many of the practices

Taylor was assumed to have invented. We would like to point out that Taylor was not the zealot that he is often portrayed; originally, he was successful in his application for Harvard Law School but unfortunately, early problems with his eyesight meant he had to change his career plans. His initial job at the Midvale Steel Works was as a laborer but, with improvement in his sight, Taylor rose through the ranks to the position of chief engineer while studying in the evenings for the degree of master of engineering.

Taylor began to appreciate shortcomings in how the plant was managed, in particular that management had little or no understanding of its responsibilities, especially as to what constituted a fair day's work or output. Taylor tried to persuade his people to step up output, which they were restricting because they thought this would lead to greater job security. He soon realized that ignorance about measurement and production planning of individual operations lay at the heart of the problem. He concluded that timing with a stopwatch offered the most satisfactory means of establishing, reasonably accurately, standards by which output could be determined. Taylor also began to appreciate that jobs would have to be divided up into their constituent elements, each of which would have to be measured several times over, to work out an appropriate set of figures that could be relied on to provide worthwhile data for management. He chose to time better-than-average employees, asserting that this was the correct approach to adopt. At the same time, he also appreciated that to persuade a first-class man to do his best he would need to introduce an incentive payment of about 30 percent above average wages. If the work was particularly onerous physically, this premium might have to be increased perhaps to 50 to 60 percent (Currie, 1977, p. 14). Taylor joined the American Society of Mechanical Engineers to exchange ideas, and the major interest was in his piece-rate system rather than on his approaches to measurement.

While Taylor's work is well known, the people who are most widely recognized for their contribution are the Gilbreths—Frank and his wife, Lilian. Frank, in common with F. W. Taylor, had an early change of career and spent some time on the shop floor before progressing up the organization. This was extremely rapid, so much so that he went into the contracting business on his own so successfully that by the time he was twenty-seven, he had offices in New York, Boston, and London!

Gilbreth concentrated on finding the "one best way" of carrying out a particular task (Gilbreth and Carey, 1949) by analyzing in appropriate detail the individual elements of which it was composed, sometimes using a cine camera to facilitate this process, as Maray had done several decades earlier (Corbett, 2006). Once the job had been recorded for analysis, the individual elements of which it was comprised could then be examined to establish whether there was a better way of carrying them out. Perhaps

Frank's most significant contribution to management was the development of a series of symbols called *Therbligs* that captured the seventeen basic elements of hand work (Currie, 1977, p. 87), in effect initiating the concept of motion study.

After Frank's tragic early death in 1924, his widow, Lilian, who had trained as a psychologist at the University of California, resolved to carry on and develop his work further. She extended and improved Frank's techniques; for example, along with medical personnel, she applied her skills and knowledge of motion study to enable physically handicapped people to do more things for themselves at home, notably developing the "Heart Kitchen" for the New York Heart Association. In 1966, when she was no less than eighty-eight years old, she was awarded the Hoover Medal, the supreme U.S. engineering award, recognition for her distinguished public service and eminence in engineering—a worthy tribute to arguably the most illustrious woman management scientist. Full of years, Lilian Gilbreth died in 1972 aged 94 (Currie, 1976, p. 30).

The Gilbreths innovated by widening the range of processes and organizations undertaking measurement and popularized the use of graphical representation of processes and the idea of "one best way" to carry out a task. These approaches became known as work study, which was the label applied to management's attempt to secure the best use of the human and material resources available to an organization. It has three key features: the most effective use of plant and equipment, of human effort and the evaluation of human work. It is defined (British Standard (BS) 3138:1969) as a management service based on the techniques, particularly method study and work measurement, used in the examination of human work in all its contexts and which lead to the systematic investigation of all the resources and factors that affect the efficiency and economy of the situation being reviewed to direct improvement. Once the "best method" has been determined for a given operation, it is necessary to measure how long it takes to perform—and the conditions under which it has to be undertaken. This means that an adequate record of observed times for carrying out the specified task has to be built up. For each set of observations, the effectiveness of the worker, who must be skilled and properly experienced in performing the given task, has also to be evaluated. The process is highly contentious as it critically affects people's skill levels and pay (Braverman, 1974). A norm is fixed giving the ideal of effectiveness a value of 100, which is designated the standard rate of working. Observers are trained to recognize the degree to which a worker's observed speed and effectiveness varies from the 100 concept. The procedure by which this is accomplished is known as *rating* (Currie, 1977, p. 148). This process requires considerable skill, training, and experience to accomplish competently. The observer has to make a series of judgments, carried out simultaneously with the timing of the task, gauging for example such factors as speed of movement, effort, dexterity, and consistency that the worker is exercising. The observer has also to recognize that workers require to take appropriate rest that ensures that they are not worn out.

In summary, measuring involves relating timing to cost and quality, and employees' work is analyzed and represented by observers using stopwatches, symbols, and charts to form an ideal standard for the activity, which often forms the basis of the person's pay and is thus highly contentious. The chapter continues by reviewing how internal systems that are in effect aggregates of ideas from the pioneers have gained popularity.

Internally developed performance measurement systems

The techniques to analyze individual processes have been combined so that some forms of measure for organization effectiveness have been derived. Abdel-Maksoud et al. (2005, p. 264) identified a list of common categories from their survey of the literature: "product quality, customer satisfaction, on time delivery, employee morale, efficiency and utilization, and product development." Much of the recent literature focuses on the balanced scorecard (BSC) that was developed by two American academics who also consulted, Kaplan and Norton (1992). Francis et al. (2005), reviewing performance measurement systems in the airline industry, noted that the BSC was the most popular approach. Pun and White (2005) have created a very useful recent review and cite the force of the technique as lying in its ability to encapsulate and tier measures, motivate people, and encode a process and improvement emphasis that should all lead to the creation of stakeholder value as opposed to short-term profits. As outlined in Figure 4.1, the "card" lists objectives divided into four categories: financial, customer, internal business, and learning and growth. It then details the measures aimed at achieving these, specifying for each the associated linking initiatives, the target level, and the actual level of the measure for the current period. The BSC was so titled by Kaplan and Norton (1992) because it attempted to balance financial performance with these other criteria (see Figure 4.1).

The idea is that the card is "scored" on a cyclical basis, with organizations building up a track record of performance. Evans (2004) notes that the length of time an organization uses the technique is positively associated with the results. Tuomela (2005) agrees with Kaplan and Norton (1992) that a balanced scorecard can both shape and deploy strategies. The "3K" scorecard he observed in Asea Brown Bovari became a source of useful interaction between people to generate improvement ideas and bond as an organization.

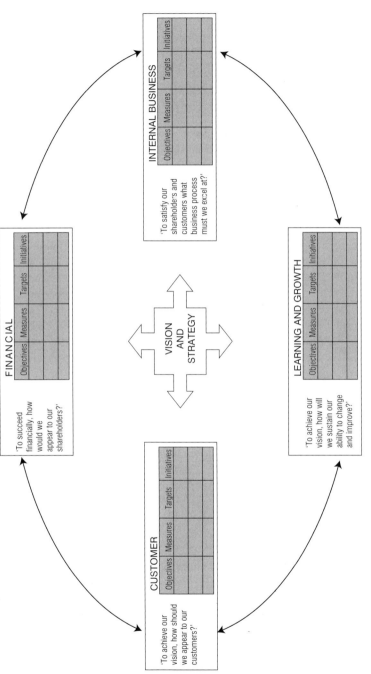

Figure 4.1 Kaplan and Norton's Balanced Scorecard. (Adapted from: *Translating Vision and Strategy: Four Perspectives,* Balanced Scorecard Collaborative Inc, Robert S. Kaplan, *Management Services,* vol 45 no. 3, p 20.)

Though it has been claimed that the BSC is a significant innovation, Bessire and Baker (2005) point out that many of its features were present in the Tableau de Bord (TdeB) introduced into French organizations in the 1930s. The TdeB, too, had emerged to redress the emphasis also given then to accounting information. The engineers who conceived it regarded performance data as the prime source of intelligence, pointing to where the organization was heading. The TdeB is based on the idea that one should select and monitor "key" variables and that these can be both proactive and reactive about controlling operations or monitoring improvements based on strategies. There can be "cascading" TdeBs, and the key variables should be reviewed regularly to ensure relevance. The academics Bessire and Baker (2005) recently produced a critical analysis of both the BSC and the TdeB, noting the similarity of both techniques in creating mutual understanding of objectives and performance. However, Bessire and Baker are somewhat skeptical that the benefits claimed from the use of the BSC will materialize without the help of consultants! They are not the only ones with reservations!

Meyer (2005) argues that the BSC does not measure what it is intended to and is the wrong tool for the application. He thinks that there could be clearer guidance for its disaggregation in organizations. Ittner and Larcker (1998) wonder whether the benefits of any system are outweighed by the cost of the bureaucracy involved in sustaining it. Otley (1999) makes it clear that critical analysis of the linkages between financial and nonfinancial performance measures as they are presented in the BSC have yet to be thoroughly researched. Moreover, target setting is not mentioned despite its prime importance for the BSC. However, it should also be recognized that this is a spin-off; the Holy Grail is to establish valid relationships between the measures, a point that Evans (2004) stresses. Only then should they properly be used for target setting. The writers seem to have a hopelessly positivist notion of the organization. The managers we have interviewed understand that true causality is very hard to establish and, at best, tentative associations form the basis of an implementation.

There are surprisingly few detailed case studies of the BSC in use. One such is Tuomela's study of FinABB (2005). The scorecard there was based on three underlying principles: the 3Ks, which stand for Kehitys, meaning development or improvement; Kasvu, meaning growth; and Kannattavuus, meaning profitability. The constituent elements of the 3K scorecard are core competence development, internal effectiveness, customer satisfaction, profitability, and growth. In the course of the 3K development process, the main objective was pinpointed as being the key importance of communicating customer focus through diagnostic control. As the true nature of interdependence within the organization emerged, a major element seems to have been the measurement team meetings held as essential and appreciated features in developing the scorecard. The use of strategic maps facilitated the clarification of what had earlier seemed to have been somewhat tentative definitions of cause-and-effect relationships. There appears to have been a desire initially to establish the 3K scorecard as a means of reviewing managerial rewards and an expectation that its introduction would lead to improved financial performance but, because managers had themselves been deeply involved in developing the system for their own learning purposes, this connection seemed to assume a less critical role.

Two other issues worthy of note were associated with the use of nonfinancial interactive control measures and emerged in one of our case companies, Organon Teknica. Firstly, these measures seem to have created circumstances wherein more information about peer and subordinates' performance became available than had been the case before. As this did not involve financial data, it was claimed that this might disrupt the power structures within the organization. It was contended, for example, that in-depth knowledge of customers implies an informal power dimension that those who possessed it might be reluctant to share! The second issue concerned the additional workload that the gathering of the extensive further information for the 3K scorecard imposed. Not only was this significant in itself but the number and length of meetings to review this and the requirement for interactive control that was an inevitable, and essential, by-product of the approach, generated issues that had to be confronted and resolved. Authors such as Ittner and Larker (1998) have noted the point about increasing bureaucracy before; nobody we know has remarked on the knowledge management issue. Understandably, Tuomela concludes that "it is not just the specific control tools (like the Balanced Scorecard) that are used but the way they are applied that should be taken into account." He emphasizes that though "The use of performance measurement systems has implications for all levels of control; the interactive use of performance management systems has some special benefits and challenges when compared to diagnostic controlling" (Tuomela, 2005, p. 314).

External frameworks for assessment

Evans (2004, 221) says, "Basically, the difference between the Kaplan and Norton framework and Baldrige is a matter of semantics." However, many organizations struggle to devise systems, and outside input can help with the definition of criteria and areas for improvement. In this section, we discuss the contribution that government and major business associations have made to performance measurement through their design and dissemination of frameworks for self-assessment: awards of prizes. Frameworks have been presented to guide organizations as to which criteria they should pay attention when designing performance measurement systems. Once they think they are sufficiently qualified, managers can enter their organization for external assessment and perhaps the award of a prize. By and large, these frameworks have been designed to improve competitive performance. Although predating the BSC, as Evans (2004) implies, they are a form of "balanced scorecard."

The oldest award is the Deming Prize (http://www.juse.or.jp/e/index.html), instigated to acknowledge the contribution of W. Edwards Deming to Japanese manufacturing competitiveness. The Union of Japanese Scientists and Engineers (JUSE) administers the prize. Any organization or clear subunit, regardless of the type of industry, public or private, large or small, located anywhere in the world, can apply for the prize. Applicant companies write a submission and are examined by the Deming Application Prize Sub-committee; on the basis of this test, all organizations that score the passing points or better are awarded the Deming Application Prize. Thus, there is no limit to the number of recipients each year.

Award of the prize is made to an applicant company that effectively practises TQM appropriate to its management principles, type of industry, and business scope. Unlike most other organizations awarding prizes in this area, the Deming Prize committee does not publicize a framework to guide organizations; it requires them to be operating TQM. The overlap between the key concepts of TQM and popular frameworks is displayed in Table 4.1.

The Shingo Prize for Excellence in Manufacturing is a comparatively recent addition; it was established in 1988 to promote awareness of "lean manufacturing" concepts and to recognize organizations that achieve world-class manufacturing status. It is regarded as one of the premier manufacturing awards; indeed, *Business Week* terms it "the Nobel Prize of Manufacturing." It highlights the value of adopting world-class manufacturing practices to attain world-class status. The Prize, though centered in the United States, is also open to business manufacturers in Canada and Mexico and to public-sector manufacturing in the United States. The award recognizes the work of the late Shigeo Shingo, the Japanese manufacturing engineer who developed the Toyota production system. The Shingo Prize Model includes eleven key elements thought critical to world-class manufacturing and bears a similarity to the other frameworks shown below. In common with all prizes, the criteria do not entail specific methods, techniques, practice, or processes. Rather, they suggest areas and leave the specific ways to improvement open to the organizations to decide.

The Baldrige Award

Concern about the decline in American productivity and loss of competitive edge in the early 1980s motivated the then President Reagan to sponsor a

Table 4.1 A synthesis of framework "criteria"

	Deming (based on 1986 book)	Shingo (based on award criteria)	Baldrige (based on model criteria)	EFQM (based on model criteria)
Leadership	Yes	Yes	Yes	Yes
Strategy	Yes	Yes	Yes	Yes
Process improvement	Yes	Yes	Yes	Yes
Customer focus results	Yes	Yes	Yes	Yes
People development	Yes	Yes	Yes	Yes
Society and environment	Yes	Yes	Yes	Yes
Innovation and learning	Yes	Yes	Yes	Yes
Performance results	Yes	Yes	Yes	Yes
Supply chain management	Yes	Yes	Yes	Yes

series of study conferences to examine why this was happening. Their final report recommended that something along the lines of the Deming Prize in Japan should be instigated. The Baldrige Award, (http://www.quality. nist.gov/) named after the then Secretary of Commerce, was established by the U.S. Senate in August 1987. The Baldrige Criteria are the bases for organizational self-assessment, for making awards, and for giving feedback to applicants. Externally set, these generic criteria closely resemble the other frameworks, although minor adjustments have been made over the years. Again, an organization familiarizes itself with the criteria, amasses a performance track record, and composes a submission. Though the applicants for the national award are comparatively small, there are a host of state "daughter" organizations using the criteria and receiving local applications. Only companies operating in the United States and in Canada and Mexico are eligible to enter for the award; they compete in one of three groups covering manufacturing, service, and small business. Assessment is carried out by a panel of about six or seven examiners skilled and trained in evaluating organizational performance. They read a formal submission and operate in teams to carry out a thorough on-site appraisal of the candidate company, scoring criteria elements out of a possible total of 1,000 points. Each year no more than two companies in each group may receive this prestigious award, though frequently fewer than that number are given. Over the years, we have been fascinated to watch how the models have impacted on one another, and it is fair to say that one of the most influential is the EFQM.

The European Foundation for Quality Management Model for Business Excellence

By 1987, several Europeans had noted the success of the Deming and Baldrige awards in driving performance improvement. In the next year, fourteen leading businesses took the initiative of forming the European Foundation for Quality Management (EFQM). Membership has now grown to around 800 organizations, drawn from most European countries and encompassing most business sectors, sharing the apparent lack of coverage of the Baldrige model; however, it must be appreciated that again there are daughter organizations in many countries spreading the use of the model. The EFQM presents a framework and a process that is theorized with improved performance. A key feature of EFQM's mission is to encourage self-assessment as a most effective means of improving business performance. The Model, introduced in 1991 to promote this approach, is also the basis for the European Quality Award. The EFQM describes self-assessment as "a comprehensive, systematic and regular review by an organization of its activities and results, referenced against a model of business excellence" (http://www.efqm.org). Whether the organization stops short with self-assessment or submits itself for an externally assessed award, the same framework model applies. The EFQM Excellence Model is based on remarkably familiar criteria (see Table 4.1).

We have prepared this table very crudely and would hate to be thought to misrepresent any one set of ideas! It is possible to see different emphases and priorities in the different frameworks; obviously, we are being unfair to the Deming award by "giving" it criteria, but if the applicants follow Mr. Deming's ideas, they will cover these areas. In the early days, the Baldrige model gave greater emphasis to, for example, partnering, and the EFQM adjusted one of its criteria to reflect this. By far the most influential

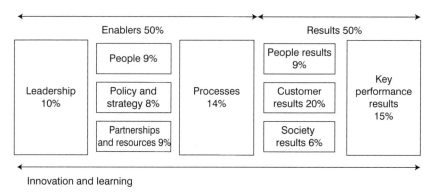

Figure 4.2 The EFQM model of business excellence (EFQM, 1999)

aspect of any model has been the EFQM's encoding of "enablers" and results explicitly adopted by the Baldrige at a later stage (Figure 4.2).

The model encodes the idea of prevention: by developing the left-hand-side criteria, the right-hand performance results will be attained. As with the Baldrige Model, the framework represents the "top" tier. Every criterion has several subcriteria that give more guidance to organizations as to what to do and also what to measure; the organization is scored out of 1,000 possible points. Blue Circle, Nortel, and Govan Initiative, mentioned in chapters 2 and 3, used this model to drive their improvements. Instead of thinking up their own particular scorecards, they examined the EFQM and tailored it to their requirements. Though each of the frameworks we have outlined is well-known, we take this opportunity to discuss two cases wherein the organizations developed their own framework, not atypical for global organizations; however, these cases detail local initiatives to develop performance measurement systems and tie in with the discussion on Balanced Scorecards:

Astra Zeneca

The site we studied at Yalding in Kent has been subject to ownership changes over the last fifteen years. At the time of our research, Zeneca had been recently merged with Astra. Again, like many of our other cases, the site's viability was precarious; for example, there had been several waves of rationalization, and a driver for improvement was to create a justification for retaining the site. The business had successful products, but the financial and operational considerations at corporate level frequently affected performance; for example, in 1994–1995, a board edict to reduce stocks, then unacceptably high, happened to coincide with an increase in sales, which meant the sites struggled to provide a satisfactory level of service, not made any easier when a new enterprise resource planning (ERP) system was introduced in 1995–1996. Its implementation was complicated by a serious loss of product and customer data. At the same time, market growth had generated higher volume sales in greater variety coupled with a more complex range of package types and by the Amistar product launch. The Yalding packaging and distribution unit was at the heart of the action taken to deal with the situation.

Mixing and packing had been consolidated at two large units, one being Yalding in Kent, UK, despite some misgivings. The unit responded positively to this challenge by beginning the Yalding Improvement Plan (YIP), aimed at improving performance while simultaneously ensuring that current standards were at least maintained. The company was experienced at improvement initiatives. When we visited the site, we interviewed a person who had worked in the area of improvement for at least two decades, and he told us that the organization had had phases of pursuing quality assurance and TQM. (For example, ISO9002 had been achieved worldwide in 1997.)

The YIP was linked to the annual business plan. One of its prime aims was to achieve a degree of focus that may have been absent in the past—perhaps the origin of comments that the organization was rich in ideas and initiatives but whose full potential was seldom realized! Its objectives were first, to deliver improved customer service, and in doing so, to achieve improved credibility; second, to maintain or improve standards of operation; and, finally, to develop action aimed at continuous improvement.

The YIP was perceived as part of a change process encompassing the whole site. It required the establishment of a project team to involve all staff from the start in generating their own improvement plans. Each team member had to commit both as an individual and as a team member. This approach marked a major cultural change. Traditionally, as part of the chemical industry, scientists and engineers have tended to develop and operate processes with a fair degree of authoritarianism. Sometimes this had meant that satisfying the customer had not been a top priority! The innovative approach was top-down-directed; its aim was to be the establishment of common levels and measures of performance and their translation into specific actions for improvement. Each department was required to present its own improvement plan to the business director.

The YIP enabled staff to focus on the supply of every order on time in full (OTIF), as a set of common measures that were relatively straightforward to monitor. The target figures for this particular measure were 95 percent leaving the Yalding site, which was not met in the first few months for reasons associated with the ERP software system. Though the full management team participated in developing measures for the whole site, individual sections devised measures that they decided were appropriate for their own departmental purposes. The way in which these measures were developed set the tone for the project, with management emphasizing maximum people involvement. Eight common measures were agreed to enable OTIF and site export order quality performance to be determined by the whole site. The first six were:

1. Section OTIF
2. Filled-pack quality checks
3. Software system stock accuracy
4. Routing accuracy
5. Number of customer complaints
6. Routing efficiency.

On the twelfth of each month, the results for the preceding month were displayed on twenty-two boards located throughout the somewhat cramped factory. To make the YIP concept real, the team had to agree on the crucial areas demanding attention.

Communication was immediately identified as one, particularly as a workforce survey revealed that one-half claimed they had at no time received any information directly from management. Lack of responsiveness of the Yalding site to the marketplace was the second area to be addressed. The third focused on the unsatisfactory site materials handling arrangements that the company tackled by putting these operations out to tender in association with an external logistics operator. (The successful firm now removes the palletized product from the end of the production line and distributes it in accordance with customer requirements, an operation it claims to carry out in partnership with Yalding.) Given how the decision was taken, unsurprisingly, this arrangement initially generated some hostility from employees whose jobs were now handled by contractors.

The introduction of the YIP included the establishment of measures in the people-management area, particularly in identifying potential and in enhancing individual skills. In a departure from the seniority-based system that had long determined promotion and progression, a skills matrix that was developed enabled individuals to add to their expertise and so attain higher skill levels. This enabled them to carry out more-complex, responsible, and highly paid tasks and was seen as a key element in the individuals' self-fulfillment. The routes by which this could be accomplished were thoroughly explained to the whole workforce. The YIP was well and widely publicized, and several ways of promoting the attainment of its objectives were devised.

A team-based short-term incentive scheme based on OTIF was introduced to inject emphasis. Though two teams (out of seven) were unable to attain the targets they had been set, nonetheless one of these succeeded in "delighting" its customers. Recognition of target achievement was given by a surprise "Saturday marquee" jazz party organized by management but only after a careful audit confirmed that the target set had been attained. Finally, a bulletin with workforce input showing celebrities as staff noted in a humorous way memorable milestones along the road.

A further illustration of the major change in Yalding culture concerned a new product introduction. Before this was set up, the workforce were given the opportunity of suggesting how this should be done. The table on which these proposals were to be placed was submerged in suggestions! As a result, the old and outmoded suggestion scheme was replaced by a more effective and relevant arrangement.

The problem of ineffective communication identified by a staff survey led to set mechanisms being put in place to ensure that people are kept fully informed. These include quarterly meetings with the whole workforce—a sizeable commitment as six meetings are needed to cover everyone. The performance targets and monthly achievement boards throughout the site also address this. Progress toward attainment of objectives generated through individual team efforts is regularly reported in person to the business director. "Listening" by senior management to what people really have to say during the performance review was linked to a drop over eighteen months of 50 percent in process absence rates. Positive feedback from customers on service levels has been reported and is publicized in the company bulletin.

Despite this, when we visited the organization, they were looking to create "YIP2," which they thought built on the "process and people" measures of YIP. It was felt that YIP did not go far enough, though managers were struggling to devise something as attractive as YIP had seemed to be. It was almost as if this were like a movie sequel. They were still at the thought stage and had come up with a Greek temple building–type drawing, with the pillars consisting of safety, health and environment, information systems, procedures, training, and self-discipline. This was intended to highlight interrelationships and assist in creating tiers of measurement points in the system. It seemed to us that perhaps the old engineering method of solving the problem might be hampering them; our knowledge of the use of the EFQM in broadening systems could have helped, but the managers wanted it to be grown internally.

Organon Teknika

Organon Teknika (OT) is one of five companies that make up the Pharma Group within the worldwide Akzo Nobel organization. The group employs some 3,000 people internationally, of whom about eighty are based at Cambridge. The company is organized into four divisions: pharmaceutical, microbiology, hemostasis, and general diagnostics,; together with support services covering technical, secretarial, financial, and marketing areas. The complex technical characteristics of the products and services that the company offers entail methodical management of its supply chain. This aspect of its operations is not only important in satisfying its customers' needs but critical to the company's prosperity. In the early 1990s, Organon had judged it important not only to improve their own performance but at the same time to demonstrate to their customers what had been achieved and how it was to be evaluated. They chose to follow a quality agenda to do so. However, the divisional managers were unable to commit themselves wholly to the form of TQM that the company advocated at that time; the initiative consequently failed.

Coincidentally, about the same time, a support group of Organon's parent company, Akzo Nobel, had completed the development of a performance improvement program—Managing Total Quality (Gilbert, 1993)—based on procedures that the consultants 3M had originally devised and applied extensively to organizations in the United States. Subsequently, the Akzo department and 3M worked together to produce a bespoke version for the Akzo group. A pilot study in early 1994 yielded sufficiently encouraging results for the MTQ program to be applied throughout Organon; MTQ is founded on four concepts termed *Akzo Basic Cornerstones* (ABCs) with which are associated ten Akzo Building blocks (ABBs). The cornerstones are management commitment, conformance to customer expectations, prevention and, finally, goal setting and achievement, wherein the emphasis is quite specifically on measurement and comparison with past results. Akzo's ten building blocks comprise seven typical components of a quality initiative: leadership, training, customer focus, measurement, communication, planning, and recognition along with three others that are rather distinctive—work = process, organization and teamwork, and projects (design, development, and execution). MTQ defines work = process as a sequence of actions and tasks that results in products or services for a customer, the symbol bringing out their interlinking nature.

At the heart of the approach that Teknika has now adopted, the company each year prepares a quality plan (AQP) to translate into practical terms its vision statement that "Superiority and speed bring survival and success." This is the mechanism by means of which the company's "in- house" or local strategy is developed and implemented. By specifying areas for improvement in each sector of the company, the plan facilitates the identification of "quality" projects to address the problems highlighted. Projects may originate from many different sources, the departmental discussion groups held six times annually being a major source. Once a project has been identified, a project leader is designated and empowered to carry it through. The leader then decides who else is to be involved (personnel are normally involved in no more than two projects simultaneously), what the project is to be called, and what timescale is to be allowed for completion. The team begins with a brainstorming session at which it will set down all the cognate issues, map their inter-relationship, and establish what can be immediately achieved. It will next determine the preproject situation against which to evaluate the extent of the improvements ultimately brought about and set down what it hopes it will achieve and how its objectives are to be accomplished. "Action points" are then chosen, and a timetable is fixed.

After deciding what resources are required to carry out the project, the team will specify, as far as it is able, measures against which its outcome can be assessed. Authorization to proceed will then be sought. In setting team objectives, the need to achieve consensus is seen as important; individual input is valued, and assumption of ownership is deemed critical. The extent to which the plan has been successfully implemented is evaluated by measures, termed *evidences of success*, which the company then uses to gauge its progress in tackling the issues pinpointed in the plan. These are single-focus goals, which reflect legitimate and measurable achievements.

Projects are "scored" by a company team, and results are well publicized for their positive impact on people.

A project from Organon's diagnostics division illustrates how the approach operates. In the 1998 Annual Quality Plan for this division, the first topic to be addressed was to develop areas for improvement based on the results of the 1998 sales performance and tracking survey. (The biennial survey prepared by independent market research consultants for the company had stressed the importance of this topic and listed where action was required.)

Accordingly, a quality improvement project was initiated with the detailed remit to develop arrangements to improve in four specific areas identified as (1) clarification of call structure and "follow-up," (2) style of communications, (3) clear delivery of information, and (4) problem and query handling. The team assigned to the project had five members (four from the divisional sales force) and was led by a member of the company's steering team. The success of the project was to be assessed by measuring, for each of the salespeople involved, the extent of improvement over a specified time period in six elements of their face-to-face customer negotiations. These were communication style; call structure; explanation of call purpose; agreement on "next call" objectives; summarizing the call messages; and lastly clarity of information presentation. The team decided that six field visits were to be made by each sales person accompanied by the manager; the outcomes of each call would be scored by the manager to reflect whether the way in which these elements were now being handled had improved and to what extent. (Where a need for further improvement had been revealed, this would also be noted and acted on.) In his report on the completed project, the divisional manager commented that during the twenty-four accompanied calls, the issue of problem-query handling had arisen so irregularly that it could not be scored. With that single qualification, the results for the other three areas (1), (2), and (3) disclosed "a satisfactory increase to maximum scores." The project had two outcomes,: the first being that the team amended the coaching plan to address the specific areas identified for improvement and the second being that a laminated "reminder" card was prepared to prompt salespeople of the revised approach.

The evidences of success enables the extent of attainment to be quantified and allows for appropriate action to be taken—perhaps by way of a project—where problems have arisen. It is interesting that, in some instances, after several years these may no longer reflect the current interests of the organization. Though it is important to have continuity in measurement, this can sometimes be at the expense of relevance. At the beginning, the employees were involved in improving the processes before they were encoded in the measurement system, and they chose to simplify and show the relationships between many processes in a way that they could be managed better. The company was part of a huge organization with access to resources and a comprehensive framework and system. Astra Zeneca was similarly resourced, but the local management was determined to create its own pattern and use it to drive improvements and market its site. There would not have been the same kudos for it in following a corporate or external framework.

Discussion

If we compare the cases to the ideas we discussed earlier, both organizations accelerated their improvements by coupling them to a new measurement system (Abdel-Maksoud et al., 2005). It is fair to say that Organon Teknika's system and improvements were far more established and so they derived more benefits (Evans, 2004). However, we would say that despite being engaged in the process for longer, the impetus was greater than the Yalding attempts, which seemed to be petering out at our last contact. The Yalding measures were still very much at the level of the pioneers: Processes were being timed, ideal routes were being developed—which is, of course, a very good place to start! We think we can safely say that the system emphasis had not shifted to a wider range of stakeholders (Ittner and Larker, 1998); the proposals for the YIP2 were developments on existing criteria and were, as such, not fully "balanced" (Kaplan and Norton, 1996). There was a very sensible emphasis on developing employees and a carefully drawn up skills matrix along which people could progress, but we had doubts about how engaged shop floor employees were in the process, judging by their response to the supply chain outsourcing. They had clearly not been involved in that decision, and any resentment had not been addressed. The picture was very different at Organon Teknika, where similar efforts had been made in developing employee skills and the relevant employees were involved in decisions about their part of the process. Employees were responsible for mapping out their processes, so much so that one person's office space was the butt of jokes as it had so many charts on the wall. OT had several tiers in the measurement system (Kaplan and Norton, 1996), and they had thought out the linkages and dependencies, though it would be fair to say that both cases had few "causal" measures they discussed with us in the way that the EFQM model is set up with "enablers" and "results"—AZ were results driven, OT had a mix.

Both organizations would say that in no way did the setup and running costs outweigh the benefits, so they did not encounter Ittner and Larcker's concern (1998). Both sets of employees could point to unintended benefits from initiating the new system, especially OT, who could showcase employees who had shown considerable skills their managers were not aware they possessed and were thus able to progress up the career ladder.

Although neither company was interested in pursuing external acknowledgment through, for example, the EFQM process, we think that some of the loss of momentum the AZ managers were feeling might have been addressed by doing so. We do not think it could have added much to the OT outcomes, as in effect the differences in the approach were, as Evans (2004) says, down to "semantics."

Conclusions

In this chapter, we have examined forms of measurement systems and how they have evolved from an operations management perspective. We have not especially unpicked the term *measurement* but, suffice to say, our cases demonstrate our concerns about overconfidence in the precision of any system that is applied to social entities such as business organizations. All measurement systems began by detailed analyzes of individual work processes, and some continue (Organon Teknika). Others are driven by "strategies" that, as we discussed in the last chapter, are even more amorphous. There are some inherent contradictions in establishing systems, as once they are set up they might be out of date. However, if systems are changed too often, they fail to assist in determining whether any progress has been made. Comprehensive approaches such as OT's and external frameworks that call for regular reviews as integral to self-assessment are the best hope of maintaining relevance, and we think that if this is addressed, the system will be sustained, because it should be generating information that can support a continuing approach to improvement.

Summary conclusion

This chapter has discussed:

- The historical roots of performance measurement
- Performance measurement systems
- How one company devised their own performance management system, which seemed to lose momentum, because it was very process-based
- How one company subscribed to a corporate system and, by translating it to their own needs, used it to implement major changes and sustain momentum
- How performance measurement systems frequently diverge from process improvement.

Discussion questions

- Why might Deming think performance measurement systems and targets are counter-productive?
- How can interests be sustained in any system?
- What system of measuring performance would you devise for yourself?

Further reading

Meyer, M.W. 2005. Can Performance Studies Create Actionable Knowledge if We Can't Measure the Performance of the Firm? *Journal of Management Inquiry* 14 (3):287–91.

Pun, K.F., White, A.S. 2005. A Performance Measurement Paradigm for Integrating Strategy Formulation: A Review of Systems and Frameworks. *International Journal of Management Reviews* 7 (1):49–71.

Soltani, E., van der Meer, R., Williams, T. M. 2005. A Contrast of HRM and TQM Approaches to Performance Management: Some Evidence. *British Journal of Management* 16:211–30.

Section 2

Improvement as damage

The second section of the book argues that not only can improvement initiatives fail to achieve their objectives; they might even be considered to cause damage. We should warn the reader that we use a very different approach to the topic than is common, again with the intention of being constructive.

As we mentioned in chapter 1, the first chapter in this section is the only one we did not create together; it is a revised version of a paper Lynne wrote with her student, Constanze Hirschhauser, (Baxter and Hirschhauser, 2004). For her research, Constanze carried out her fieldwork in two business units of an automotive company and coined the term *pink factory* to describe the façade that organizations can construct to convey the impression of being engaged in improvements rather than actually making a material difference. To assist our consideration of improvement processes in general, we use the "communities of practice" ideas from Lave and Wenger (1991) and Wenger (1998). We discuss where their ideas assist in change processes in organizations and then discuss where the automotive companies created the impression of improvement and for whom. It was thought important for the company to maintain relationships with their customers, and individuals' career progression, to know the latest trend in improvement more than actually constructing anything meaningful. Delusions are not limited to people in the automotive sector company. A site has featured as a good example in a performance improvement book because the writer was superficial in his or her investigations. The contradictions between the excess capacity in the sector, the reference of manufacturing excellence, and the fabrication of improvements strike us as well worth discussing.

The next chapter is this section explores ideas related to who is the employee and how this affects the day-to-day dynamic of improvement. Most books and articles in the area have a very general approach to the employee. It is almost as if trying to treat everyone the same has clouded fairly obvious differences. It was a feature of our research that organizations that were successful in improving processes and had a balance of men and women to begin with were places wherein women could succeed. Several women progressed up the organization thanks to their participation in improvement initiatives showcasing their skills, leading to a displacement of some men. In the chapter, we discuss how some men lost out in the process but were used as "totems" of the old regime to foster the improvements. The organizations were still controlled by men but men who embodied a different form of masculinity. There is not a "feminizing" of the workforce, but more facilitating men are still in charge. The point of the chapter is to open up discussion on how people as individuals relate to improvement processes and how in future managers hoping to improve processes may well need to have a more subtle conception of the employee as an individual.

The last chapter explores a massive improvement process at a major European airport. The airport had absorbed the current business wisdom of acquiring more and more customers and channeling them through their "hub." Coupled with the increase in travel, it faced a huge capacity problem. It chose to restructure its operations using business process reengineering (BPR), with a "big-bang" approach developed with the premier consultants in the sector. The approach was rejected by the staff, and a modified alternative was introduced much more slowly. We use the analogy of diet and fitness and between BPR and cosmetic surgery, especially liposuction, contrasting this with the more incremental approach of continuous improvement. BPR was appealing as a quick fix; however, it did not really address the underlying problem. We hope the use of the metaphor encourages people to think about the long-term implications of initiatives and the role of consultants in creating visions of what might be, which prove impossible to realize with the material at hand. Improvement approaches might appear to take longer if a more incremental approach is used, but frequently big-bang approaches end up being incremental!

5 Superficiality

Summary introduction

This chapter discusses:

- How improvement suffers from approaches that are superficial
- An approach for ensuring an improvement is well implemented
- A case drawn from two sister organizations in an automotive company, highlighting how and where managers can create superficial responses to improvements
- An explanation of what managers learn about how to respond to improvement initiatives
- Some conclusions on how observers should take care when assessing so-called improvements.

Introduction

This chapter discusses superficiality in performance improvement. We explore one aspect of the lengths to which managers can go to appear to have implemented improvements when there is no material difference in performance that can be identified. The next chapter discusses our visit to a "prize-winning" site where no improvement had been carried out but a report had been fabricated for submission; we have not included details of visits we made to organizations where managers made presentations about what they were intending to do rather than the completed improvements we had asked to research. In addition to our own frustrations at failed research visits, superficiality was an issue for some of the managers and many of the employees we interviewed. Most of the guru texts do not "unpick" the concept, preferring to stress the amount of effort required and the futility of a superficial attack on improvement. Critical writers do point out instances of superficiality whereas a substantial part of the literature cites the totalitarian and highly threatening aspects to improvement methods (Dawson, 1998; Wilkinson et al., 1998; Parker and Slaughter, 1993).

Each form of improvement activity has its own lexicon and prescribed set of activities but, despite the accompanying rhetoric intended to differentiate them, it still can be difficult to distinguish one from another. Commentators argue over the effects of embracing such initiatives, for example whether they lead to the desired improvements and criticize the set of ideas when objectives are not fulfilled. More recently, there is wider acceptance of the perspective that maybe the ideas are not being implemented properly. This chapter contributes to the idea that improvement initiatives rarely become totalitarian or extreme because they would take enormous effort to implement, which in our case company was spent creating a façade of success; the actual changes were very superficial. The chapter examines an attempt at implementing total quality management (TQM), which has numerous definitions but usually is focused around involving everyone in improving processes continuously in line with identified customer requirements. The conclusions drawn are not concerned with prophesying the fizzling out of individual initiatives (Dawson, 1998), but they provide a possible explanation why organizations seem to have a strong appetite for engaging in these activities in the face of mounting evidence of their lack of success. Briefly, we argue that many performance improvement initiatives are intended to represent competence to the outside world and may never be really intended to revolutionize the workplace; some are strongly coupled to individual managers' careers. It is in subsequent managers' interests to denigrate and undermine activities while creating a new modus operandum associated with them. Rarely do others (including academics) penetrate the representations, but individuals subject to the initiatives are fully aware of their hollowness and lack of meaning. This is a somewhat different position to that adopted by Zbaracki (1998, p. 602), who argues that the rhetoric associated with the implementation of total quality initiatives creates "an overly optimistic view" of total quality, though it does have an extremely important role in implementing it, an aspect that we will explore more fully later.

Using the ideas of Lave and Wenger (1991) and Wenger (1998), the chapter explores the complex relations of participation and reification that contribute to the learning process an organization undergoes when implementing sets of ideas. Briefly, Lave and Wenger's ideas relate to and build on Nonaka and Takeuchi's concept of tacit knowledge (1995) and organization learning. From this, Lave and Wenger develop the ideas of "communities of practice" and "learning by peripheral participation." They suggest that there are many communities of practice within an organization and that individuals learn through participating in these communities. Improvement initiatives represent attempts to engineer new communities of practice, which are claimed to be better than the existing ones. The learning community is a form of organization wherein people carry out activities and learn new activities using the "tools of the trade." Improvement initiatives are explicit attempts at changing these communities.

The chapter is based on an analysis of detailed material Constanze Hirschhauser (Lynne's student) obtained for her Ph.D. degree (2001). She conducted two detailed, longitudinal case studies of sister sites in a multinational automotive sector company, one based in England, the other in Germany. The company supplies engineered components to major car manufacturers. Over extended periods, Hirschhauser carried out participant observation, interviewing and analyzing documents to gain an "in-depth" ethnographic feel for the sites. Through interviewing and analyzing documents, she was able to build a picture of the organizations and how they had evolved over three decades, as many of the employees had considerable periods of service.

Both sites had a degree of autonomy over how they ran operations, and both decided to improve them. The UK site had been highly profitable until a patent ran out in the early 1980s; since then, a series of initiatives have been undertaken. The German site had a broadly similar history but was at the time of the research engaged in winning accolades from Japan for one such approach: its total preventative maintenance. However, visits to the shop floor established that despite waves of performance improvement initiatives, with new technology and alterations to working practices, a wide range of people said that very little tangible progress had been made in the performance improvement of manufacturing processes or organization.

Lave and Wenger's theories are used as a framework to analyze the forms of representation and reification involved. We begin by outlining their theories and relating them to performance improvement. The chapter then details the change attempts at both the sites, which we have chosen to label the *pink factory*. Crosby (1980) uses the term *hidden factory* to describe the intricate operations organizations create to deal with errors in their processes. Constanze coined the term *pink factory* to describe an organization creating the superficial impression that the sites were improving processes. We provide explanations for the development of the pink factory by relating it to the framework. An entire community of practice, including customers, was created to maintain this impression. The community of practice has little to do with real improvements to the performance in the sites as such but more to do with being seen by others to be doing so; management had endless commitment for this particular community and was highly successful in maintaining the fiction. We do not think this organization was an isolated incident. The next section of the chapter outlines Lave and Wenger's theories.

Communities of practice

Lave and Wenger's primary concern (1991, 1998) is to examine learning in working environments. We do not think it is too much of a leap of imagination to describe the processes of improvement as learning processes, as previous authors in this area have cited Senge (1990) in this context. These initiatives are supposed to engender continuous improvement—indeed, create a learning and responsive organization. Wenger (1998, p. 5) further developed his and Jean Laver's ideas on a social theory of learning, arguing that it has four components:

1. Meaning: learning as experience
2. Practice: learning as doing
3. Community: learning as belonging
4. Identity: learning as becoming.

The community of practice (CoP) refers to a dynamic social grouping with an activity and set of relations, rules, and the like. Any given individual is involved in several—at the workplace, at home, socially, and so on. The work setting has several overlapping CoPs. Each of these groupings involves interplay between the four components outlined above. Meaning as learned through experience, Wenger claims, is developed through the "interaction of two constituent processes ... participation and reification" (Wenger, 1998, p. 52). Participation is defined as a coupling of action and connection. Reification means literally to make something a "thing" or making something abstract into an object. "We project our meanings onto the world and then we perceive them as existing in the world, as having a reality of their own" (Fig. 5.1; Wenger, 1998, p. 58).

It is possible to relate this to the ideas in Table 4.1 in the previous chapter. Participation is taken by most writers to mean increased involvement by employees, and the connection part of Wenger's use of the term can be assumed, which we think is wrong. Reification can thus be applied to teaming as a process, statistical process control charts, the labels applied to the process, the corporate mission statements, the procedures in ISO9000 documents, the documentation surrounding performance measures—indeed, performance measurement as an activity. Improvement initiatives usually entail modifications to the way individuals participate together with a new array of reification possibilities. An employee carries out tasks, belongs to a work group, has a sense of identity through his or her skills, and derives meaning through his or her experiences. Effective implementation of TQM is assumed by authors to require a "cultural change" (see Oakland, 1999; Hill, 1991), in which a new CoP is established through using the new tools, determining the critical success factors, and designing procedures in a way that sets up new interactions and forms of membership of the organization.

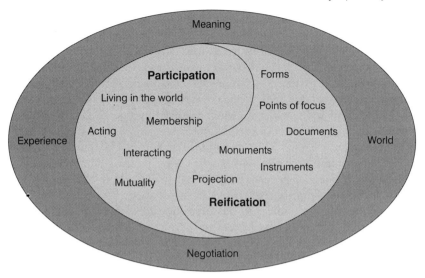

Figure 5.1 Participation and reification (Source: Wenger, 1998, p 63.)

The second aspect of learning—practice—refers to both the overt carrying out of tasks and the tacit knowledge (see also Nonaka and Takeuchi, 1995) that inform this. The machine operators in a cell know not just how to work the machinery but also to acquire knowledge about the operations in depth, which enables them to perform their job better. The third aspect of learning—community—Wenger suggests, consists of three interrelated dimensions: mutual engagement, joint enterprise, and shared repertoire. He suggests that it is the mutual engagement that separates a community of practice from other social groupings such as networks or teams. A community of practice is not a formal organization structure or a set of people who know each other or are physically near. There have to be prerequisites to make interaction possible, whether it is an office, a workplace setting or, a computing facility. The community embraces a wide range of possible roles, different people on different personal trajectories, who are more or less central to the community. Though there is an element of commonality, this does not mean that each individual is identical; each is part of a set of mutual relationships that encompass both the good and bad features of life. Wenger (1998, p. 77) cites "success and failure," pleasure and pain, as just some of the dual aspects of sustaining relations with others in the community. In this thinking, it is possible to recognize echoes of studies on informal work groups that cut across formal organization structures (e.g., Mayo, 1933).

The forms that mutual engagement take are the outcome of collective negotiation as defined by the participants who have ownership of it.

Though there might be an overarching goal of the CoP, the ways of working are discussed and worked through by participants. This is shaped by the context of the CoP. CoPs are always "'situated" within a context that affects aspects of the CoP, but Wenger asserts that they are fundamentally "indigenous enterprises." Despite its activities being seemingly shaped by external objectives and structures, the CoP grows and endures. It sets its own rules, and individuals are mutually accountable to each other for their actions. This is seen most obviously where breaches of these rules occur (frequently reified into texts and rituals).

The community stays in existence as long as this remains. External events can frame the process but not kill it entirely if its interests are being developed. Intermittent checks are made to see whether individuals are carrying out their role and, in some instances, this accountability is formalized into grant-review bodies and report-submission procedures.

Another element in the cohesion of a CoP is its shared repertoire. What constitutes the repertoire can be extremely varied; it can include "'routines, words, tools, ways of doing things, stories, gestures, symbols, genres, actions, or concepts that the community has produced or adopted" (Wenger, 1998, p. 83). The repertoire embodies the history and practice of the CoP and, through its interpretation by individuals, is changed and supplemented. It is crucial that individuals can have access to and enact this repertoire, as it is the CoP's main resource and, indeed, Wenger goes on to define a CoP as possessing "shared histories of learning" (Wenger, 1998, p. 86).

In any learning organization, people mobilize participation and reification in such a way that some elements are remembered and some are forgotten. An updated form contains more information on some areas and less on others. Finding something from the past sometimes helps us to develop new ideas. Participation helps to fix memories and interpretations in our minds, however partial these may be. Artifacts and events are introduced, perceived, rejected, and changed through our individual and shared histories. These have features, some of which are sustained through time and others of which are dropped. While individual identities remain quite fixed in an established CoP, to change it is often necessary to participate in a new one.

This brings us to the last element in learning, that of learning as "becoming." Persons are changed by their learning experience; they become different persons with the acquisition of knowledge. Through learning, employees become different people: a skilled—as opposed to an unskilled—worker and a team leader as opposed to a team member. Quality improvement initiatives such as "six sigma" have gained popularity through their ability to mark these changes by using the Japanese martial arts system of belts. Six sigma seems to couple a project management method with process control techniques, and proficiency at the techniques and experience gained in projects are marked with a change of "belt" color.

It is within this context that organizations try to implement TQM and, contrasting with this, it has been commented that managers want TQM to be implemented quickly and with little inconvenience (Wilkinson et al., 1992). Companies that have a quick-fix attitude toward TQM are more likely perhaps to concentrate on visible changes so that there is something to show. The CoP ideas offer a way of analyzing the organization undergoing improvement, yielding many areas on which to focus in a way in which some of the "culture change" writers do not (see, for example, Oakland, 1995).

Autoco

As mentioned above, Hirschhauser visited two business units of the same organization. The company had been manufacturing similar products for about 100 years, although ownership of the organizations had changed. Both factories made components for the car industry, and supplied the major automotive original equipment manufacturers (OEMs). The research was originally designed to explore national cultural differences in implementing TQM, but it emerged soon after the second site was being researched that the similarities between the sites outweighed any national cultural differences. The research revealed that the companies were not willing to commit fully the effort necessary to drive quality improvement but, to retain the TQM image, they went to the extent of creating what might be likened to Potemkin villages. Potemkin, the political advisor of Catherine II of Russia, showed her, on a trip through the Krim in 1787, villages that were mere facades. This is explained more fully in the next section of the chapter.

How factories become pink

Superficiality and the creation of facades occur in other areas. For example, the "farm" at the palace of Versailles and film and television sets are all created impressions to fool onlookers. Potemkin villages were constructed to create an impression of wealth in the country; the case companies paid a lot of attention to the "appearance" of their factories to show competence to customers or casual visitors. The following section explores "pinkness" in this context by focusing on three elements in this category: visual appearance, the use of tools and techniques, and people management. In each case, activities and reifications that were able to be identified were intended to represent competence in TQM but could be argued to have not such a positive construction.

Pink is for girls; sugar and spice and all things nice; pink and fluffy is insubstantial; pink has homosexual overtones; it is also the color of the chapter on which the *Financial Times* and the sports supplement of the

Edinburgh Evening News is printed! The idea of pinkness in this context has been derived from a German saying that can be translated into "looking at the world through rose-tinted spectacles" because, in doing so, everything appears much "nicer." This has been discussed by Marchington (1995, p. 65) in a similar context before "Caution [is needed] in assuming that all has changed in British industry just because a few well chosen examples paint a rosy picture of involvement or empowerment in action," but we will develop it further. Just as the pretences of Potemkin's village, the pinkness will reveal only the desirable image to the spectator. Therefore, a pink factory is one where a facade has been created but does not live up to scrutiny.

Schaffer and Thomson (1992) compared the impact of performance improvement efforts that many companies introduced on operational and financial results to the effect a ceremonial rain dance has on the weather! *"This 'rain dance' is the ardent pursuit of activities that sound good, look good and allow managers to feel good—but in fact contribute little or nothing to bottom-line performance"* (Schaffer and Thomson, 1992, p. 81).

A pink factory will concentrate its efforts on creating an image instead of changing things fundamentally; therefore, a program incorporating such an approach cannot get beyond being an ephemeral phase. De Cock and Hipkin (1997, p. 667) said in one of their case studies that *"... the desire to 'look good' to significant stakeholders in the wider organizational environment was perceived as more important by line managers than improving internal processes."*

In particular, if workers and management have learned to create a veneer of efficiency without changing the status quo, they are unlikely to change their habits when implementing TQM. So even though a company engages in TQM and keeps it "alive" for a considerable time, it need not have taken root in the company. Feinberg (1996, p. 8) gives some examples of how managers can undermine TQM. For example, to appear busy they become involved in only "'non-substantive, mostly-for show sorts of events' to keep up the image, in order to survive until things can go back to normal and TQM will have become just another large three ring binder cluttering up the shelves."

The next sections explore three of the elements that contribute to the construction of the pink factory. The first and most obvious is that of visual appearance. Hackman and Wageman (1995, p. 329) define meaningless change as "window dressing:" "... as in a programme that exhorts people to alter their behavior but that requires managers to do little other than issue the exhortation." However, as window dressing is used as a marketing communications device to entice customers into shops, we would argue it was used in this way by the managers at the research sites to impress visiting customers and researchers that they were competent and innovative.

Both sets of managers directed their efforts toward visual changes (e.g., the production area of both factories were painted as part of the improvement initiative). In one site, the production area was painted green and the walkways red. The image was spoiled relatively quickly; at one site, the paint flaked off; at the other, a special floor coating that was used was actually slippery to walk on! These initiatives also incorporated wall hangings, mainly in the shape of display boards with graphs to create a sense of transparency in providing information. A colorful floor or graphs that are read mainly by visitors are unlikely to exert any influence on bottom-line performance or show that a deep-rooted change has occurred. It was particularly true of the German site that those units that appeared to keep up with the set targets on the wall charts were respected, but those that took more time were denigrated because they changed things fundamentally deep down but displayed less exciting performance statistics in the interim. Thus, the foundations for a "fad" were laid.

Another visual display of performance improvement is the story board, which is a wall chart portraying an improvement initiative in text and pictures. Smith (1990) praised story boards because in his opinion they linked directly to teamwork and team discipline and as a discussion focus for managers "'walking the talk." He did admit that they also could be used to impress visiting customers. Both sites had all sorts of boards to display what they did, and one site had a story board of which they were particularly proud and showed to every visitor. It transpired that this depicted a much earlier improvement; indeed, the change it described had actually been introduced at the behest of a customer.

Presenting an image to the outside world appeared to be important, as they hosted many visitors at the respective factories. One even had a specific "quality center" on the production floor, and people working there felt they were part of a museum or showcase, as the center had goldfish bowl–like windows. The employees on the line thought the center a joke and referred to the people working in the center as being like animals in a zoo. At the other site, the managers installed an actual fish tank in the factory floor, which was intended to symbolize "Japaneseness." Shortly after it was installed, the top cover had to be nailed down to avoid sabotage. Several areas were set aside for seating with monitors at which one could watch monthly company videos. The lavish space allocated for this purpose could be contrasted with that on the production floor where a key factor in deciding whether to buy a piece of new technology for the line was size, as space was in short supply!

In addition to the painting and new quality centers, the factories had been spruced up so much that the workers at the German site confused the total preventive maintenance (TPM) program with "cleaning": To them, this was all TPM meant in practice. Despite being used in the literature as being a good example of TPM, some of the production process machines had been leaking oil for months, and slicks were simply wiped up prior to any visitor touring the company. The underlying problems were not solved but instead were covered up to enable a good image to be portrayed to any outsider.

Some of the visual changes had been introduced at the behest of the customer: One Japanese customer wanted a triangle with a letter *A* in it on top of critical machines! The factory floor employees had seen many "programs" and managers come and go, while their working lives remained largely the same. The changes to the visual appearance of the work setting served to make the managers and customers seem childish in their eyes. A recurrent theme in interviews was the questioning of the costs of such activities and whether it would affect profitability and employment. The next subsection investigates a more substantive aspect of TQM—tools and techniques; they can form part of the pink factory and overlap with the visual aspects of implementation, depending on how they are implemented.

There are within TQM tools and techniques that help with demonstrating competence in a visual way to the outside world without any significant improvement in performance necessarily being realized. The ones on which we will focus are performance statistics and suggestion schemes.

Customers and senior managers were interested in performance statistics in areas such as scrap and defect rates. One Japanese manufacturer, renowned for its TQM and general manufacturing excellence, insisted on 100 percent inspection. Both sites had targets for scrap that were "met." However, these statistics were acknowledged to be bogus, as it was possible to dispose of scrap in a variety of ways other than in the designated receptacle. For example, conveyor belts designed for swarf could be used for disposal, as could pockets of overalls. In one subunit, an employee noticed that factory input did not reconcile with output, so the scrap rate had to be increased above the target figure!

Many customers required the sites to produce statistical process control charts for each batch of parts. It was pointed out that graphs meeting the appropriate standard could be prepared by monitoring the process at certain points as opposed to others. Accident statistics were displayed only when none had been reported. One employee said that when there had recently been an accident recorded, the board displaying the statistics would simply disappear until the period within which the accident had occurred elapsed. Downtime was measured, but one could avoid recording a stoppage if one labeled it as planned through TPM.

Similar falsification was evident in the use of suggestion schemes. Suggestion schemes are often taken as indicators of employee involvement (Evans, 1999). Although some suggestions that had been made in the companies did result in improvements, there was a set target for number of suggestions, and failure to meet this target led to unwelcome management scrutiny. This led to "pseudo" suggestions being made or the falsification of suggestions by team leaders on behalf of line workers. A team leader admitted to recycling suggestions as a way of generating interest. Management were not likely to investigate this, as for them the scheme was realizing the objectives they had for it; for example, one of the sites came fifth in a nationwide competition for competence in suggestion schemes, despite widespread acknowledgement by employees that the scheme had no impact on productivity.

The last element of the pink factory we will discuss here is that of people management—in this case teamwork and training.

Reorganizing work groups into teams under team leaders is one of the sine qua nons of TQM (Oakland, 1999). One feature of teamwork that is omitted by the literature is the pink factory. Although implementing teams and achieving performance improvements take time, a company might choose to introduce teams quickly, as an immediate benefit would be to "show" to the outside world that the company "operates teamwork." Similarly, merely introducing teams because they are an integral part of TQM without determining whether they have any relevance in the production setting helps to construct a pink factory, because invariably the company operates teamwork by numbers, as the actual number of teams in operation is more important than their performance! The teams may exist on paper; in reality, it is different (Walsh, 1995). Teams can be introduced to create or comply with an image (Feinberg, 1996).

Training and leadership are often said to be important factors in any quality program, but these two characteristics have been identified as those that show the largest gap between theory and practice. Within this context, training programs will be considered, because a successful TQM program will need an educated workforce that is in a position to make decisions.

Training has to be an integral part of developing a TQM initiative (Benson, 1993); moreover, successful companies may win an award, such as Investor in People. Training is similar to teamwork as a useful attribute to display to visiting customers or researchers. Numerof and Abrams (1992, p. 10) wrote that "...*the most common response to the quality imperative is a structured and often comprehensive training effort, kicked off with substantial hoopla, pomp and circumstance.*" Training may well merely lend itself to pinkness, because even with an exemplary training program that is well documented and has received an award, it is difficult for an outsider to ascertain how much is actually put into practice.

Both sites developed training programs as part of their quality initiatives and had folders to show for it, but these were not always adopted or even regarded as adequate training by those being instructed.

The UK site had won an Investors in People award, and individuals had personal development plans. Yet again, boards were mounted showing skills matrices and degrees of competence for each worker. However, the training was seen to be nothing more than learning another job, one team leader pointing out that in some instances the worker did not have an opportunity to carry out the new task for years, by which time they had forgotten what they had learned. Therefore, it was easy to present a picture symbolizing that the workforce was multiskilled, which was not the case.

Managers were unwilling to release workers from the production line to attend training courses, so many of the courses had to be run in overtime. Employees were skeptical about management's attitudes as, for the majority, training was in-house, cheap, and not in production time, whereas for management, budgets were more extensive though not necessarily well spent. Indeed, employees at both plants could cite expensive courses abroad that managers had attended without much subsequent impact on performance.

There were employees who were illiterate or innumerate, which meant basic training in those areas was needed before anything more advanced could be attempted. There was a high percentage of foreigners at the German site, some of whom could not even speak and understand German properly, so training here meant a German language course. The company did arrange for German language classes to be run, but because they had to be taken in the workers' free time, many employees chose not to take them. This makes the point that it cannot be assumed that as long as management offers a training plan everybody will participate.

The human resource (HR) department has an important contribution to make in developing and evaluating training programs. However, the HR department at the German site was seen more as a cause of quality problems than a help, because their employment policies meant that workers were employed on a short-term basis, which made training difficult.

The previous section outlines three areas wherein elements of TQM were implemented so superficially that they did not have the effect of improving performance. They did manage to "hoodwink" outside observers into believing that the organizations were competent in manufacturing. Both sites had long-standing relationships with their customers, who audited the sites regularly, a process that usually involved examining performance statistics and touring the facility. Both parties were aware of the importance of appearances; indeed, a worker mentioned that a Japanese customer had not been interested in a certain quality problem: He had been exhorted to "move the curve on the graph up!" Customers were not the only outsiders to visit the sites; two sets of academics carried out research on both sites. In one case, the researcher circulated a survey; in the other, a cross-section of management was interviewed in the offices.

Shop floor employees found these studies amusing and were sure that a suitably false impression had been created. The next section relates the above to Wenger's model of learning and then to Lave and Wenger's theory of the community of practice.

Analysis

We began by asserting that critical authors tended to regard improvement initiatives such as TQM as either sinister or superficial. The analysis of the two cases and emergence of the pink factory as a theme in the data can be viewed perhaps as both or neither. In the current climate of Western European manufacturing contraction, it is disquieting that managers in these cases were more engaged in the "impression-management" community of practice than the "performance-improvement" one. The attempts to implement TQM did not lead to any totalitarian regime of employee brainwashing, because the shop floor employees could identify the superficiality of the attempts better than either the customers or visiting academics; therefore, the engineering of their community of practice did not engage them in the way it was intended.

Wenger (1998) suggests that learning involves interplay among experience, activity, belonging, and becoming. Our work reveals that the way in which management implemented performance-improvement initiatives actually developed worker resistance to new initiatives, as the activities they carried out were shown to be largely meaningless. They did not forge a new sense of being an employee in a single status organization; the pinkness reinforced the traditional class schism in the organizations. The cumulative result was for them to become more cynical so far as future projects are concerned.

Referring to Figure 5.1, our discussion of the pink factory included descriptions of many elements of reification and how they failed to promote an internal dynamic with elements of participation but succeeded with customers. The clearest demonstration of this were the "monuments" of the story boards, which in one instance were actually at the behest of a customer. The managers were not using them to gain employee participation but were using them to mobilize the participation of customers in the business relationship! Another example of this was the documenting of performance statistics, such as control charts or waste. Again, the people these reifications engaged were not the employees in improvement initiatives but customers in the business relationship. A visible quality center might be intended to serve as a point of focus for meetings and resources, but the way in which the employees referred to it served to highlight its failure to spur their participation. We think the physical painting of the factory floor might be a form of monument signifying change; however, the lack of thought surrounding the type of paint and its safety characteristics and longevity indicate a lack of understanding of the content and process of TQM on the part of the managers (Zbaracki, 1998).

Our work highlights that the second component of learning—"learning as doing"—again did not involve the shop floor employee but the managers, customers, and outsiders. The German attempts at TPM gained the organization much kudos and brought managers into contact with other organizations and an ability to present the site as competent but, for the shop floor employees, TPM performance-improvement initiatives were essentialized and trivialized to mean cleaning, as this was the only element that resonated with them. Furthermore, it was necessary to do this only when visitors were around.

An important aspect of learning and one that Lave and Wenger (1991) stress is that of learning as "belonging" to a vibrant community of practice. What was startling about the two companies was again how the three subelements were not directed at the workforce but at visiting customers and, to a lesser extent, academics. The examples we choose to use here are those of suggestion schemes and performance statistics. Both of these are intended to provide some focus for mutual engagement, some joint enterprise and hopefully shared repertoire. Ideally, points are put forward through negotiation, vetted by superiors, discussed, and rejected or implemented. They are signifiers of employees having an input, taking part in a dialogue. They are widely discredited means of doing this; however, the same kind of process underlies the preparation of total quality performance statistics. Employees monitor the process and input the information, the information is shared by shop floor and management, and both parties gain something from this. This was clearly not the case at both sites, where team leaders fabricated suggestions; scrap and accident statistics were manipulated so that far from creating a shared repertoire and joint enterprise, the workforce was alienated from the improvement initiative. The outputs of the fabrications, however, were taken on by the customers.

The final component of the theory of learning we are using to analyze our cases—that of learning as becoming—also had different outcomes for shop floor employee and manager. The training given to enhance skills did very little to change the identities of the employees but served to present the managers as enlightened. Knowledge was not used and lapsed. But, the training grids remained on the walls. The way in which training was carried out, frequently in overtime in a context wherein short-term labor contracts were being operated, meant that an employee did not sense that the organization was trying to develop them as individuals. Rather, the organization was developing itself in the eyes of the outside world.

However, the pink factory acted as a lure to customers and researchers who engaged in the image of competence CoP with interest. The manipulation of the visual appearance, construction of the monuments of story boards and fish tanks, provided a backdrop signifying competence.

Points of focus such as TPM projects helped to generate elements of mutuality and set up positive dynamics between management and the outside world, enabling the organizations to win certificates and accolades. The form filling and performance indicators allowed management to practice the appearance of controlling the process and demonstrate this to their superiors. The ability to construct a pink factory enabled them to progress up the organization; on the German site, the leaders of the performance-improvement initiatives were referred to as "popes," reinforcing the symbolic nature of the process. New managers learned quickly to embrace a pink approach to improvement, as this was the best way to succeed in the organization. The purported focus for learning did not work, the ancillary pink CoP operated beautifully: From our studies, the process had been going on for more than thirty years, both as a learning process for management and as a reassurance for customers.

Discussion

Many of the references we have quoted assume that superficiality or pinkness is wrong or dysfunctional and attribute the blame to the managers who embrace improvement halfheartedly or incorrectly. Zbaracki (1998) addresses the introductory stages of TQM and notes that managers are introduced to it through "rhetoric" and essentialized sketches of "best practice" that overlook the problems and difficulties of implementing and sustaining initiatives. He thinks the rhetoric is almost all they have to go on and can be useful in creating interest within the company. Our position is slightly different. We share his view that rhetoric or, in our terminology, pinkness, is all they have to go on. Many of the texts in the area are hopelessly pink, and government sponsors of improvement are some of the worst culprits. The Department of Trade and Industry (DTI) guides of the late 1980s and early 1990s come to mind, with the pictures of the smiling case study participants and the reported successes: "The first circle in the company 'The Systems Sizzlers' began by introducing a voluntary performance indicator sheet and then went on to redesign their area' ... The result was a ... saving to the company of £5,000 a year' (DTI, 1990, p. 12). The publication concerning the quality gurus gave thumbnail sketches of the gurus' work, carefully downplaying the amount of dull process control work that they advocate, preferring to focus on the pinker issues.

It is not just these kinds of texts that are pink; one of our sites appears in a case study book for excellence in TPM, and one of us visits an electronics organization famed for its "Just in Time" purchasing (Schonberger, 1982), which it has yet to implement more than twenty years later. Reading about improvement initiatives might be hazardous; what about visiting sites? Our material demonstrates that it is possible to be taken in by a well-constructed tour, even if one employs the rigorous approach advocated by Upton and Macadam (1997). They suggest that people engaged on factory tours establish precisely their objectives before they begin and use a form of the improvement cycle as a guide to making sure that information is noted systematically. Visitors should make cross-checks so that views expressed in interviews are corroborated with data from process measurement and so on, rather like a European Foundation for Quality Management Assessment process. We would argue that both our sites would pass this scrutiny. One has to delve beneath to understand how the process measurement was constructed, who was involved, and especially the history and context of the operations. The sources of information for managers are glossy rather than properly informative.

We would like the cycle of pinkness to be broken because of its debilitating effect on manufacturing performance, but we argue that often academics collude in sustaining this because we too are members of the pink CoP. We embrace the new three-letter acronyms as areas in which to become prominent. Research methods such as questionnaire surveys and one-off interviews enable both parties to negotiate a pink view of the organization and a semblance of competence to funders. Many academic texts are anodyne because the authors use methods that are easy for people in the organization to respond to in a pink way. We need industrial collaboration to obtain grant funding; whereas producing work that is "useful" is very laudable, the slant toward best practice can veer dangerously to pinkness, because it is very difficult to draw a distinction between consultancy and independent research. We construct quick sketches of "excellence" and move on to the next set of ideas before adequately critiquing the existing ones. We pride ourselves on the practical nature of our discipline; however, our proximity to the subjects we research makes us liable to the same kinds of problems the accounting profession has encountered recently with the demise of a major consulting organization and Enron. It is difficult to maintain a critical stance if we rely on our research organizations for consultancy contracts.

How then are managers to obtain a clearer perspective of what improvement initiatives entail? As Zbaracki (1998) noted, most of the tools exist; what our work would suggest is that the CoP refocus away from the outside world and create more of an "indigenous enterprise" (Wenger, 1998). This would make it possible for a dialogue to begin so that the elements of reification that managers enjoy so much are constructed in such a way as to help employee participation rather than deter it.

Conclusions

The chapter set out to explore forms of superficiality in implementing performance-improvement initiatives. We described case material from two sister sites of a large manufacturing organization and put forward the term *pink factory* to describe the elaborate representation of quality management performance-improvement initiatives in the work milieu. We would conclude that for our cases, the forms of superficiality were complex and interlinked—indeed, far from superficial in their effects!

We introduced and related our material to Lave and Wenger's CoP theory, in that quality-improvement initiatives can be construed as a form of organizational learning. The theory helps us to explain why, in the face of repeated attempts at improving processes, limited success was achieved. The way in which management attempted to reify aspects of TQM failed to spur participation; rather, it created more distance between themselves and shop floor employees. It did, however, create closeness and identification between the managers and outsiders such as customers and researchers. The more successful, sustained learning CoP was between these parties. We would conclude that over the years, people in industry have become adept at embracing new initiatives, creating reifications, and presenting images of competence to the outside world, irrespective of the impact of these initiatives on manufacturing performance.

The material we have presented shows how deep-seated, interconnected, and socially constructed is this pinkness or superficiality.

Summary conclusions

This chapter discussed:

- Improvement processes are similar to knowledge management and organizational learning processes
- The existence of a strong connection between participation and reification
- The analysis of the case material helped to coin the term *pink factory* to describe the factory within a factory dedicated to creating the impression of improvement
- Specific examples exist in the areas of performance statistics and training
- The point for many managers is to convey the impression of performance improvement rather than improving performance.

Discussion questions

- Of which communities of practice are you a member? Do they help you to participate in improvement?
- Can you think of any other forms of symbolic improvements that have had no material effect?
- Can you think of an example where you were "pink" at work?

Further reading

Oliver, N. 1990. Employee Commitment and Total Quality Control, *International Journal of Quality and Reliability Management* 7 (1): 21–9.

Wenger, E. 1998. *Communities of Practice, Learning, Meaning and Identity.* Cambridge: Cambridge University Press.

Zbaracki, M.J. 1998. The Rhetoric and Reality of Total Quality Management. *Administrative Science Quarterly* 43 (3):602–36.

6 Considering the gender aspect to involvement

Summary introduction

This chapter discusses:
- How organizations typify the employee in improvement initiatives
- Whether improvement initiatives represent a "feminizing" of organizations
- Definitions of masculinities, including a rare positive one!
- Two cases wherein women gained—and some men lost—status through an improvement
- That the improvements represented a shift in the form of male domination of the organizations.

Introduction

Though it is widely acknowledged that involving all the people concerned is critical for the success of any improvement initiative, Soltani et al. (2005) found that lack of involvement was one of the principal barriers to success! In common with many other aspects of improvement, the various ways to involve people are relatively well understood and have been discussed for years. One aspect that is not discussed but remains a feature of every organization we have encountered is gender and how people relate to one another as individuals. Gender is typically viewed as concerning relations between men and women; we use the word in its fullest sense and hope in this chapter to show that improvement initiatives can be shaped by the relations between women and men and also between men.

Two of the most successful organizations we studied had noticeable participation of women in the changes. These women made career gains, sometimes at the expense of men. A form of behavior usually associated with traditional masculinity was deemed inappropriate; these people were marginalized and more appropriate ways of interacting were valorized. Books on performance improvement do not typically contain a chapter discussing this topic, and our treatment of the subject is rarer still; however, we think that consideration of gender might be a useful addition to the debate on improvement because it is an important aspect of how people experience organizations and will affect how people can become involved in improvements.

There has been work that examined whether organization change can represent a feminizing of the workplace (Itzin, 1995; Wajcman, 1998), but this did not fully make sense of our findings (it was still the men in charge), and this led us to investigate the concept of masculinity. There is a growing literature on masculinities (Whitehead, 2001), but this work has developed conceptualizations that we perceive to be largely negative (see, for example, Collinson and Hearn, 1996, and Kerfoot and Knights, 1993) and, again they are of limited use in explaining the processes in our cases.

In this chapter, we explore how involvement was enacted focusing on two organizations, discuss the forms of masculinities that others have described, and use the unusual conceptualization of testicularity put forward by Flannigan-Saint-Aubin (1994), because it allows us to incorporate both positive and negative dimensions to a form of masculinity, and we think it helps to explain the shift in the ruling forms of masculinities deployed in the organizations that created opportunities for women, which in turn helped the improvement initiative succeed.

Employee involvement

There are many terms circulating in this area, and we could date our book immediately by using an inappropriate acronym. The ultimate objective is to have keen, committed people, and it is argued that if they are trained, engage in two-way communication, and are given responsibility within a context where they feel valued, people are more likely to participate in improvement initiatives, and these initiatives might actually lead to improvement (see, for example, Rahman and Bullock, 2005). The organizations we studied used frameworks to provide a more elaborate structure (Martin, 1996) to support and channel employees into being more involved (Oliver, 1990). The European Foundation for Quality Management (EFQM), the Business Excellence Model, the United States Baldrige Award and, indeed, internally devised "balanced scorecards" (Kaplan and Norton, 1992) encode more benign human resource policies and require organizations to measure their success in practice and gauge whether employees share this perception. For example, the EFQM model subcriteria (see http://www.efqm.org) against which organizations are assessed encourage the planning of human resources, the development of employee competences, the empowerment and involvement of people, and the consideration of recognition and reward, and this has to be established within the context of employees having a contribution to the design of these activities and having a sense of continuity and care in their employment contract.

Organizations using the former two models have to be able to prove to external judges that they have in place activities to support the above, that these have achieved results, and that the employees share this view. To accumulate a high score, these have to be embedded for a sustained period. The form of employee involvement in the organizations resembled a re-badging of familiar participative approaches to organizing, representing a move from direct control to responsible autonomy (Friedman, 1977). Operations management writers (e.g., Schonberger, 1979) with whose normative texts managers in organizations are more familiar usually construct this approach differently to organization theorists. Though the idea has been around in one form or another since pre–World War II, it has been given added impetus with popular texts promoting it as an element in performance improvement exemplified by the success of Japanese manufacturing organizations of the 1970s and 1980s (Ohno, 1988; Imai, 1986; Schonberger, 1979; and Oakland, 1995). Academics may question the validity of this perception, and Kondo (1990) provides a more considered account of organization life in Japan, but the ideal typical Japanese worker as contributing ideas and being involved in a constructive way in the labor process has many industrial subscribers in the United Kingdom. The managerialist texts choose to portray employees as having not been "involved" in the past and thus that the culture needs to be changed so that this can be brought about (see, for example, Oakland, 1995).

It would seem obvious that different people might respond individually to the various mechanisms, though an important difference is gender; however, we have not found much discussion of this in the literature. The mainstream-operations texts do not consider gender, and the opportunities afforded to women by so-called Japanese manufacturing methods have been noted by writers whose primary focus is gender (Wajcman, 1998).

Wilson (1996) notes that organization theory is gender-blind or, at very best, gender-suppressed (Linstead, 2001). We were blind to this perspective in our initial analyzes of the organizations but were forced to consider it when gender emerged as an important element in our analysis of the organizations that had been more successful.

The use of the very term *employee* is intended to remove class and gender from this area of people management; however, as Due Billing and Alvesson (2000, p. 145) note that men occupy the top positions of organizations, whereas if women are employed, they usually occupy lower status, more marginalized positions (see also Gherardi, 1995). Due Billing and Alvesson's paper (2000) discusses leadership, and our chapter earlier in the book can be said to be presented in a "gender-blind" fashion. They consider whether the change in emphasis from management to leadership marks a "feminization" of the workplace, in that some traits of the ideal leader have been labeled "feminine." We would agree with them and Pease (2000) that using "trait" theory is inadequate in both leadership- and employee-involvement contexts. There is a theme within the literature exploring whether women who do progress in organizations end up performing as "men" (see, for example, Metcalfe and Linstead, 2003; Wajcman, 1998) or shifting the nature of the performance to that more associated with the feminine (Rosener, 1990). We would go so far as to agree with Segal's finding (1990, p. 64) that "the variation within each sex far outweighs any differences between the sexes," which is also supported by Ramsay's detailed review (1996). Segal goes on (1990, p. 96) to quote Connell's assertion that there are three main structures underlying relationships between women and men: labor, power, and desire. Our chapter does not address the third structure, although it would be possible to extend our analysis to include this. We chose to examine the labor and power relations in work contexts, focusing on the discourse of masculinity (Kerfoot and Knights, 1996).

Butler says,

> Terms such as "masculine" and "feminine" are notoriously changeable; there are social histories for each term; their meanings change radically depending upon geopolitical boundaries and cultural constraints on who is imagining whom, and for what purpose. That the terms recur is interesting enough, but the recurrence does not index a sameness, but rather the way in which the social articulation of the term depends upon its repetition, which constitutes one dimension of the performative structure of gender. Terms of gender designation are thus never settled once and for all but are constantly in the process of being remade
>
> (Butler, 2004, p 10).

Forms of masculinity

"Men and masculinity are usually *implicit* but central/*centred*" (Hearn and Collinson, 1994). Masculinities have a central role in organizations but this is rarely acknowledged. These authors in another text (Collinson and Hearn, 1996, p. 2) note that feminist writers have failed in the past "to name men as men, and that writers who do tend to assume a unitary conceptualization of the masculine, which is also inadequate. It is easy to see how this oversight is sustained in different contexts. Books and papers on performance improvement assume a form of masculine viewpoint, and this is reproduced in many more highly esteemed texts, as Segal notes

(1990, p. 85): "There are not two sexes in Lacanian writing, but only one: one and its Other—Woman does not exist."

Many authors have now explored the masculine and identified discourses of masculinity in the workplace. The most cited is Collinson and Hearn's five competing discourses of managerial masculinities. These encompass first, paternalism or the rule of the father, with its moral overtones—a family metaphor; second, authoritarianism, a subcategory of which reinforces masculine management style with rules and practices; third, entrepreneurialism, the self-made thrusting man with its association with "laddism"; fourth, careerism, the confident pursuit of advancement; and last, informalism or "locker room" banter and bonding (Collinson and Hearn, 1996). The terms used to describe the discourses do not always mean the same thing, or different terms are used to describe similar processes. For example, McDowell (2001) would argue that Kerfoot and Knights' patriarchy label (1993) corresponds to Collinson and Hearn's paternalism and that these last authors put forward another term—*strategic masculinity*—that contains elements of authoritarianism. What can be commented on is that the discussion of these discourses almost always focuses on the negative and repressive. It seems to us there must be some positive aspects of masculinity worth investigating?

Flannigan-Saint-Aubin (1994) would categorize these discourses as adopting a "phallic" view of masculinity (i.e., they portray an active, invading, penetrative, and unstable form of masculinity). Flannigan-Saint-Aubin's chapter is concerned with widening the range of metaphors in use for maleness beyond the phallic. He argues that the almost exclusive use of the phallic metaphor fails to account for the range of possible masculinities; indeed, causes masculinity to be conflated with patriarchy; and proposes a variation: that of testicularity (1994) as a way of spurring alternatives. The "testicular" form of masculinity encompasses a "nurturing, incubating, containing and protecting" way of interacting (Flannigan-Saint-Aubin, 1994, p. 250). It could be seen as a positive variant of the paternalism discourse outlined above. The negative counterpart is "testeria," characterized by "stagnation, stubbornness, petulance,... fretful, ... morose [behavior]" (Flannigan-Saint-Aubin, 1994, p. 250). There is an obvious parallel with hysteria, so named as the ancient Greeks believed an extremely upset woman was subject to her womb's moving around her body and influencing her mind, and Flannigan-Saint-Aubin notes that there is no corresponding term in common usage to describe a man overcome with hormones. He thinks it important to acknowledge that the male embryo comprises both the X and Y chromosome and that "masculinity is experienced as constant insecurity in the face of feminine absorption" (Flannigan-Saint-Aubin, 1994, p. 245). Though he is concerned with extending the repertoire of acknowledged ways of performing masculinity, his arguments are broadly in sympathy with those who oppose dualisms, such as "male and female" "mind and body."

Though the most common site of gender relations is thought to be between men and women, increasing numbers of authors have noticed that relations between men are gendered. Indeed, Martin (2001) noted that many of the ways men have for mobilizing masculinities have male, not female, audiences (e.g., she identifies "peacocking" or showing off one's achievements as a largely male activity targeted at a male audience).

And just as women are acutely aware and sensitized to the effect their gender has on work relations (Wajcman, 1998), gender relations are a source of alienation and anxiety for some men as individuals (Guttenman, 1994; Seidler, 1997; Hollway, 1996). We would therefore want to avoid conceptions of masculinity that are too shorthand, to acknowledge that what constitutes masculinity in the workplace takes many forms that change over time and can encompass so-called female characteristics (Ashcraft and Mumby, 2004).

It is within this context of overarching masculinist strategic change (Kerfoot and Knights, 1993), wherein power relations are constitutive and repressive and present multiple possibilities for masculinities, that we introduce our case studies and go on to analyze them in relation to the concept of testicularity.

Company A

This is a global organization with a range of business units covering their industrial sector. It took over several sites in the United Kingdom in the early 1990s and inherited a workforce that had been subject to rounds of hiring and layoffs. We studied one site in a geographically peripheral location. The local senior management set about implementing a local initiative to transform the organization, using the EFQM framework to guide them. They implemented a number of changes, including delayering the hierarchy, forming process flow–oriented teams, altering the production process, and enacting a much more visible and personal style of leadership. A new organization structure that had been designed by management had also delayered, with line management responsibilities going to team leaders who in turn managed larger teams than before. The fewer tiers of management meant that the team leaders had a more direct relationship with the top of the organization.

The team leader role was seen as key, and a formal assessment process was set up to identify people displaying "leadership" traits. Some existing managers migrated into the new posts, other people from the shop floor progressed, and some people were hired from outside because they had displayed competence in a similar role. Some individuals were given additional training in the hope of acquiring the desired traits; others were reassigned elsewhere.

As we mentioned before, when we visit an organization, we ask to speak to a range of people, though in some cases our entreaty to speak to shop floor workers is ignored. Company A managers were very enthusiastic for us to talk to a wide range of individuals, including people who had been both advanced and displaced by the changes. We met a former line manager who was now working in the procurement function. It would be very difficult to exaggerate the disaffection one sensed in this person. His body was slumped, his speech was unenthusiastic, and he was far from animated when he talked. He told us about how he had liked his old job—he had been in it for several years and enjoyed running a part of the production process—but the selection process for the new team leaders meant there were fewer line-management jobs. He had participated in the selection process but was not selected to be a leader: He was considered to be too autocratic, so he was offered a different job. He felt the job was fine but not as good as his previous one. The procurement role does give the opportunity to manage suppliers, and there was some rationalization of the supply base, but he did not find this as enjoyable as the day-to-day management of a section.

His whole demeanor was that of an unhappy person, and he projected this onto the people nearby. We had an opportunity to gain this impression both from his demeanor in the interview and in more social settings, such as lunch in the canteen. When we quizzed the host manager about this, he concurred about our reading of this person's demeanor and mentioned again that the company was keen to reassign staff where possible—the previous owners had a history of laying off staff, and they wanted to avoid this as far as possible. There was a sense of pride that the old, almost thoughtless layoffs were a thing of the past, that employees did have some security if they were prepared to change roles.

This could be sharply contrasted with the five female employees whom we interviewed and who had been the subject of layoffs during previous regimes but now were much happier in teams; indeed, two had gained academic qualifications with the encouragement and support of the company and had been promoted. We also spoke to a new female team leader who had been hired from another organization because she displayed the required characteristics; her whole demeanor was in sharp contrast to the former line manager discussed above. She too loved managing people and spoke extensively of the improvements that the team had come up with together.

A much quoted and symbolic event was the demolition of the old senior management office tower block that was situated in a building separate from the main one. The senior management were now situated near the production floor and could be seen. The most senior manager was known universally by his first name, as if he were well known to them: "Colin." People discussed him as if they knew him well; they could recognize his voice, talked with him, and felt they knew him as a person. Employees thought the organization far more committed to the plant and the individuals working there. We never spoke to Colin, but we almost thought we had, from our interviews with female staff. His name cropped up on a regular basis: In an organization of well more than a thousand staff, he seemed to have a personal relationship with these employees, given the amount of times his name cropped up in the interviews. They clearly had warm feelings for him and had stories to tell of going to off-site presentations with him, which described his personal behavior patterns. There appeared to be an atmosphere of positive familiarity between them. They seemed almost "bewitched" by the person and by the processes, as in Knights and McCabe's use of the word (2000). (Knights and McCabe, 2000 are alluding to employees being duped by TQM.) The people we talked to had good memories and a healthy skepticism, but they really got on with Colin.

The HR policies of selection, training, and development might have left some formerly powerful people feeling marginalized, but the employees whose jobs had in the past been marginal felt more integrated and had gained more personally from the changes. The plant's key performance indicators were being achieved, and shortly after our visit they became an award-winning site of "excellence" and act as a model site for the rest of the company.

The processes, activities, and outcomes described above can be construed in a number of ways. The company could be accused of replacing expensive male labor with cheaper more docile female labor as part of their strategic intensification of the labor process, but though this might help to provide an explanation for the loss and dislocation experienced by the former line manager, it fails entirely to capture the real gains made by the female employees, who were far from docile. Indeed, Colin was clearly being subjected to far more questioning, "'piss-takes," and interchanges than he had ever had from the more status conscious male manager, who was at the same time not only trying to conceal his feelings but projecting negativity! The person did not feel involved; the mechanisms traditionally associated with involvement had served to displace him so that he was less involved than before. His presence served as a signal that things had changed in more ways than one. We will analyze this further after we discuss the similar case of Company B.

Company B

This is another global organization with multiple sites all over the world. Over the last decade, the organization has been structured into a series of business units and support units. We first approached the organization's support unit for TQM for an improvement process to research. We visited the support unit and interviewed three of the permanent staff in the unit and the long-term consultant who had helped to shape the approach that the organization as a whole took to total quality management. It emerged that all business unit managers could avail themselves of resources, such as training materials, consultants, and advice, from the support unit. However, it was the business unit managers' decision as to whether their units participated; across the organization as a whole, implementation was patchy, which made the support unit feel vulnerable. Indeed, its head felt that being given that job was a demotion: He appeared highly defensive. The unit also ran an annual prize competition and, after some discussion, the support unit manager suggested that we study the management improvement project, which had won the prize last year, whereas the consultant suggested we examine one of the finalists—what was termed "the secretaries" project—which we chose to do first. The consultant had been very pleased with the head of this unit, as after the initial training on the approach to improvement that included briefing on the key concepts and additionally playing Scalextric and getting drunk, the head had embraced the ideas wholeheartedly, implementing and facilitating them to great effect.

On "the secretaries" site there were around seventy sales technical and administration staff who managed the business unit's activities in their specific country. The nature of the business was base "support" to the itinerant sales force and distant customer. The organization was more balanced in terms of numbers of men and women as compared to others we studied, with the technical staff and senior management being men and the administrative support and sales representatives being women. We were treated royally, with access to everyone and anyone at the small site—except the finance director, whose office was between the managing director's office and the conference office in which we were based (whom we will discuss later).

All site personnel had undergone training in the preferred method for "managing total quality" with the assistance of the support unit, and the site leader was particularly enthusiastic about the method and its results. Through equipping people with problem-solving techniques and enabling them to form teams, the staff themselves had redesigned several aspects of the site's key processes in a way that reversed the traditional hierarchy. The secretaries had identified problems with the current way of working with the sales staff, which had left both the sales staff and the secretaries frustrated. A reorganization and change in the working practices resulted in improvements from both perspectives. The secretaries reorganized to be more responsive to the sales staff, and the sales staff changed their working practices to fit in more with those of the secretaries. Customers were reported to be far happier with the new system, and the organization's "evidence of success" performance indicators were moving upward. Several female staff had won promotions, and the secretaries' function was now recognized as being more core to the effective running of the unit. Again, a similar enthusiasm and constructive interplay could be witnessed between the male leader, "Richard," and the female staff, who had gained much from the transformation. His name cropped up in the interviews and transcripts far more regularly than did those of other "bosses" in our extended sample.

With this case, it was Richard who was our main contact, and his personal assistant made most of the arrangements for our interviews with the stakeholders. Again, there was a higher representation of women than was normal on the list of people we spoke to, but again, though these women had progressed, they were still not senior.

Richard and his PA had offices in the corner of the first floor of the building, and we were greeted there and went back in between our interviews, which were conducted in a meeting room two doors along. The next door along was the finance director, and we were never introduced to him, nor could we see him, because unlike the other offices, his was curtained off so it was impossible to tell whether he was in or not. We learned about this person from others: they mentioned in interviews that he did not participate in improvement activities, and they were in some ways proud to say that was his privilege. Richard admitted that he would have liked everyone to be involved, but it had not slowed things, as the finance function did not intrude on everyday operations, and he thought the man would leave of his own accord as he seemed very out of place now. People had told us about him before we ever remarked about the curtains being closed around that office; when we spoke to Richard and his PA about the oddness of the drawn curtains, they viewed it as consistent with the finance director's negativity.

We were never introduced to him. Merely because he did not "participate" did not mean that he did not influence activities and—vicariously—the thoughts of others. In one way or another, he cropped up in most interviews. Again, this person was labeled as a bit of a "throwback," but there was never any question of his leaving. He was quoted as being completely against the new way of working, not joining in at all, despite the nature of the changes that were supposed to include everyone in improving processes and measuring outcomes.

We arranged to visit the site where the prize-winning improvement had been implemented; there we found a very embarrassed senior manager and a group of stakeholders who did not know to what we were referring. The improvement project was a new method for carrying out post mortems on all projects, and the all-male team that the contact person arranged for us to speak to did not know about the method and certainly did not use it. Other than in the report submitted to the TQM support unit, the project did not really exist, yet it had won the prize in competition with the secretaries project, which was very real and contained a series of examples wherein the support unit's resources and working practices were implemented to material effect.

Analysis

Both cases constitute representations of change processes wherein attempts were made to involve employees (Oakland, 1995). There is very much a sense of "before" and "after" and some radical intervention. Our analysis would suggest that far from the aspects such as delayering, training, and development leading to a holistic form of involvement, involvement seems to have taken place along gender lines. Marginal women became core, and men who were core and high-status became less involved than they had been before. The women did avail themselves of the opportunities to contribute, as the various mechanisms provided a space for them to show their interest. The involvement was not total, but not being involved did not mean being fired in these two organizations. Instead, the men were labeled as throwbacks and referred to as demonstrating undesirable characteristics. The literature (e.g., Oakland, 1995; Ohno, 1988) attributes lack of involvement to ignorance and lack of effort in implementation, but neither of the men was unaware of what the organization was trying to do or of current management ideas.

The gender relations are important when trying to analyze the cases in more depth. Both cases contained instances in which women developed as individuals and had progressed up the organization hierarchy; in Company A's case, we know for certain at the expense of men. However, the ultimate leaders of the organizations were not only male but far more secure males than before, through generating loyalty and support from the women and by marginalizing some men.

It is possible to explain some of this by drawing on existing discourses of masculinities. Both cases represent attempts to use more-rational, control-based strategies to move away from authoritarian paternalist regimes (Kerfoot and Knights, 1993). The gamut of Collinson and Hearn's (1996) discourses can be identified in the Company A case, as there was a "'change" program that was designed by a coterie of men and imposed on the rest of the company because it would be at one and the same time good for the organization and the individuals in control. It served to promote the site and the individuals making such an improvement effort. In some respects, it resembled elements of the strategic masculinist discourse outlined by Kerfoot and Knights (1993).

There is less evidence of the full constellation of previously articulated discourses of masculinities at the Company B site, as Richard was far less authoritarian from the outset and capitalized on the accomplishments less than a more entrepreneurial form of masculinity would allow. Nonetheless, there was a patriarchal overtone to the changes; it did boost his career, and this was going to maintain his power position for the long term.

Curiously enough, Company B's support unit that was designed to be a catalyst for change displayed a failure to move from paternal-autocratic forms of masculinity in its devaluing of the secretaries project and what appeared to be unjustified recognition of another project's worth. The social processes for allocating prizes reflected an enactment of a fratriarchal (Hammer, 1990) element to the masculine system of domination (Martin, 1996), wherein the project that included a large female element was evaluated as being less worthy. They picked a bogus project because they wanted to impress one set of managers higher up the organization. The demeanor of the support unit's boss seemed more consistent with testeria, and his allocation of the prize to an intangible project had more to do with choosing the audience to whom he was performing (Martin, 2001).

These discourses of masculinities fail to explain fully the constructive aspects of the change, the supportive behavior of the male leaders, and the retention of the managers labeled deviant. To our minds, mobilizing the discourse of testiculary helps to account for these processes, both the testicular masculinity of Colin and Richard and the testeria of the displaced managers. We would argue that Colin's and Richard's version of masculinity is similar to Flannigan-Saint-Aubin's (1994) "testicular" metaphor. They both provided the structures and resources to help incubate the change processes, nurturing the improvement initiatives and staff that developed and yielded considerable dividends. This can be juxtaposed by the managers who lost out in the changes, whose behavior resembles what Flannigan-Saint-Aubin would term "testeria" (1994, p. 250). The Company A manager was morose and fretful; the Company B man was petulant, stagnant, and intractable, but it is part of Colin's and Richard's testiculary that these men held any position in the organization.

Hollway (1996) is useful in reminding us that the positivity of testiculary enabled the managers to defend and promote their own position and that this is an accomplishment requiring repeated attention. Equally, the testeria displayed by the disaffected managers would perhaps further marginalize them.

Exploring the relationship between the leaders and the female staff, the change processes served to bolster each side, and this was displayed in playful banter in a way that would have been totally inappropriate before; these instances of intimacy triggered visible displays of alienation and anxiety. A form of Collinson and Hearn's informalism (1996) is occurring between genders, which is difficult to capture in writing or texts but was evident in the tone of voice used when we watched interactions between Richard and his female coworkers and heard Colin described by his. In some subtle way, this is supported by the "losing" men's obvious social dislocation.

The two cases and the relationship of Company A's support unit to the case site illustrate the insecurity of the masculinities enacted in the organization, how they shape and are shaped by events. The cases highlight several areas wherein gender difference is maintained, though the power relations have shifted and, in some instances, enabled women to progress. Disaffected managers displaying signs of testeria provide more readily acknowledgable forms of splitting as a defense against anxiety (Hirschhorn, 1988). More positively, Colin's and Richard's testicular response to the pressures to intensify the labor process is perhaps a response to their having a personal history in which gender difference was seen to be a creative force and positive relations between themselves and women provide a more secure defense against the anxieties of maintaining their masculinities.

The role of the disaffected

In both cases, the disaffected people might have had a role in delaying or dragging the improvement process, which is consistent with the many authors who suggest that everyone needs to be involved and that cultures need to change to facilitate improvement. Several managers we interviewed in other organizations placed great store by encouraging the disaffected to leave the organization. There might be an argument for retaining some of the disaffected staff, as they have a role in relation to the improvement process as the performance of genders outlined by Hollway (1996) above. Creating and sustaining an identity of keenness might require having "the not keen" present to highlight differences in behavior and serve as a totem of what is inappropriate behavior.

The managers who were not involved appeared to us not to be hindering things, although the Company B manager was not peripheral to operations or geographically in the building. The closed curtains signaled a person shutting out the changes, marking him as distant, and refusing to engage socially. He could have refused to resource initiatives, but we were not told about this, only that he did not participate in teams and that it was hoped that he would either come around or leave, but it was not part of the new way of doing things to force the issue.

Conclusions

We think that like other areas of management, the ideas about employee involvement are overly simplistic. Writers such as Deming (1982) have for long enough highlighted the damage that disaffected employees can cause and prepared the way for taking each individual seriously. There is no doubt in our minds that the management in both the organizations we discuss in this chapter attempted to "drive out fear."

The means by which our study organizations attempted to involve workers had some success for some, largely because it afforded them opportunities for personal advancement. The programs were not, as such, designed for their individual needs, but they could tailor what was on offer in such a way that it served a mutual purpose.

Involving people by having a unitary conception of the individual and assuming what might motivate the individual based on what might motivate oneself is unlikely to be successful. The models of business excellence do require organizations to be aware and to manage diversity, but too often this seems to us to be a "bolt-on" activity and not integral to improvement efforts. In this chapter, we have chosen to explore the concept of gender, although ethnicity and sexuality might well be used as other examples. For example, one of our students noted that in a presentation given by a major fashion retailer to one of our classes, every single "reward" for outstanding performance contained some form of alcohol—from a bottle of wine as an ad hoc gift to a hotel trip with champagne reception. The student did not drink alcohol and would not have been spurred to greater performance by such rewards. Whoever designed them did not have religious observers or alcoholics in mind as employees.

To return to the topic of gender, this chapter examines changing power relations in two organizations undergoing periods of radical change. Well-established, "masculine" management practices were labeled ineffectual and had to be changed to improve performance. Considerable effort was vested in outlining and projecting new practices. These new practices could be seen to be a move away from traditional enactments of masculinities through largely hierarchical interactions and formal and informal evaluations (Martin, 1996) to a less hierarchical yet still masculine style. We argue that the male leaders enacted a form of masculinity that was subtly different from paternalism or other forms described in the literature, known as "testicularity." Flannigan-Saint-Aubin's ideas (1994) constitute a rare portrayal of masculinity in a positive light. The main losers in this shift were other men.

Summary conclusions

This chapter discussed:

- That employee involvement is crucial, but relations between employees is under-researched vis-à-vis improvement
- That some people argue that more-modern employee involvement approaches lead to a feminization of organizations

- That masculinity is not well explored either, and there are few conceptualizations, mostly negative
- Two cases highlighting instances wherein women progressed up the organization as a result of their participation in improvement, also highlighting the loss of status for some men, although other men were still in charge!

Discussion questions

- Is there an ideal employee?
- How do different genders behave in meetings? Does this affect improvement?
- How would you encourage a reticent, but competent employee to contribute?

Further reading

Flannigan-Saint-Aubin, A. 1994. The Male Body and Literary Metaphors for Masculinity. In *Theorizing Masculinities*, edited by H. Brod, Kaufman, M. Thousand Oaks: Sage.

Hollway, W. 1996. Masters and Men in the Transition from Factory Hands to Sentimental Workers. In *Men as Managers, Managers as Men*, edited by H. J. Collinson D. London: Sage.

Martin, P. Y. 2001. Mobilizing Masculinities: Women's Experiences of Men at Work. *Organization* 8 (4):587–618.

7 Continuous or "big-bang" improvement

Using the analogy of the body

Summary introduction

This chapter discusses:

- The case of an airport that used careful research to develop a "big-bang" improvement initiative
- How the big-bang failed and resulted in considerable damage
- The similarity between big-bang approaches and cosmetic surgery
- The similarity between continuous improvement and bodily "fitness"
- The difficulty of reaching any image of the ideal improvement
- That the apparent speed of a big-bang approach does not materialize in reality.

Introduction

This chapter was inspired by something one of the managers we interviewed said to us. At the time we were visiting a major European airport, which had decided to go for a "big-bang" approach to improving operations. Briefly, the airport is extremely successful, but it is a victim of its own success. A surfeit of customers, in the shape of both passengers and planes, was clogging up the system. The decision was taken to business process re-engineer the hub, and the "experts" were called in to assist the existing management. A large team consulted widely, and an ideal type of the fully functioning new organization was presented. We visited shortly after the big-bang had been attempted and was unsuccessful, and the manager responsible said this in the interview:

> We have given thought to where to *cut the organization* to divide up the process. The most visible cut was in the aircraft turnaround process. The people on the ramp and the others in the terminal are highly interdependent.

The design is about delimiting processes and *creating a repair* mechanism. With each *cut* you make you are making a choice for operations or strategic or financial reasons. What is the 'repair', the monitoring process, the bonus, the appraisal? We are still in the process of doing this, and there is *scar tissue*, with every cut there is scar tissue.

There is a sense wherein the senior manager sees himself as a surgeon. The organization was not perfect, and some repairs needed to be carried out. In the course of doing this, some other cuts were carried out on "good" parts of the organization, which are then in need of repair. The change process leaves scar tissue (i.e., tissue that will never be as flexible again, but is perhaps stronger than what was there before).

In this chapter, we contrast approaches to performance improvement with those to improve the body. Imai (1986) contrasted the Eastern holistic, gentle "kaizen" approach to the Western "big project" method, and it strikes us as very similar to how we now attempt to manage obesity and lack of fitness. The options available now are the slow fitness method and the fast cosmetic surgery tactic. We liken continuous improvement to the fitness method and business process reengineering to cosmetic surgery. For both approaches, there is some kind of "ideal" to strive for, varying sets of ideas and consultants available to help, but the organization is left to deal with the consequences.

Continuous improvement is based on Shewhart's pre–World War II Plan-Do-Check-Act (POCA) cycle (1931), wherein processes are analyzed in careful depth and incremental changes are implemented, monitored, and altered. Business process reengineering (Hammer and Champy, 1993), a fad of the nineties that is echoed in some of the improvement projects we have witnessed, requires a vision of the ideal process, reorganization of the workforce, information systems, and a dramatic shift from the old system to the new.

We would argue that this bears strong resemblance to an individual's approaches to the body. If one's body is perceived to require improving (e.g., it is seen as too heavy), there are two possible routes to follow. The first (continuous improvement) is to embark on an exercise and diet-weight-loss regimen, monitoring performance and making local adjustments with the help of one's nearest and dearest. The second is to book oneself into a plastic surgeon to have the offending globules sucked out of the body, returning home in the desired shape. Clearly, both approaches do not necessarily start and finish at the same place. Both often end up as quick fixes: Seldom do diets or plastic surgery work for long.

Drawing on the work of Davis (1995, 1997), we argue that choosing the "plastic surgery" approach implies an attitude to the body that thinness is the ideal and that one can adopt a variety of processes to achieve it. It is possible to use the metaphors of the body and cosmetic surgery to explore the process of organization modification, most obviously paralleled by operations management writers embracing "leanness" and "agility." In addition, we draw out the similarities between how managers construe the identity of the organization, and the decision-making processes determining the choice of the improvement activities selected. In addition, there is a moral issue about the application and practice of management techniques and research on body modification. So-called improvement techniques are rendering the "fat" anorexic and the "fit" less fit.

Continuous improvement

It is generally accepted that Shewhart's statistical study, *The Economic Control of Quality of Manufacturers' Product* (1931), was a seminal work that stimulated the thinking of the quality "gurus," notably Deming (1992); Juran and Gryna (1988); Crosby (1980); and Feigenbaum (1991). During the World War II, Shewhart's methods were used in the U.S. industry to a limited extent to aid manufacturing problems. After the war, Deming, as head mathematician of the U.S. Bureau of Census, had been assisting General MacArthur, at that time the head of the U.S. Government of Occupation, in preparing for a national census in Japan. MacArthur knew of his work in improving quality levels in American industry during the war, when he had explained his methods through the medium of courses held throughout the land. By 1947, Deming was convincing Japanese managers and engineers of the value of his quality approach, basing his messages on advanced statistical quality-control techniques. "Deming did not, as many Westerners think, introduce the Japanese to statistical quality control. These concepts...were well known to the Japanese long before he went there. However the Japanese were struggling with the problem of conveying the mathematical concepts to their people... Deming's contribution was to help them cut through the academic theory, to present the ideas in a simple way which could be meaningful right down to production worker levels" (Hutchins, 1990, pp. 26–7).

Statistical process control requires measurement points along a process to be set up and data to be gathered on either the process or the product. These are recorded on a chart that has control limits marked. These mark the limit of what constitutes acceptable scores, and if the data fall outside the limits or are patterned in a certain way, this should trigger concern. The idea is use the chart to identify problems before they lead to damage of the process or product. The technique can be used on any process or product; for example, Imai (1986) quoted an example from telephone answering. If a process is understood and in control, it is possible to improve it. Additionally, confidence in operating existing processes makes creating new ones seem less of an adventure. We have to say that in the processes we researched, there was precious little use of control charts, especially for prevention. Where they were used was for corrective action. To be effective, they need to be part of daily routine and tied to analyzes of causes and the PDCA cycle.

Deming (1982), Juran and Gryna (1988), and Crosby (1980) all believed in process control (who could not?) and thought it needed to be supplemented with employee involvement and customer requirements to create total quality management (TQM). There is no point in having processes in control making good product if the product is not what the customer wants, and it is far more cost-effective to do away with separate control organizations and have the people near to the process managing it.

Although TQM shares the emphasis on customer requirements and process improvement with business process reengineering (BPR); as it is intended to be a holistic but incremental approach; therefore, if it is implemented properly, it is much less dramatic than BPR. It takes time to facilitate, and the outcome can be more far-reaching. Any TQM approach requires stamina; Juran and Gryna think it needs at least five years to implement (Juran and Gryna, 1988). The EFQM business excellence model requires organizations to sustain upward trends in data for several years to score well in any assessment. The success of Japanese organizations, such as Toyota, has resulted in the interest in TQM becoming global. Given what it consists of, it is not surprising that Wilkinson et al. (1998), among others, cite several articles that indicate a high failure rate of the approach.

A revamp of TQM called "Six Sigma," which originated in Motorola in the 1980s, has become popularized recently with the success of General Electric in the United States (see Welch, 2003), which in essence is a new version of statistical process control tied to a new version of the PDCA project-management support. A bolt-on addition is the organization support structure, which adopts a Japanese martial arts hierarchy of belts that are obtained through gaining knowledge of techniques and experience in managing projects. The essence is the same: Detailed understanding of what is going on is used to decide which areas to improve, and the requirement is to monitor that any activity does actually have some material effect. The whole process is time consuming and laborious but can yield substantial financial benefits in the long run if pursued diligently. It strikes us as surprising that the analogy of the body has not been used more extensively in this context. In the next section, we discuss how similar "body" improvement can be to continuous improvement.

Improving the body: exercise

The insurance industry has produced ideal weight tables, and what constitutes a fit body through exercise is also well understood. Everybody knows that some exercise is useful in improving the length and quality of life; here are three excerpts from fitness books on one of our bookshelves:

> ...The secret of aerobic training is that through regular exercise at an output level that is high enough to raise the pulse to a certain level over an adequate period of time, the heart will become stronger and can pump more blood through the veins per heartbeat. This tends to lower the resting pulse - making the heart last longer and its owner live longer.
>
> (Van der Plas, 1990, p. 8)

> Thus we face the contradiction that we have enhanced nutrition that is not matched by an enhanced workload. Worse still, the [sic] modern man and woman have the additional problems of coping with the foodstuffs industry, from which a large amount of advertising is aimed at persuading people to eat for pleasure—a very different proposition from taking a normal, healthy pleasure in what they eat.
>
> Modern society also tends to regard all problems as having technological solutions. Every doctor knows that many of his patients no longer regard sound advice as therapy, and without recourse to drugs or even surgery they do not believe they are getting good treatment. There are innumerable jars, bottles, tubes, capsules and syringes contained alleged cures and reliefs for ills that arise solely from the way we live. Consider how much orthopedic trouble has arisen from fashion shoes alone. Think how many people insist on medicine and treatment rather than stop smoking. We owe it to ourselves, as well as to society, to try to live in a more natural and healthy way. There may not be much we can do about our employment, but there is a lot we can do with our diet and our leisure.
>
> A carefully worked out running schedule, coupled with a good diet, will not only help us to achieve fitness, but it will also be one of the best pieces of preventive medicine that we ever undertake.
>
> (Coe and Coe, 1983, p. 8)

> "Fitness" is *your* ability to do what ever you ask your body to do.
>
> (Jackowski, 1995, p. 12)

The quotes above seem to us to describe the circumstances at the airports aptly. The airport did function well as an operation; nevertheless, managers chose to stimulate demand by creating a hub at the time that external factors, such as deregulation, were leading to an increase in air travel across the region.

None of these authors suggests that a person starts off with a clean sheet; all are concerned that people check their health with a doctor so that appropriate programs can be designed for them. Jackowski, (1995), who advocates skipping as a primary method of achieving fitness, goes so far as to analyze skeletal types and suggests appropriate methods that will improve the heart rate of these individuals. Coe and Coe (1983) provide indicative training programs, as does Van der Plas (1990), but all give information so that individuals can devise their own.

The focus of the books is on the internal workings of the body and preparing the various muscles, organs, and the like to cope with the exercise that will improve cardiac and other functions. The surface of the body is not really discussed, and certainly not the facial features. The approach is similar to the Buddhist one:

> In this very body, from the soles of the feet up, from the crown of the head down, surrounded by skin, full of these various mean impurities; there are in this body: hair of the head, hair of the body, nails, teeth, skin, flesh, sinews, bones, bone-marrow, kidneys, heart, liver, membranes, spleen, lungs, large gut, small gut, gorge, dung, bile, phlegm, pus, blood, sweat, fat, tears, skin-grease, spittle, snot, oil of the joints, urine (and brain).
>
> (Khema, 1987, p. 62)

There are many similarities between this and Deming's (1982) idea of the organization. Everything is important, especially the inner workings and less fashionable areas of the body. It is foolish to concentrate on the surface of things because the underlying problems are likely to be systemic.

Bauman, (2001, p. 82) contributes a useful argument. He thinks that the modern identity is like a palimpsest: that new identities are inscribed over old, that forgetting rather than learning is the continuous aspect, and that people "enter and exit the field of vision of a stationary camera itself is like video tape, always ready to be wiped clean in order to admit new images."

As the medical professions developed, they were charged to provide "healthy" bodies for the labor force; however, now things have moved beyond this to require us to be "fit," which is a looser epithet, certainly at the higher ends of the spectrum.

Business Process Reengineering

BPR was popularized in the nineties by Hammer and Champy (1993), with their book becoming a best seller and spawning an industry of conferences, spin-off technologies, and consultancy opportunities. The authors placed great emphasis in asserting that their methods were consistent with a U.S. ethos, in contrast to the Japanese initiatives of TQM and JIT (just-in-time). Citing the "successes" of the approach in well-known companies, the authors argued that it was a radical departure in thinking about organizations in process terms rather than as task factories, although some writers had been doing so since the 1930s (see below).

Hammer describes BPR as "fundamental rethinking and radical redesign of business processes to achieve dramatic improvements in critical, contemporary measures of performance such as quality, speed and service" (Hammer and Champy 1993, p. 32).

What could be claimed to have a flavor of originality was the "clean sheet of chapter" mentality. BPR is not about improving existing processes but starting from scratch to achieve customer fulfillment. Specifically, in an easily digestible set of four key words, the authors say BPR is "fundamental"—the organization should go back to basics; "radical": Reengineering is about business *reinvention*—not business improvement, business enhancement, or business modification" (Hammer and Champy, 1993, p. 33). It is "dramatic" in that it should be used when substantial change is required; and finally it "concerns processes," tracing what they are, making sure they are consistent with what the customer wants; the division of labor, it is argued, frequently hinders progress.

To realize BPR, an organization has to address core processes thoroughly, be ambitious, break traditional rules, and support this with judicious use of Information Technology (IT). (One of the spin-off technologies might explain why enterprise resource planning systems have become so popular, as the "benefits" sold by vendors of this software are consistent with BPR).

Hammer and Champy are at pains in their first book to differentiate BPR from TQM. BPR is a top-down redesign of an organization. TQM, as is discussed later, is to do with improvement of what exists.

There has been a whole stream of criticism of the concept, from both managerialist and critical authors. Hammer (1996) chose to address the managerialist's criticisms in his subsequent book (not coauthored by and with no mention of Champy) wherein he admits that the prognostication that BPR fitted in with the U.S. "zeitgeist" might be mistaken. There are numerous cases of organizations attempting BPR and creating an unpleasant mess. Hammer argues that in these cases, the management stopped half-way because they lost their courage. Whatever the reasons for the mess in practice, critical authors have devised several very interesting theories to explain its appeal.

Case (1999) argues that managers engage in these approaches on a symbolic level, that there are religious overtones to the owning up to being imperfect, and that salvation can be achieved through embracing the new ethos of BPR. Grint and Case (1998, p. 557) discuss the approach as being an attempt at "reverse colonization": The United States was sick of hearing about and being told to implement TQM as a Japanese success story. The BPR approach, they argue, has many similarities with the Wild West in its use of quite violent techniques. On a more positive note, David Buchanan (1997) details a project at a hospital, describing circumstances in which the managers in the organization perceived that it was necessary to carry out a more dramatic change. Targeting the process was less troublesome than focusing on the individuals; he charts the improvement in operations turnaround resulting from the ideas.

Ideas on the body

There is a wide range of perspectives on the body and its place in society. Davis (1997, p. 2) discusses how "the meanings surrounding the body have changed," from a former emphasis on work thrift and sobriety to a more recent one of leisure, hedonism, and consumption. Allied with this is the notion of the body itself as a "means of self-expression." The body is a "malleable organism" (Burkitt, 1999, p. 7). This can be organic or mechanistic: Several authors draw the analogy between the body and a machine or even a form of cyborg (Shildrick, 2002).

There have been a number of texts written on how females relate to their bodies in particular ways (e.g., Young, 1990). Bordo (1993) argues that the female body is a metaphor for the mind-body split: The male is the mind, and the female is the body. However, there is some evidence that an increasing number of men are relating to their bodies in a way that has been historically considered female. Rudberg (1997, p. 195) discusses the "staging" of the body and argues that whereas in the past it was just women who were scrutinized, "men have achieved a new character of 'to-be-looked-at-ness' e.g., David Beckham". There are undoubtedly social pressures both to look a certain way and to "improve" any particular deficiency. A radical and increasingly popular means of achieving this is surgery.

Cosmetic surgery

"It is possible to transcend age, ethnicity and even sex itself" (Davis 1995, p 18). This author has written a very detailed study on cosmetic surgery and carried out empirical work with "patients" and surgeons. It was not until the Crimean War that body interventions were legitimized. Before this, interfering with nature was viewed as blasphemous. War and accident victims required plastic surgery to protect or ameliorate injury, and techniques that were developed for that reason became used for cosmetic purposes. Major advances occurred in the twentieth century, culminating in the variety of techniques that are practiced today. Various tucks, face lifts, abrasions, eye surgery, implants, and the like are all possible ways of changing the appearance of individuals, usually to make them more youthful or to conform to some "ideal" shape. Initially, cosmetic surgery techniques were not seen as a substitute for dieting, but then liposuction was developed; combined with more traditional methods, it is possible to get rid of "saddle bags, bums even pudding knees ...liposuction is the most popular and fastest growing area" (Davis 1995, pp. 26–7).

One of Davis' main arguments is that people who avail themselves of cosmetic surgery are not "cultural dopes" but individuals with many reasons for doing so. She (1997, p. 12) uses the term *biographical agency* to consider the ambivalent relationship that a woman has to cosmetic surgery "as both an expression of the objectification of the female body and an opportunity to become an embodied subject." Later, she comments, "Cosmetic surgery is a complex dilemma, problem and solution; symptom of oppression and act of empowerment all in one" (Davis 1997, p. 176). In her own research, she found that, far from using cosmetic surgery as a way of "improving" the body, women used it to become ordinary. Countering this, in a later chapter Davis discusses the case of Orlan. Orlan is preoccupied with a series of surgeries that she views as performances and is attempting to move toward her "'ideal" body, which is not the Western norm; other commentators might consider that she has made herself more "ugly." The point Davis is making is that, irrespective of outcomes, cosmetic surgery is a mode of expression; the women obtain "control where there was no control" (Davis, 1997, p. 175).

The consultant

Davis (1995) is one of the few authors to discuss the role of the surgeon and the doctor-patient relationship. One particular man described the cosmetic surgery relationship as being the reverse of the usual one. The patient knew what she wanted; the surgeon was supposed to carry it out but often had difficulty seeing the "problem." This research was carried out in the Netherlands, where the government will pay for the surgery if the patient can show a "medical" reason why it "needed" to be done. The surgeons had to come up with a set of criteria to establish this, but had difficulty doing this and applying them. Some even thought the women wanted surgery to retain husbands—a procedure that the surgeons saw as futile!

Computer technology enables the surgeon to show the individual how they might look after surgery. "The patient is photographed and the image is projected on the screen. The surgeon (God and artist, all in one) uses an electric pencil on a special board to make the desired changes while the patient watches. Flesh is added and taken away, shape is transformed. The malleability of the body and the power of medical technology are visually sustained in each demonstration" (Davis, 1995, 17).

At this stage, patients feel as though they are making an informed choice; however, Davis goes on to describe in detail that if the procedure is relatively quick as compared to normal dieting, it may be far from painless afterward and does not last:

> Pain, numbness, bruising, discolouration and depigmentation frequently follow liposuction, often lingering up to 6 months after the operation.... Fat which has been removed from thighs or buttocks may return, requiring another liposuction, or the skin may bag and have to be cut and reshaped... Following a liposuction, the skin can develop a corrugated, uneven texture so that the recipient looks worse than before.
>
> (Davis, 1995, p. 28)

> Cosmetic surgery involves a surgical intervention in otherwise healthy bodies. It is a painful and dangerous solution for problems which are rarely life threatening and seldom evoke physical discomfort.
>
> (Davis, 1995, p. 29)

The alternative to this invasion is the prosaic and more time-consuming method of self-modification. The next part of the chapter describes the change program at our host organization, an airport.

Hub in transit

The organization we are discussing is a major European airport hub, employing 1,000 people outside the terminal building servicing the departure gates alone. The airport has experienced considerable expansion of capacity and demand over the last decade (9–10 percent growth in traffic per annum). The key processes are outlined in the following figure (Figure 7.1).

Around 70 percent of the throughput it handles is transfer passengers, and problems were being incurred with delays and baggage transfer. Information management was poor; they did not use "through ticketing" because in the past, when they allocated tickets at the original airport and a plane was delayed, it caused havoc. There is also a big problem

1 Turnaround of planes

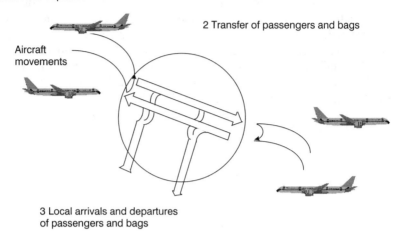

Figure 7.1 Main processes carried out at the hub

with parking planes. One of the repercussions of this was that a new bus terminal had to be created to transport passengers to the planes. One of the people we interviewed, whose job was to train ground staff, said that the way in which the operations were managed was very militaristic.

The managers had a range of possibilities open to them as to how they improved operational performance. They chose a BPR approach developed with the assistance of a major consultancy with experience of managing projects in the airline sector. The following section of the chapter explores the nature of the change, how it was selected and designed, and the effects on the organization. We interviewed jointly a range of "key stakeholders" in the change and toured the facility. The following year we made a follow-up visit to the airport and were brought up to date about developments. This year, we made a phone call to enquire as to progress, and only one of the then nine key stakeholders was still working for the organization!

What to change?

There were more than 100 people on the "change" team—external consultants, internal consultants, management, and employee representatives—at the mandatory works councils who reviewed the reengineering process.

The external consultants drove the early stages and, depending on whom we talked to, the job was either very thorough or superficial. Contrast:

> During the redesign phase the team conducted a quick scan of the processes. They analyzed them through putting people and bags

through the processes and used this as a basis for redesign....the main bit was done by NYC [a pseudonym for the consultants] and mostly their ideas were realised in a couple of phases. The Orientation phase specially focused on benchmarking to find out performance indicators. We intend to strive for World Excellence, to be the best hub in the world, so you have to know what the rest are up to. We visited 8 other airports, and NYC did the writing up (which was a condition for the other hubs participating). This gave us a good insight of processes and helped define our own targets. Phase 2 was an analysis of our own core processes, for instance the check in process, waiting times etc. NYC charted the processes. Time studies were conducted and passengers and employees interviewed to find out what was positive and what the passengers want to be improved—we used the employees to think through whether that could be done. A lot of measuring using critical path analysis to determine the bottleneck was carried out with a stopwatch. They studied 80 turnarounds.

(middle manager, change team)

From all this, they developed their own ideas for improvements. The project team numbered eight at that time. NYC also invited groups of employees to contribute every month. A workshop was organized with fifteen to twenty employees, at which findings were presented, reactions sought, and further ideas solicited.

The senior manager thought NYC had performed a key role, though another interviewee judged it a minor one, a view that a subsequent person we talked to endorsed. Her view was that NYC had an agenda and used the airport staff as "gofers." In any case, it was the senior manager who made the choice: He decided on what he termed "the split up" supported by two consultants. He admitted that it was not an analytical choice but more down to "gut" feel. His priorities were to make sure that the proposals were not too outlandish and to form a coalition of other managers. He "secretly" got three or four people to "remain" on board [but he's not sure how secret this was]. The next layer, he argued, will be much more a team decision.

The whole project is a *process* redesign which was apparent in the organization construction ... to go to a customer type form. I've given thought to where to *cut* the organization to divide up the process. The most visible cut was in the aircraft turnaround process. The people on the ramp and the others in the terminal are highly interdependent. The design is about delimiting processes and creating a repair mechanism. With each cut you make you are making a choice for operational, strategic or financial reasons. What is the 'repair,' the monitoring process, the bonus, the appraisal.....? If you make a cut you must monitor goals etc. and feedback performance. Making employees accountable for local and global performance indicators is the most important tool you can give them. Lots of 'repairs' have to come from the flow of information from IT systems.

In the end, the main objective derived from the analysis was that the minimum cycle time it took to service an aircraft from when it landed to when it took off was to be cut by a half and to be accomplished at 30 percent of the cost. This everyone considered "very stretching." Current performance was between 10 to 15 percent on time and, rather like other transport providers, there was a bit of slack built in, e.g., fifteen minutes late was still on-time!

Performance measurement to monitor progress was going to be team-based, and outcomes would be fed back to them. The top management identified key result areas and areas for teams to address, such as punctuality and on-time performance. Some of these were customer-related, such as "first bag on the belt." Teams would have some autonomy to optimize the process. For example, the "dolly" cart can wait to be filled, which is efficient, or you can split the carts and improve customer satisfaction; the teams can decide which. Initially, the teams would not be given a budget; they would be managed on performance and then given budgets.

How to change things

It was at this stage that the "change team" expanded tenfold. The team's responsibilities were to handle the HR aspects, such as change management, basic HR, and communications.

The change team had to consider which elements were of most importance to employees. This was new to this airport. They did not formerly measure motivation but only people satisfaction, which is retrospective. They thought they needed to know what motivated people who are receptive to change. They generated lists of points derived from interviews, which yielded twenty-five issues. The top five were always the same. The first was work recognition, second was freedom to manage their own roster, third was leadership style, fourth was working for the airport, and the fifth the interviewees could not remember but were sure it was not money.

They tried to encode as many of the top five in the new job designs and developed a flatter organization structure based around "turn-around" teams that transcended the inside-outside divide. At this stage, employees had not been trained for wider tasks and, unsurprisingly, the forty-five- to fifty-year-olds were particularly apprehensive about the future.

Jobs in transit

After analyzing staff motivation as a way of smoothing the migration to the new structure, a new organization was set up to process the employees. People were put through a battery of tests to ascertain their likelihood of performing well in teams or leading them. Every layer was involved in choosing the layer below.

Though the company involved the workers' council as each stage of their proposals developed, there appears to be some uncertainty as to how far and how thoroughly the actual workers were actually informed about the changes envisaged. The workers' council had been expected to be the prime communication route to the employees. It seems open to question whether its members really acted as representatives of the whole workforce. More often they now appear, in retrospect, to have been acting more in an individual—as distinct from a representative—capacity. Nevertheless, regardless of whether this was the case, the company firmly believed that their people were continuing to be informed about the broad shape and emphases of the project, but in retrospect some slippage might have occurred in autumn of the second year. By January of the third year, the ways in which the new arrangements were to be implemented and how these would affect individuals' jobs, salaries, working patterns, and the like had been sufficiently clearly drafted for a major exercise to be mounted to communicate the whole project to the entire workforce.

Accordingly, over a three-day period in that month, a marquee was erected within which six or seven stands detailing the new organizational structure and operational methods were set up. All employees were invited to go along to learn about the new arrangements. There was some fifty staff on hand to explain the plans in detail and how they would apply to individuals. Though each of these staff were expert in one change process, they were frequently asked questions about the plan in general or about aspects with which they were not personally sufficiently knowledgeable to be able to answer authoritatively (or both). Perhaps understandably, the answers provided confused rather than clarified the situation. Consequently, rumors then began to circulate about the nature and character of the changes, inevitably embellished with unverified perceptions. Two days later, there was a strike.

The "marquee" approach was different in concept in that it tried to communicate to everyone, more or less simultaneously, the essence of the new ways of working and how these would affect each employee. It was concluded that it had actually resulted in contradictory messages being conveyed and the real import being apparently misconstrued.

The events of that month represented a communications watershed for the whole airport. Now, whenever there is something of substance to convey, line managers begin the process by informing their first-line supervisors; worker representatives are then advised and thereafter each individual employee. Comprehensive information is provided in written form at every stage, accompanied by a consistently positive approach. Continuous operation always makes effective communication demanding, but now employees' questions can be answered by a supervisor who has been thoroughly briefed.

After the strike, a cooling-off period or "time out" followed. Work resumed but under the working conditions prevailing before the stoppage. During the "time out," negotiations took place to resolve the dispute. At the airport, one of the outcomes of these negotiations was that the trade unions would be active participators in all future discussions; "social" conditions would be given especially close consideration.

Implementing the changes

Once the organizational design was completed, the first team was planned to be up and running in November of that year (nine months after the tent event), with the rest of the teams in operation in the following year. It was anticipated that it would take four years to redesign and reorganize to incorporate the new working methods into the new organization and the new working methods [with 4,500 employees]. BPR takes a long time, don't you know!

Senior management commented that North Airlines (a pseudonym) had a big-bang approach and "it worked," but they have now undone some things. The reason why the big-bang worked for North was because they had more control. They had their own terminal, whereas this airport has stakeholders, work councils, and unions; North had only the unions. This airport has an egalitarian approach to people; it was argued that in the United States, the boss rules. Actually, the airport managers were relieved to have the additional control factors.

This project has turned out to have been spaced over four years; in the future, managers hope that the process should be much quicker with the second stage of implementation being carried out in one go. Incremental approaches may appear to leave the organization in control, but the management thought there are different kinds of risk because the longer it takes to implement the changes, the greater the dangers there are in operating two systems in parallel. Continuous improvement was seen to be the next step. It will take four years to catch up on not having change before that. The managers felt that the lesson was that a big program is not always the best way to proceed.

Despite authorizing benchmarking and comparisons with other airports, the managers realized that the approach they took was perhaps too analytical. They later acknowledged that it is possible to overanalyze things. Goal setting needs to be appropriate for the particular context, and they commented that they would analyze a person differently if they knew they were going in for the marathon rather than a sprint.

Though the four pilot studies went well enough within the teams, other parts of the organization were not supportive or cooperative. Managers acknowledged that this would always be the case, especially when the organization was not used to such major change.

The workers' council was very suspicious. The project team came up with new ideas that received adverse reactions; council members initially thought there would be less money, harder work, and redundancy. This made things hard for the managers, despite the publicized basic guarantee that everybody had been assured a job at the airport, though not necessarily in the hub. Managers dropped a couple of the more controversial suggestions to smooth negotiation of the social conditions. However, the workers council proved to be if anything under-representative of the resistance they eventually encountered.

Analysis

In the following section, we will address first the effects of the initiative, second the relationship between the management and the consultants, and third the utility of the analogy we are drawing.

It would have been embarrassing to ask the managers whether they had hit their stretch targets, because they clearly had not. They had taken the decision to go for radical change, and the outcome was an element of it; the control center with accompanying information system was implemented. On our first follow-up visit a year later, the body looked only slightly different. From "wholesale liposuction" in lots of different areas, they had ended up with a "tummy tuck." The most striking thing was the absence of many key members of the change team. When we telephoned three years later, the only manager the person who answered the phone could put us in touch with was the skeptical manager, the one who had had experience of TQM and the organization's love of "change" programs. The rest had been sucked out—they had gone.

The management was convinced that it needed to address the problem quickly with the assistance of outside people. They would then deal with the effects. The more mundane incremental approach was not considered as a credible alternative. The body analogy fits particularly well when looking at the consultant's role. The use of "outsiders" to "improve" an organization is a conscious decision that has unconscious implications over which managers have almost no control. The patient-consultant relationship is usually privileged and singular, but the organization awards a contract to a consulting company that supplies a plethora of different consultants.

Exploring the manager-consultant relationship, the managers chose which type of "new body" they wanted and proceeded both to sign the consent form and instigate the surgery. The airport's most senior manager interpreted his role as a surgeon, but he did not do much cutting himself; the change team did that. We find it difficult to ascribe either the surgeon or the patient role to the senior managers. They acted as the patient in the initial phases of the change, they identified a consultant, they selected the type of change, and they agreed with the procedure's going ahead. However, the patient body is both themselves and at the same time not themselves: It is other people who are operated on and who rebel.

When we examine the analogy between the organization change and body improvement, we find there are a number of areas wherein the organization body has been cut and where layers have been taken out. The NYC team examined the corporate body with the help of the airport staff, presented the managers with a vision of what the organizations could look like, and assisted with instructions as to how to draw up a plan. The plan was very aggressive: half the turnaround time at 30 percent of the cost. The organization would be cut and joined together. Management layers of fat were to be sucked out from selected areas. The external skin would be cut and sewn together, but scar tissue would be inevitably created.

We have been accustomed to change being seen as inevitable, rapid, but painful in the business sector. The use of the body metaphor, its unknowns, indeterminate reactions, and healing processes helps us to undermine simplistic theories of organization change prevalent in many texts on improvement. It provides a way of showing how potentially damaging invasive change projects can be: In our case, the organization body "vomited" its rejection, bled, and ached. The fitness-regimen analogy provides us with a way of explaining why activities designed to improve the internal processes of the organization lose out to activities that are supposed to lead to faster surface effects.

The top-down design approach failed as a "fad" in the wider business community and specifically in the airport, as it reinforced the Taylorist view that the mind equals the manager, whereas the workforce equals body dualism. The managers failed to appreciate that they were in fact carrying out an operation on themselves; the "fat" they were attempting to suck out might well be themselves! The token "incorporation" of the representatives and surveys failed as they were the surfaces of the organization body of employees; they were only samples, and they turned out not to be representative. Above all, contrasting liposuction and fitness approaches to body modification helps to explain why one can have the appearance of being fit without actually being so (see chapter 5; Collinson and Collinson, 1997). The use of information systems to assist BPR interventions is well documented (Hammer and Champy, 1993; Buchanan, 1997); perhaps they can be seen as the equivalents to the introduction of implants to the calf or breast. It is hoped they are "incorporated" properly, but again, they can remain a parallel system within the body, which can leak and render the rest of the body unhealthy.

Both approaches have models of what are ideal, largely based on financial indicators, perhaps relating this to quality management or defect levels. However, continuous improvement requires systematic engagement with customers and employees to enhance processes. The equivalent for the body analogy might be monitoring vital signs, such as heart rate, blood pressure, sugar levels, liver function, and the like, with the help of practitioners to meet some life goals in conjunction with relevant stakeholders. The continuous improvement-fitness metaphor starts from what is; the BPR-liposuction one starts from what might be. The shared elements between both approaches are the modernist assumptions that one can actually improve processes and that people can get into a mess when they try to implement either!

The dull, worthy, time-consuming, continuous improvement approach can "hook" people on the endorphins, but it takes a while to become addicted to these to such an extent that they become an everyday need.

The airport case demonstrates, we would argue, that using the BPR approach on what was essentially a healthy but fat operation upset the balance: The management failed to achieve its objectives and, in many cases, lost jobs. The activities failed to make the organization function better either in terms of the current socially defined criterion of "thin" or from the perspective of the manager-surgeon or the "operated-on" employees.

Cosmetic surgery is an elective option; one chooses to do it; and it is normally a commercial transaction. The clinic where the liposuction is performed commissions or is owned by doctors who have a professional duty of care, but patients sign a waiver acknowledging that they understand that problems might occur. No such waiver exists for management consulting. The surgeon usually is not tainted by postoperative complications, rather as consultants are rarely damaged by failed organizational interventions, such as BPR or TQM.

Modern life places emphasis on consumption and capital accumulation. The body analogy enables us to suggest another way in which increasing consumption can create problems. The approach taken by the organization was that the managers perceived the airport to be "unwell" or choking and they needed to process things more effectively, burn calories faster but, to do that, they tried to suck out fat and rearrange the process. An alternative would have been to manage the process so that less input was entered. The hub concept creates greed. Southwest airlines does not have a hub and, as a result, is more "lean and flexible." Instead of the mad rush to accumulate customer numbers, organizations might be better served to improve the operations for the existing customers so that they are in a position to process new ones to a satisfactory standard.

Above all, whereas the TQM-fitness appears to effect modest changes across industry as a whole, the BPR-cosmetic surgery approach can "Orlanize" the organization (i.e., make it "uglier" than before).

Conclusions

We think that drawing this analogy helps us to understand some of the difficulties of sustaining performance improvement. Initiatives fizzling out are not peculiar to organizations trying to make things better. What needs to be done is obvious and well understood; however, we want a faster route to getting it. Any form of change can have both negative and positive consequences, and it is sometimes extremely difficult to trace any linkages or causality. There are some well-known addicts of cosmetic surgery who demonstrate this in a way that is not possible for organizations; however, we would argue that the effects of repeated initiatives have a similarly scary effect.

The managers who wanted to eliminate layers and change the organization were victims of their own plans. Perhaps if they recognized more clearly that they were part of the "body," not detached, their choice of remedy and how they enacted it might be different.

Just as Davis (1997) questions whether women who want surgery do so for improvement or merely to feel normal, the stories and images of organizations in popular management texts—and in some senses encoded in critical writers' ascription of knowledge and purpose to management—present images of the ideal organization as fit, lean, and competitive. The ideal organization is presented, together with snap shots of other organizations that apparently have undergone transformations. Whether these organizations ever constituted models for others, or still do, is open to question (see chapter 5), but they are seductive images for troubled managers to dream of attaining.

The analogy also gives rise to the possibility of seeing customers in a different light: They might be food to be processed or might be fat. Cutting fat as a way of processing more food seems an activity doomed to failure.

Summary conclusions

This chapter discussed:

- The appeal of fast approaches to improvement as similar to the desire for plastic surgery
- Continuous improvement, especially statistical process control, as like a detailed fitness regimen

- The airport case management, which followed a perfectly reasonable route for the sector
- The long time it took to develop their big-bang approach, which backfired when management try to implement it
- The thought that they had represented staff views, though staff disagreed!

Discussion questions

- How would you go about improving airport processes?
- What other aspects of the organization are like the body?
- What improvement shortcuts prove successful?

Further reading

Case, P. 1999. Remember Re-engineering? The Rhetorical Appeal of a Managerial Salvation Device. *Journal of Management Studies* 36 (4):419–41.

Davis, K. 1995. *Reshaping the Female Body: The Dilemma of Cosmetic Surgery.* London: Routledge.

Shildrick, M. 2002. *Embodying the Monster.* London.: Sage

Section 3

Repair

This section explores performance improvement using a word not normally associated with the area: repair. The preceding chapters have discussed some examples of the role of traditional topics in improvement in our organizations, and more recent chapters have taken a nontraditional, more critical perspective. To summarize: Unintended or not, improvement activities can lead to damage. In other contexts, damage is usually followed by an attempt at repair.

Almost every book we have read in the area adopts a forward-looking, modernist perspective on improvement. A set of ideas is presented, not in relation to deficiencies in previous attempts but rather as *ab initio* methods to deliver similar objectives of dramatic improvement and market domination. There is no acknowledgement of past failure. There is no acknowledgement that there might be different attitudes to improvement, that some people might not see that their job needs improving at all, that people other than poorly paid workers might be recalcitrant and in need of "culture change."

There is a consumerist culture with management ideas: Initiatives are adopted, used for a while, and disposed of in shorter and shorter cycle times. There are in the organization elements that exist before any initiative and will continue afterward as forms of continuity. For example, many people work in the same job for more than a decade, and it undermines credibility if past mistakes are glossed over and remain unacknowledged.

If we were to sketch the approaches, writers in the modernist vein characterize performance as being poor and in need of improvement; critical authors tend to view improvement attempts as intensifying further the labor process; and even those who hold a more complex view of power seem to see this as a zero sum game with gains primarily for the management. We would argue that this is too simplistic; the relationship between the past, the continuing, and the "new" is ill explored, but it seriously affects whether an improvement activity will be a success. Authors fail to acknowledge the similarities between their approach and older ones, preferring to package their ideas as novel. Consultants shadow these activities, having vested interest in appearing up-to-date and being able to generate income from tying in to initiatives.

As the manager at the airport we studied in the last chapter argues, change can cause scar tissue, and maybe there is a case for extending the body metaphor to suggest that repeated interventions to improve something can weaken it beyond repair. We are not new in pointing out the layering or the damage caused by the bombardment of initiatives, but our contribution is to suggest that it might be an idea to consider the concept of repair and how repair as a process might have a useful role in achieving performance improvement. Organizations have prominent and not so prominent activities, although all are necessary in performing the task and improving. Maintenance and repair is an example of a less-heralded area that does not, for example, form headline modules on university courses but is essential to the smooth running of any operations. We think the processes of organization improvement can include an element of repair, and we consider the facets of this in the next two chapters. The first chapter in this section explores some of the individuals we met and interviewed and how their relationship with their work was in a sense repaired. The second chapter looks at the role that frameworks have in repairing and restoring faith in improvement activities.

8 Repair at an individual level

Summary introduction

This chapter discusses:
- Elizabeth Spelman's concept of repair
- The role of the apology in repairing relationships
- The role of money in repairing work relationships
- The case of Blue Circle Cement
- How apologies can be given in subtle ways
- The usefulness of the repair concept for improvement.

Introduction

Previous chapters have highlighted some of the dimensions of individual relationships that help or hinder improvement. In essence, every author discusses how people relate to each other; however, it is usually couched in management concepts of motivation, involvement, and so on. Drawing on the analogy of manufacturing-process activity, the product (improved performance) is the target rather than the process (relationships), and perhaps addressing the relationships directly might yield more long-term, flexible results. The nearest managers come to articulating these are through implementing ideas such as team work, flatter organization structures, and single-status organizations that are intended to create the conditions for people to interact more directly and track relationships but not directly address how individuals relate to one another. To put it another way, improving relationships is always a means to an end rather than an end in itself. Where we think our case organizations were more successful, there was clear evidence of some kind of "'repair" of fractured relationships, albeit indirectly.

This chapter outlines what we mean by repair. We draw heavily on the work of one individual, Elizabeth Spelman (2002), who has written concisely on the topic. We are indebted to Dr. Elaine Swan of Lancaster University for bringing Spelman to our attention. The first part of the chapter summarizes Spelman's ideas, and we draw out their relevance for performance improvement; the second part relates the ideas to one of our case organizations; and the third and concluding part discusses some of the implications of this approach for managing other organizations. However, first—what is it that we found so appealing in Spelman?

Repair

Spelman defines repair as "maintaining some kind of continuity with the past in the face of breaks or ruptures to that continuity" (Spelman, 2002, p. 4). She draws a distinction between repairers and creators, who she says start from scratch; destroyers who eradicate; and bricoleurs who assemble existing materials to form something new. Most appealing to us, she states, "To repair is to acknowledge and respond to the fracturability of the world in which we live in a very particular way" (Spelman, 2002, p. 5). To be able to repair is a very skilled activity.

Spelman identifies three approaches to repair; the first is "Willie," the country general "Mr. Fixit" mechanic. He is presented with a variety of machinery by people from miles around, and his job is to try to get the machinery to function again. He does not pay attention to the appearance of the machinery he repairs, but cannibalizes materials and fashions new parts so that the car or tractor functions again without paying too much attention to esthetics. Over the years, he picks up additional knowledge of materials and machinery and can see the same item repeatedly. The second is Fred, the car restorer who returns old models to their gleaming original condition, using his extensive network to acquire original parts while remaining faithful to the original look and function. Esthetics is all—his work is dictated by the intentions of the original designer, and he too employs a network of contacts to locate parts. The likelihood of a piece coming back to him is smaller. The third mode is described through Louise and her team's work at an art gallery, where the job is entirely about "invisible mending" of works of art housed in the gallery. The pieces are permanently located except for releases to other exhibitions. Careful research is carried out into materials so that the restoration process is as unobtrusive as possible because earlier, clumsier attempts at repair can have created additional damage. Louise has narrow margins within which to operate.

Spelman discusses the methods used by the three approaches, noting that Willie can go beyond the intentions of the original designer if that helps him to get the car on the road; he can fashion a better part. He and Fred can be as radical as they like; they can replace the majority of the items. Fred, however, is bound by the intentions of the designer, his work is much more constrained, but he can visibly make his mark on the artifact in a way that Louise and the artwork team cannot. Louise and her team work *in situ* and, over the years, will build up a bank of knowledge about an item and the materials known to have been used in the repair in a way that Willie and Fred cannot. Their skills lie with having knowledge about the methods of repair used and materials.

There appears to be a zone wherein repair is possible. Spelman quotes Elgin (1997) in saying that some damage is either too minor or even too major to attempt repair; indeed, some of the effects of time are to be desired—it is the "ravages" of time (p. 17) that should be addressed. She uses this to highlight that what constitutes damage is highly context-specific. One person's damage is perfectly acceptable to another. We might cite the example of alcoholic drinks: While the ageing of whisky is desirable, this does not apply to beer.

Spelman concludes that part of her book by discussing the emotional ramifications of repair, specifically consolation. Willie offers no consolation to the visual senses other than some joy of new combinations: It is partly a creative process, and the consolation is to be able to use the machinery, however interesting it may be in its new appearance. Fred's restoration offers the consolation of the "material memory"—an emotional link to the past—and that the effects of time can be eradicated. Louise's team have the consolation of continuity in caring for the pieces over time.

Repair of individual relationships

Spelman's next chapter explores where we learn about repairing human relationships: the household. She begins by drawing a distinction between men's and women's spheres of repair. A form of masculinity is performed through domestic repair; do-it-yourself, decorating, minor plumbing, and the like have traditionally been seen as man's domain of competence. Tradesmen with panoplies of tools can be hired to perform these repairs, and women are actively discouraged from entering these trades with the use of pinups in garages and so on. There is an increasing market in courses for women and books helping someone to learn skills directed specifically at women, but the inference is that she would not be availing herself of these if there were a man available to carry out the task.

When the scope of repair is extended to include relationships, Spelman argues that this is a female domain and that the home is not only a "haven in a heartless world" (Lasch, 1979) but a kind of dry dock and repair facility. Day-to-day feeding and sleeping are unmistakably forms of maintenance; one learns at an early age that minor repairs are carried out at home and that there is a medicine cabinet for such tasks. (Children are sometime accused of feigning injury to trigger the emotional repair process that accompanies a cut or fall. The fuss is worth the damage.)

Relationships can be damaged to a greater or lesser extent, and the home is where we learn or fail to learn how to repair them. Spelman quotes Klein's theory that we dream about destroying our all powerful mothers, "conflate the desire with its accomplishment" (Spelman, 2002, p. 34), and then counter it with restoring fantasies. Babies tear apart, then attempt to mend, and Spelman notes the healing role of children for relationship problems. She argues that there is a gamut of repair roles performed in the home, although increasingly tasks are outsourced, and house members are "deskilled" (Hochschild, 2003). She also points out that it is impossible to tell whether a person can be said to be "repaired" and that outside agencies have jurisdiction over which kind of interventions can take place (e.g., the use of "smacking" to discipline children is now proscribed). It is important to acknowledge that the home can be the site of relationship damage and repair.

Spelman uses the analogy of a "demolition derby" to illustrate her point that the home repairs people for the workplace so that they function in a restricted number of ways. There is a psychological repertoire operating that limits the individual, and this is learned in the home —we learn a range of responses and actions that we use to shape our interactions at work and how we interact in society. The nurturing of these skills is quintessentially female-dominated activity. Men frequently invoke women as mediators, and it is considered "non-economic": it is not acknowledged or particularly valued (e.g., subject to the trade organizations and certification that are male-dominated activities).

Spelman then goes on to discuss more societal levels of repair, stating that women and men operate to different "ethics of care." She uses Gilligan's argument that men are likely to invoke rules and women to focus on the individual, using an example of a pregnant teenager. Gilligan typifies a male response as considering which rules govern activities (for an unwanted pregnancy, this involves whether the person is underage or overage, timescales for abortions, and the like), whereas the female response is typified as being more child-centered, focusing on what can be done to alleviate the situation for the individual.

There is not the same well-acknowledged panoply of tools, publication of approaches, and well-acknowledged industry as for mechanical or electrical breakdowns; however, relationships break down on a daily basis, and an ability to repair them is extremely valuable socially. The lack of panoply means that the skill is undervalued and mundane, which can result in the repair workers' skills and processes being overlooked and isolated when they are in need of repair themselves.

Social repair

Restorative justice provides examples of social attempts at repair, but the history of its use shows that some kinds of damage are irreparable (e.g., the holocaust and apartheid). The majority of justice systems are retributive, but Spelman argues they have evolved from more restorative ones and that there have been many recent attempts across the globe to reintroduce restoration. The truth and reconciliation process in South Africa is an example of employing one-time perpetrators of damage in the repair process. It provided a forum for accounts of the victims to be aired, and consequently there was more of a chance of healing taking place than the traditional retributive justice process afforded. The aim was to enable people to live together later, not apportion blame with the focus on the perpetrators, like the vast majority of Western legal systems. "The overriding aims are the restoration of social equality among the participants, not the retributive punishment of the offender; the reintegration of both victim and offender into the community, not their isolation" (Spelman, 2002, pp. 65–66). We almost hesitate to point out that this phrase has strong echoes of W. Edwards Deming (1982)!

One of the traps of restoration is to concentrate on specific individuals and circumstances, which can lead to unfairness across cases. Improvised solutions can mean that similar problems are addressed in different ways, leading to the type of repair and the consequence being different. Another trap is where it is assumed that repair is desirable; perhaps there is a probability of recurrence (e.g., where a relationship was abusive). Although Spelman thinks that the wholesale incarceration of prisoners on the assumption that they are not repairable is wrong, there are some instances wherein it is very arrogant to try: The skill set available to tackle the repair is too low and the probability of failure too high. Lastly, what constituted the predamage state is open to question; similarly, the completeness of the repair. Some indication of the damage might actually be desirable; it could serve as a warning sign for others.

Next, Spelman turns her attention to what might constitute the tools in the human-relationship repair business—"words and money" (Spelman, 2002, p. 79). She argues that a verbal apology entails an admitting of responsibility that many wrongdoers find difficult to make. It is easier to make a monetary payment that "means from the side of the payers not having to say you're sorry; it also means from the side of the payees not being called upon to forgive, not being pressed to forgo resentment" (Spelman, 2002, p. 82). The process of establishing reparations can enable victims to take an inventory of where they think they are damaged and can provide an avenue for individuals to realize they have something to apologize for.

An apology is complex; there are social obligations on both sides. It is required in situations wherein the damage is significant. Apologizers lay themselves vulnerable and, by offering the apology, expect a response. "An apology is an invitation to share in a ritual of repair, in a dance that takes more than one dancer" says Spelman (2002, p. 85). The person who accepts the apology is obligated to forgive;, the problem lies with them if they cannot move on from there, and they are socially in the wrong if they continue to harbor resentment.

The intentions of apologizers and their comprehension of what they did have an effect on whether the apology needs to be taken seriously. Spelman uses the example of white Americans apologizing to blacks for slavery; the apologizer is too removed from the damage and the people causing the damage for the apology to have much force. "Apology is more about the wrong doer than it is about the wrong done and the person to whom the wrong was done" argues Spelman (2002, p. 96). So if the apologizer is tied closely to the wrongdoing, the apology is an admittance of guilt, and no excuses can be made to shift the blame; the person is in a fit state for rehabilitation. The victim, in turn, cannot revisit the harm done or question the wrongdoer more. In this curious way, the apology both links and distances the person from the wrongful act. The person publicly says he or she was involved but socially creates the conditions to move on. It is in this way that the apology then shifts the social responsibility to the victim so that he or she become part of the repair process. Apologizers admit they caused pain and open up the possibility that the victim will cause pain for them.

Spelman then goes on to discuss the role of ruins. She draws a distinction between ruins and rubble: Ruins have a degree of coherence and are sought out as being instructive. Notably she quotes John Ruskin's phrase, "to restore is to destroy": There would be something destructive in restoring the Parthenon; the ruin serves as a symbol and a lesson in itself. We can become overly concerned with ruins. Spelman uses the term *ruinenlust* to describe where a love of the esthetics of the ruin blind us to the horrors that may have created it, and nothing can repair some horrors, such as the holocaust. She quotes Langer (1991), who says that scars are different from ruins in that scars are a sign of a "curable condition, a past injury healed in the present. What we are really speaking of ...is a festering wound, a blighted convalescence" (Spelman, 2002, p. 116). Ruins are damaged artifacts, and the damage continues.

Memories are perhaps even more permanent monuments to ruins; they are passed on through generations and can become more geographically dispersed. Langer would argue that if there were not the language of repair, the hope of an opportunity to repair, we might intercede before or in the early stages of an atrocity and stop it. In this sense, repair can be bad. Perhaps some organizations are ruins, and attempting to repair them would not serve any purpose? Some people working in these organizations might have *ruinenlust* and like to conserve the "brokenness" as it makes them feel good about themselves.

Returning to repair's relationship to the past in her final chapter, Spelman writes that to carry out a repair is a conservative act that returns an item to a past moment. We would add that this can go beyond physical appearance. Spelman notes, "In its service to the past and the pre-existent we find reasons to distinguish repairing something from creating it or replacing it" (2002, p. 126). She argues that there are three impulses that humans have— to create, to destroy, and to repair—although repair is often juxtaposed with creating rather than with destroying. What constitutes repair is what a person does that is different from creating, although repair quite often contains an element of creativity (e.g., Willie the car repairer employs other models' doors to mend a faulty one because of the limited finances of his customers). However, some acts of creativity would never need repairing; music is used as an example. It would seem silly to tinker with the perfect, even if the perfect is not technically correct. This returns Spelman to the link between repair and destruction, noting that by repairing for example a book, some of the desired aspects of ageing are lost (the imprints of people and the like). In some cultures, traces of the repair are valued. The repair offers consolation of a return to the past when things were fine, but an element of destruction is required to do this. Visible repairs retain the link with brokenness, invisible ones do not: A scar shows that the skin gaped open; there was a wound, however created. "Repair is the creative destruction of brokenness" (Spelman, 2002, p. 134). However, it lacks the drama of creation or destruction, so it is not as feted. In some ways, repair is anti-capitalist: The fetishization of the new and the minimization of opportunities for repair are the driving forces behind much competitive behavior.

Repairing can be uncomfortable because it brings us into relation with the concept of brokenness, the ways in which things can be broken, and our own skills at mending them. *Homo sapiens* might be in vogue now but, owing to the finite resources of the world, *homo reparans* may yet have her or his day!

The area of operations management is full of stories of initiatives wherein ideas have been tried and are perceived to be a success. The longevity of the results can often be questioned. Although many of the activities are about repairing poorly running processes to make them function, the language is couched in terms of improvement *ab initio*; there is no acknowledgement of history other than a sketchy casting of the past as being a mistake. The language is more analogous to, for example, an athlete striving to achieve world-best times, rather than one with an injured ankle trying to restore fitness.

As far as we know, the language of "repair" is not used. The damage is not acknowledged; indeed, in chapter 4, we present an argument that people are caught up with presenting images of success. There is little recognition that a repair job might be necessary. Certainly, whereas we have heard of attempts to learn from previous mistakes, repair and apology do not feature in the aftermath.

Spelman highlights the conservative aspect of repair that could imply a negative or retrograde process. We think that this has relevance to the study of work relations in the sense that it is the relationship that needs to be conserved. People choose to work in companies and at some point they are positively disposed to them, but this attitude is eroded by damaging activities. Repairing them is a constant and strategic activity.

In the following case, we focus on the elements of an initiative that had the effect of repairing the brokenness of the past. What constituted brokenness was a fracture of the relationship between management and employees, and this manifested itself in poor financial results. The next paragraphs describe what happened in the organization; then we use Spelman's ideas to highlight where we think the individuals succeeded in repairing the relationships and, most important, continue to succeed in financial terms.

Blue Circle

As we discussed in chapter 2, Blue Circle had had two previous attempts at improvement. These were unsuccessful; indeed, employees did not think much of the competence of the management (e.g., they thought they were "like headless chickens"). They thought the third attempt was different because they were included in the process at an early stage and even invited to attend to hear what was proposed! People were asked, not told to participate; they went and agreed. There was a different manager using the same old words of "'trust," "commitment," "improvement," and the like, but the employees decided to give it a try and "go for the hat-trick."

Slowly, they started again and decided to get to know something about total quality. There was a widespread sense that thirty years of autocratic management had not gotten anywhere. The site was in danger of being closed but, on the positive side, there was plainly energy to be released. The trick was to get it channeled in the right direction. Everybody without exception was trained. Respect and pride became the new norms, commitment absolute, people safety treated as paramount—again, these words had been used before, but this time it seemed different to the employees.

All this was decided by brainstorming with all the workers; the art work used at the site was designed by a worker and a manager. The lampooning continued with the naming of business unit managers as BUMS: "BUMS take a back seat" was the legend on a cartoon illustrating empowerment. The site employs 210 people; soon after starting, two-thirds were involved in teams. Usually there are twenty teams at any given time; they operate by talking, helping, and trusting one another. One of the early successful projects was to improve the shower block, and this became a metaphor for the improvement process that included BUMS. The process was described as a shower combined with upward bidet effect!

Previously, if managers wanted to communicate with the rest of the workforce, it concerned bad news: either redundancies or sob stories to lower expectations before wage claims. When such a meeting took place, nothing was really explained: A statement was read out by a charge hand who parroted what he had just heard himself. Communication was obviously not viewed positively. The new communication system was far more intense and two-way; the volume of information quickly snowballed (e.g., there were six monthly briefs, weekly meetings, graphs, reports, newsletters, fact sheets, profit sheets—the variety was great). One of the reasons for this was that it was learned that one method did not necessarily achieve the desired aim. For example, one manager thought he had been over-repeating himself by saying to the people he was about to announce the twelve-month results showing the recovery was underway and that the initiative was thriving, announcing this and then summarizing by reviewing this. However, people said they thought it was a very good brief but what was it supposed to be about?

Part of the initiative was to connect everybody with working on customer satisfaction more explicitly. They used questionnaires to establish their position in the marketplace and areas for improvement, and this has resulted in the development of new products, training for employees, and forms of customer support. They have found that they have the major market share and intend to maintain and improve it.

Some of the projects that were supported by the steering group included one wherein men who were reputedly not renowned for changing a toilet roll redesigned the toilet buildings. Capital investment patterns, shift patterns, subcontractor employment, equipment purchase, and the like were all subject to review and improvement. The involvement did not just include the quarry and the production facility; more marginal areas, such as the depots, joined in.

The process was clever insofar as everyone was included; ideas were not passed on for someone else to process. Everyone had the knowledge that he or she was eligible to put forward ideas; all would be listened to, action could be taken by one another, and all learned to appreciate one another.

One of the managers was supported to do further education in management, and he was delighted that his organization was operating to the theory. It was not difficult to pass the exams because this meant writing down what he was doing during the day; it was not about learning a separate stream of knowledge. Understandably, this added to his sense of its being rewarding working with the company.

The shift in relations can be exemplified by the focus on safety. Before there were about fifteen accidents a year, which was the industry standard but not acceptable. There were procedures in place, but they were not really addressing the problems, and there was no scope for improvement. It was thought unacceptable to expect a certain level of accidents. A safety improvement team that was set up was multidisciplinary and tasked with increasing safety awareness and reducing the level of the rate to zero. Some of the issues the team tackled included employees who had regular eye problems. The team made it mandatory to wear safety spectacles on site, which eliminated the problems. They now have safety-protective equipment for all other parts of body, and the model to show how this should be worn is a cartoon of a naked manager. The plant will stop for a safety problem. £250,000 was allocated for a safety project, and efforts resulted in a 60 percent drop in incidents in the first year. During one of the times we visited, everyone was very upset because someone twisting an ankle at the rail depot meant that a single accident had been recorded that year.

A process operator who had joined the site straight from school described how he thought things had changed. When he first joined the company, he felt obliged to follow older workers, which was to go along with the "us and them" relationships, the management hierarchy was very autocratic, and so on. The only person who communicated with him was his direct line supervisor; managers were distant, untouchables, and did not know your name. Chances of promotion and recognition were very low. Lads who joined enthusiastically soon became entrenched in negative behavior. Now he thought attitudes had changed radically; for example; there were one-level meetings and team-building activities. Simply being heard had had a dramatic effect on his attitude.

He was pleased to participate in the local open day to show the people he lived alongside the pride he felt in his job and industry. The organization had been working for thirty years at Dunbar, and it was only now that there were open days. At the open day, hundreds of locals arrived and praised the site. People came in and worked on a Saturday unpaid, which was an attitude unthinkable in years gone by. For the day, people worked to create an exhibition of projects on posters supplied by everybody, which was another way to give recognition to those involved. It was "our exhibition, our achievement and done by us."

The process worker thought the potential was always there but never tapped. He considered the employee questionnaire a genuine attempt to gain views, because action had been taken on the findings, whereas problems had been ignored in the past. The works manager who usually stayed in his office wearing his suit changed into overalls and helped out on a production problem to help sustain production.

From a management perspective, key business processes were identified, benchmarking was carried out,; and more facilitators were trained to develop ownership. Families were encouraged to become involved, and different things were tried to keep things interesting. In the early days of change, it was thought that trust was fundamental; however, you cannot trust people you do not know. Ross, the leading manager on the site (see chapter 2) advocated stability in the management team: He required managers to be there for sufficiently long to develop their skills and, most important, work in pace with developing trust so that people progressed together. He considered his highest achievement was then possible: everybody working together. His objective was to develop a culture resistant to reverting to how things were before.

Physical changes in the workplace happened everywhere. They upgraded the control technology, meaning that seven workers could do the job that twenty-five did before. Now seven work together, fully cross-trained and paid a stable wage. The results of the workforce questionnaire were encouraging for management, too: on average, a 50 percent improvement on last year's scores. Employees appreciated management's taking such care: They felt they knew what the customer needs and had a family feeling of security.

Improvements led to more good things (e.g., they doubled the profits in a difficult market). The successes helped to make the decision to improve the terms and conditions simple. There is a statutory income plan for everyone. In the packing plant, they changed the working hours so that they covered a bigger range of the day, enabling the site to take advantage of cheaper fuel and improve its service to customers. After some encouragement, teams evolved and emerged. It was easy to raise awareness and carry out training. The subtler aspects of the environment and culture were more difficult to engender. It was all very well to say, "We trust you!" Managers said that it was not actually that difficult to give information such as budgets and forecasts and then empower people to do things (e.g., all three trade unions supported it). The stability in the workforce that others may think of as a problem was to the company a great thing. Many people had twenty years of service, and turnover is low, which proved useful to us as researchers. Some of the initial support committees have been disbanded, and now they have lunch every couple of months to take things forward. There are still only two-thirds involved; something to work on is how to encourage the one-third who are not engaged.

Managers do question whether the improvements would have happened anyway. They think not; the process, for example, caused a problem at the depot. This was addressed in a way that could never have happened before. The main reasons for the profits increase were the benchmarking activities and the management of power and fuel (e.g., simply looking after the vehicles better saves money). The teams spend less money on capital equipment; for example, the repair bill is down 40 percent, the hire bill is down 50 percent, and subcontractor bills are down 60 percent, all because people have been trained and understand the concept of cash flow and so make sensible decisions.

Analysis

Relating the case to the ideas described in the earlier part of the chapter, what constitutes "damage" at Blue Circle? We would say there were both physical and psychological components that were interrelated. The site was performing poorly, and the working conditions were shabby. The lack of attention to the environment reinforced the dangerous aspects of the job—a quarry and a very hot process, with grinding resulting in dust, could damage an employee in multiple ways.

The employees describe entrenched positions that new people had to learn. Enthusiasm had to be reduced if one was going to fit in with the group. As Hirschhorn (1998) describes, the vulnerabilities of the workplace meant that to cope with the anxieties of a physically precarious and long-term insecurity of job tenure, the management and employees projected "blame" onto one another, preventing them from addressing the threats from outside. The damage was the lack of maintenance on the relationships, the assumption that it did not matter, and the routinization of what could be described as "class-based" working relations.

There was no formal apology for this by the management. We would interpret the way that the managers were able to be lampooned by the workers as near to an apology as there was likely to be. In presentations that the organization gave, a cross section of the workforce participated, and managers were the subjects of cartoons and the butt of jokes. The jokes were targeted at how things were in the past and the manager's ideas of the future. The driving force behind the way they were doing things now was comfortable with being part of the banter that went back and forth. Through being vulnerable in this way, the manager was able to become a person to the workforce and promote concern with the true source of "danger"—the central management and market competition. This is in accordance with Hirschhorn's view (1998) that leaders have to balance engaging people with showing themselves to have vulnerabilities with providing strategic direction and impetus.

The repair process did contain Spelman's tools of words and money. A dialogue was opened up, with regular opportunities to have a say in changing things and serve on project teams. The exchange of information was very intense and, in our experience, the topics covered were extremely rare. Financial and production information were aired for discussion, and although money was allocated to support initiatives, the management was surprised at how, once the projects were being completed, money was saved. This shows how in its heart of hearts, the management had thought the improvement initiative would cost money. The decisions that cross-status and functional teams made were better than the ones that management took in isolation—again a source of jokes and humor. The cumulative effect of this was for employees to redouble their efforts at improving things and for management to trust their decision to involve everyone.

The people from the organization would say that both the physical environment and the relationships within the organization were repaired and, like some broken bones, this repair seemed stronger than the first arrangement. The "consolation" that Spelman (2002) refers to was, if anything, the much more intense feeling of pride and joy. The site felt confident to go in for external awards and hold open days for local public scrutiny. The latter is perhaps more indicative of how "real" the participants considered the changes as the local town would contain people who did not appreciate the site, ex-workers and the kinds of harsh critics who would be happy to evaluate the changes as being negligible or meaningless. The improvement is always presented as "work in progress," and the external exposure was also seen as a means of obtaining other ideas; however, no external ideas were ever as trumpeted as the internal ones were. It was much more a source of pride that the rest of the business units in the group visited and drew on Dunbar's lead, and one of the authors was involved in creating a corporate "good ideas" database wherein other sites could add reports of local improvements.

It could be argued that the view of how bad things were in the past was caricatured, but we are not in a position to say. The jokes could be interpreted as a form of ruinenlust—the ancient ruins of the disgusting shower blocks, the horrors of the production plant. However, these were changed beyond recognition, not retained. No physical evidence remained.

We deliberately chose a male-dominated workplace as our case for this chapter, as although other organizations might illustrate Spelman's point about the gendered nature of repair, we wanted to underline our point in chapter 6: that too sweeping generalizations are made about male and female characteristics. Very few women are employed in this organization; however, some of the changes to working conditions would make the site more amenable for them to do so. The recognition that everyone might appreciate advanced warning of working hours, job stability, and a work-life balance is important. Evidently, the male interest in tools and "things" featured prominently in the process. The momentum was accelerated with the visible, tangible improvements. If we were to attempt to try to categorize the organization as repairers, the type of repair is more radical than those of Louise and combines the functionality of Willie's mode with the esthetic appeal of Fred's. There is a powerful combination of the old and the new, *bricolage* and "split" new.

The ability to take up and thus invest in courses of study gained very positive response and an appreciative take-up. As in other organizations that we studied, there were totemic individuals who availed themselves of the opportunities and were well regarded by others, who read into the efforts the significance of the organization commitment. It was perhaps a signal of how the relationships were working positively that this individual development was not viewed with resentment, though again there were the requisite jokes about it.

Interestingly, despite Ross's protestations that the management should not move on before the job was completed, it was he himself who moved on to a bigger role within the U.K. organization before becoming responsible for an entire continent (the last time we heard about his activities). Unlike some other initiatives, the process at Dunbar continued, and that is why we are comfortable using it as an example. The initiative did not stall but continued apace. The repair held fast without the "scaffolding" to support it.

What is the proper way to characterize Ross? He was a facilitator with a forceful personality. Though he let people get on with things, he was not slow in putting forward ideas. One of the authors had further experience with him on an industrial advisory board; she has experience of him in meetings. There was no question who was the leader, though he would listen, too.

Ross achieved the correct balance between personalism and role (Hirschhorn, 1988). People could identify with him, but he did create momentum. The site was like many others in our experience—marginal and struggling to survive. The emergence of people who were focused on this, instead of the mutual antipathy and resentment, meant that the site was transformed to a reference one. There is a narrow line between pride and complacency; however, the jokes and marginal location of the site reinforced a continuing sense of risk. The organization was taken over, again creating a risk to survival if the performance statistics were not correct; however, there was a collective rather than an individual response. The cartoons and presentations are examples of Hirschhorn's point about the necessity of managers sacrificing apparent authority for substantive authority, enabling Ross to lead as a follower! The readings in this area are reminiscent of Deming (1982). The repair is perhaps the recognition of interdependency.

Managers seldom have a blank canvas in any shape or form. An organization may be new, but the individuals have experiences that shape their attitudes and behavior. Too often an initiative is layered on top of these past experiences without an attempt to repair any "damage" that might exist, in physical reality or in people's heads. We have heard managers talk of "preparing the ground" for wider involvement, but never have we heard them talk of repairing the damage caused by previous initiatives; the temptation is to "start" to improve things. We would argue that Blue Circle shows a form of attempt at repair that led to the relationships in the organization moving on instead of entering a repeated cycle of failed initiatives.

They did employ the conventional methods of words and money; however, we would want to draw attention to some specific aspects to this. Achieving a sense of the collective was helped by rallying under their sense of "Scottishness." The business unit was the only one left in Scotland, and it is not difficult to identify the proper enemy as being that outside the site when almost everyone there is Scottish and the rest of the organization is not. It cannot have harmed the attempts to involve everyone in this context, and the trick is identifying the most appropriate way of connecting with people.

Though people from the organization made light of the "shower-bidet'" approach, we think it useful as it highlights that repair involves at least two parties and requires response. What is distinctive is the amount of bidet as compared to other initiatives we have witnessed.

Conclusions

In this chapter, we described Spelman's work (2002) on repair and would argue that it is understandable that it has been overlooked as a concept in the improvement process, as most people do not acknowledge that initiatives can not only fail but cause damage to organizations. They prefer to assume that the organization is a fit place to begin a new implementation of a similar kind of initiatives and overlook that some kind of apology, or "truth and reconciliation" process, might be useful in helping to take things forward.

Some might argue that organizations and people are not like the internal walls of a building, that it is not possible to repair even the surface, let alone the depth, of a company so that an improvement can be made. However, with Blue Circle, we have some confidence that this is what they did, and it worked.

A feature of Blue Circle was the repair to the relationships achieved. They developed their own structures to guide and promote their improvement; the next chapter looks at the role of externally developed frameworks to carry out this task.

Summary conclusions

This chapter discussed:
- The existence of many different forms of repair and relationships in need of repair
- Apologizing and devoting resources as necessary components of repair
- The manager in the cement case and the use of humor as a form of repair

- The manager's resourcing of employee ideas over an extended period
- The effect of repairing the damage caused by previous failed improvement initiatives.

Discussion Questions

- With which forms of damage as a consequence of improvement processes are you familiar?
- Have you ever heard a manager apologize for a failed initiative?
- Do you have any evidence of broken work relationships? How might you repair them?

Further reading

Spelman, E. 2002. *Repair: The Impulse to Restore in a Fragile World*. Boston: Beacon Press.
Hirschhorn, L. 1988. *The Workplace Within: Psychodynamics of Organizational Life*. Cambridge, MA: MIT Press.

9 Repair at the level of the organization

The contribution of external frameworks

Summary introduction

This chapter discusses:
* Maintenance and repair, not for processes but for organizations and
* self-repair
* Aspects of frameworks that assist repair
* The case of Nortel
* The case of Organon Teknika
* Some key points to assist with the successful development of a framework to repair previous damage and promote improvement.

Introduction

This chapter continues our discussion on the topic of repair, focusing on the use of performance measurement frameworks as repair tools. The chapter explores the aspects of external and internal models of excellence that have enabled some of those organizations that we have researched to "repair" the failings of previous quality improvement initiatives. As we have pointed out earlier, there are often repeated claims that some four of five performance improvement initiatives, entered into with high hopes, appear to fail either completely or, more commonly, because of their sponsors' disappointment or frustration in yielding only limited improvements. Frequently, companies are left with the real feeling that the key to unlock more substantial benefits remains unturned. Some of the reasons for this state of affairs have already been noted, such as leaders failing to engage with other employees, little coherence or impetus to the strategic direction of the organization, or performance systems that are detached from improving processes. However, there may well be other possibilities that are less apparent. It is also puzzling that, other than as an entry in a set of statistics compiled to present a generally pessimistic view of initiatives, we have been unable to find in the literature any systematic review of what has subsequently transpired in those organizations whose first attempts to improve their performance have been unsuccessful.

In this chapter, we identify and elaborate on the area of repair we introduced in the previous chapter to re-analyze our Nortel and Organon Teknika cases from a different angle. Like Blue Circle, both of these organizations had participated in at least one previous attempt at major improvement, and their use of different frameworks illustrates our point that the frameworks themselves had a material effect in repairing the damage of past failures, generating a shift in perspective that helped to create and sustain some form of momentum. First, we recap on the available frameworks' affects on organizations; then, we go on to highlight which aspects are particularly useful.

Frameworks as drivers of continuous improvement

The frameworks we have studied, such as the European Foundation for Quality Management (EFQM) Excellence Model, the Baldrige, and the Akzo-Nobel MTQ, create a potentially helpful format for addressing damage that we think helpful. The use of the word *excellence* within these models is unnecessary hyperbole and off-putting, as is their complexity, but the frameworks themselves have their useful aspects. As we described in chapter 4, the criteria encapsulated in the models encourage holistic thinking, and the process they suggest fosters accountability. We will now go on to discuss the model we are most familiar with: the EFQM.

Fountain (1998) notes that the bulk of literature on self-assessment (e.g., Porter and Tanner, 1996; van der Wiele, 1995) proves that there is no "best" framework but only one that is appropriate, with the choice of model often being dependent on individual preference. Bearing in mind the plethora of available "off-the-shelf" models, Fountain then goes on to ask whether it really matters which model is used. He reports that a network of international quality managers evaluated in detail more than forty familiar and unfamiliar models to assess what would make a worldwide "best practice" model. From their review, they derived what they call the *target assessment* model that they freely admit includes elements "stolen" from many sources. The selected criteria embody assessment of people, leadership, empowerment, process control, change management, supplier development, business performance, customer perception and, finally, communication. How widely this hybrid model will be adopted in practice is a matter for conjecture.

Stone and Banks (1996) examined the contribution that quality frameworks, or models such as the EFQM Business Excellence Model and the Baldrige, have appeared to make in driving "new" measurement practices, especially in the use of "soft" measures (i.e., those with a particular emphasis on customers and employees). A total of forty-five companies whom they claimed represented a highly strategic perspective of the *U.K. Times* "top 500" were surveyed to assess the contribution that the use of the EFQM or Baldrige models made in driving new management practice (as distinct from the application either of the philosophical approach laid down by the quality "gurus" or of no specific set of principles). They concluded that, though the use of frameworks or models seemed to have spurred measurement of customer and employee related activities, it guaranteed neither best practice nor improvement in internal trends. The authors further commented that the measures of quality that their forty-five companies had used fell into five categories: financial, operating, customer-related, employee-related, and other. The business strategy in those companies—just under half of their sample— who use, or had used, a quality framework for measuring their quality levels was notably customer-focused. This contrasted with non-framework users who favored a financial focus. Stone and Banks (ibid) point out that a significantly higher number of framework users came from the Top 200 most profitable organizations. In their view, this suggested a possible link between the adoption and competent implementation of a framework approach and profitability. Gadd et al. (1996) have also reviewed the reasons prompting organizations to use models for self-assessment. They concluded that this course of action acted as a driver for the organization's continuous improvement initiatives while enabling areas for improvement to be identified.

The EFQM model has always drawn explicit links between the nine criteria. Some are "enablers" wherein activity is intended to lead to improvements in the other "results" criteria. Within each criterion there is a dual aspect to assessment. Each are scored, initially for the enabler criteria there were "approach and deployment" scores (i.e., whether the initiatives taken were sensible and whether they were rolled out fully). The results criteria had a measure both of attainment and of scope across the organization. Each criterion has subcriteria, so to obtain a good score, a broad range of initiatives have to be showing some effect. It is impossible to obtain a good score if the initiatives are not mature and widespread.

At the turn of the millennium, this method was strengthened in the "RADAR" process, which stands for "results, approach deployment, assessment, and review," perhaps another way of phrasing the POCA cycle. The point remains that activities have to be assessed and reviewed. Organizations are encouraged to measure for effectiveness regularly to see what learning opportunities exist. They are encouraged to benchmark with others (e.g., competitors' industry averages or best in class). We found Govan Initiative (see chapter 3) to be particularly good at this aspect. Yet, it is obvious that the nature of the market will dictate how willing organizations are to benchmark. The EFQM wants to see links between the output from learning and performance measures and improvement activities.

The performance measures themselves should give a holistic picture of the organization's operations and encompass all appropriate stakeholders. An organization should be comprehensive in measuring all the relevant approaches and their deployment using both perception and more quantitative indicators. The framework encourages the organization to develop a history of improvements, so that should it enter an award process, it can show positive trends or sustained good performance, ideally for several years. This implies that year on year there should be targets, despite Deming's long articulated caveat that the development, management, and implementation of targets create performance problems in themselves, because people cut corners to meet the targets and the performance indicators might not be related to what the organization's range of stakeholders, including the customer, want. The model requires the targets to be achieved, with comparisons with other cognate organizations presented to show that the levels are meaningful and the improvements significant. Ideally, cause-and-effect linkages should be demonstrated with these approaches, though we have found that companies often find it difficult to identify these, whereas methodologically it is impossible to isolate the results of approaches from extraneous factors. Measures the organization puts in place should not be just of current operational utility. Rather, some indicators should relate to the future health of the organization. A specific scoring matrix is divided up into quarters: People trying to score do not have to worry about reaching an actual number, which might be not representative anyway. The matrix has the guide words trends, targets comparisons, causes, and scope to help self-assessors.

The interrelatedness of the model criteria is designed to promote consideration within the organization of the complications and ramifications of improvement. This seems all very well, but it is difficult to achieve in practice. We once had a guest speaker talk to a cohort of students from a major UK retailer. The retailer sold vegetables, and the speaker acknowledged that the performance measure that required staff to keep full shelves sometimes countered customer satisfaction, because the employees stacked the shelves with alternative lettuces, and the unobservant shopper would pick up what they expected to be on that shelf, rather than what was actually on the shelf.

A key aspect of the EFQM model is how far approaches are rolled out. The organizations in which we had faith did not have isolated patches of successful improvement but had deployed their ideas fully, and the initiatives had for the most part flourished beyond expectations. This is in line with the exhortation that approaches should be both innovative, flexible as well as sustainable and measurable.

Frameworks encourage people to be systematic in the implementation of initiatives and, as employees are integral to their development, it is assumed they will understand and agree to them. Clearly, obtaining this level of detail across the organization requires cooperation, and if the organization has soured the employee relation with past failed initiatives, a repair becomes essential.

Aspects of frameworks useful for repair

The following section examines some of the concepts of repair in relation to improvement frameworks. Important concepts to bring forward from the last chapter are the "apology" and the "truth and reconciliation" process in attempting to repair past damage. As we pointed out in the last chapter, apologies in a business environment are extremely rare. Though we remain open to hearing of examples, we have yet to hear of any managers apologizing directly for the damage caused by previous attempts at performance improvement. As in Spelman (2002), there are instances of words and money being circulated within the organization as if to repair— but seldom any overt apology—we have had to interpret that something stands for an apology. The truth part of the truth and reconciliation is perhaps part of the corrective action or review process; however, there is seldom any overt attempt at reconciliation. An interesting and novel perspective on the "corrective action" and repair process is presented in Graham and Thrift's paper (2007), which we will discuss now. We are indebted to Dr Richard Williams, University of Edinburgh, for bringing this to our attention.

Graham and Thrift (2007) discuss the way in which cities, another form of social grouping, both reproduce themselves and improve. They are primarily concerned with the day-to-day processes rather than the more glamorous "improvement" programs, which is unusual in itself. We did not approach researching our organizations in this way. When we visited organizations under the auspices of researching improvement, we framed the discussion so that it was slanted to improvement rather than maintenance and repair operations. However, we can see from our research the important implications for improvement of differentiating operations between "foreground" and "background" activities as Graham and Thrift (2007) use from Heidegger. Maintenance and repair are ongoing activities that usually take place in the background and are then viewed as dull and not "strategic." When there is a major breakdown, they cease to be part of the background and have their short time in the spotlight before returning to obscurity. Background activities do not seem to have the inherent attractiveness of, for example, new product development or manufacture; they are invisible for the most part, and people are happy with this. The major breakdown makes them a visible nuisance. In manufacturing, a production line breakdown can cause an entire factory to grind to a halt. In the service sector, a computer booking system failure can cause an entire airline to cease to function. Improvement activities share many of the characteristics of repair and maintenance, analyzing processes, and devising solutions. Maintenance requires skilled people who have bespoke tools and take pride in using them. Graham and Thrift (2007) note the volume of people employed in supposedly background activities in industrial societies.

What we believe is that frameworks have a role in foregrounding traditionally background activities in an organization and that this enables them to be "scaffolding" for improvement. Frameworks draw attention to a holistic range of areas and encourage sustained attention to their development. For example, the EFQM model "enabling" criteria contain many areas that could be considered background and are intended to help organizations to implement preventative measures and to draw causal links between improvements in these criteria and performance-results ones. Usually, it is the performance indicators that are foreground, not the enablers. Like the model, it is possible to argue there are foreground and background activities as parts of individual criteria. The results criteria include business results and impact on society, and with the best will in the world, the business results are more in the perceptual foreground than the impact on society criterion. It could be argued that the balanced scorecard could be seen as an attempt to foreground criteria other than financial to create "balance," which is argued to be more beneficial for the organization in the long run.

In the previous chapter, we discussed how failed attempts at improvement can be labeled as forms of damage. They are a breakdown of management processes and can lead to a damaged employee relation. Even successful improvements can lead to such events (see chapter 7). Our criticisms of the existing literature, both pro– and anti–performance improvement, stem from their oversimplification. Any type of improvement can carry with it multiple meanings. Graham and Thrift (2007) would argue that an initiative can be seen as transductive (i.e., it carries multiple meanings for individuals and groups, and this can be extrapolated further in the different settings within the organization). So, for example, Akzo-Nobel tried to have a corporate system for improvement, but it had many disparate business units producing a huge variety of products, from the relatively simple salt to some highly complex pharmaceuticals. Is it any wonder that the framework had more resonance in some units than in others? We should not need to point out that the growing complexity of organization forms and ways of running them will mean that an element of translation is necessary with frameworks.

Graham and Thrift (2007) quote Lotringer and Virilio's (2005) argument that when we create something, we create the possibility of ancillary negative repercussions. They refer to the invention of the train leading to the train crash. New products lead to new corrective action and maintenance routines for new processes. Perhaps this makes the longevity of the core methods of performance improvement all the more remarkable? Some products now come with built-in "maintenance and repair" mechanisms. A remote auto-teller will signal to the central bank that it has no money to give out. Some products "heal" themselves: the computer into which this book has been typed into frequently downloads patches for its programs without any intervention from us. The framework taken to its logical conclusion perhaps points to new avenues for the healing and improving organization. Most of the improvement texts assume that organizations are deeply flawed before an initiative is mounted. Activities take place as a supposed remedy and life moves on. Although the gurus of improvement have long stressed the need for continuous improvement, it is that aspect that organizations find the most difficult to enact.

It is curious that in Graham and Thrift there is a sense of W. Edwards Deming's point that system faults are management's responsibility and sporadic ones are the fault of human error; yet, most management approaches stress the management of the employee as a way to improvement. Frameworks are good at helping organizations to spot faults and decay. Though this is not acknowledged explicitly by Graham and Thrift (2007), it is perfectly possible for damage to get so great that a part of the organization or process rots and "dies." Rather than struggle on, an organization's managers might think about getting rid of that particular business, product, or locale. Supposedly repressive quality systems help to pinpoint where these opportunities lie. The literature portrays static images of the past and present and does not capture organization life and history in a way that recognizes that some parts of the business might reasonably be dropped.

Similar to Spelman (2002), Graham and Thrift stress that a repair to a process might not be perfect. It might not be invisible mending. Like the scar analogy used by the airport manager, it might actually create a stronger bond and be useful in being seen: a totem of learning. The act of repair can generate new ideas; there is no need to ignore damage, as there seems to be! As we mentioned above, for one thing, many people work in the area. The maintenance and repair functions serve as a safety net so that output can be maintained, and it is not fatuous to try to improve the mesh. If damage can be seen as a disconnection (Graham and Thrift, 2007), repair can be seen as a reconnection, and this describes beautifully what happened in Blue Circle. It is also what the framework helps to do, by setting up a series of connections for the organization to discuss and address.

As an initial step aimed at widening the study of these issues, we now describe the experiences of how two companies whose initial attempts at introducing and implementing quality initiatives had enjoyed only limited success succeeded in achieving major improvements in performance at the second attempt. These cases suggest that initial failure, or only limited improvement, need be no bar to major progress once the reasons for the early problems have been identified and repaired. In each of the cases, we summarize how the companies concerned took their major step forward by following a structured approach, employing a model framework to do so. One company adopted the standard EFQM Excellence Model; the other, Organon Teknika, developed a bespoken model incorporating performance measures particularly appropriate to its own circumstances, and it is this company we will discuss first.

Organon Teknika

Organon Teknika (OT) had failed in its first major attempt at performance improvement but had its large parent organization's support unit promoting a holistic method. To recap, the Akzo Nobel's Managing Total Quality (MTQ) is founded on four Akzo Basic Cornerstones (ABCs) of management commitment, conformance to customer expectations, prevention and, finally, goal setting and achievement, wherein the emphasis is quite specifically on measurement and comparison with past results. The corner stones are supported by ten Akzo Building Blocks (ABBs), comprising seven typical components of a quality initiative along with three others that are rather distinctive: work = process, organization and teamwork, and projects (design, development, and execution). MTQ defines work = process as a sequence of actions and tasks that result in products or services for a customer, the symbol bringing out their interlinking nature. This framework, although different from either the EFQM or the Baldrige, shares some of the characteristics (e.g., there is a hierarchy, it is complex, and there was a detailed method for implementing it). The method was both iterative and inclusive, as the following diagram outlines. The diagram shows how organization and teamwork are established and reflected in the design, development, and execution of projects (Fig. 9.1). This diagram is important, as it shows the looping for cyclical improvement and the range of people involved. The diagram also transgresses traditional hierarchies: The project teams are a subset of the work groups, not something separate and disconnected. The OT approach entailed a cooperative approach to defining processes, improving them, and measuring the changes through evidence of success statements. As we discussed previously, the site radically altered its processes as a result and reorganized. The improvements in performance were very gratifying; however, the most precious aspect to the attempt was the coherence of the employees, in comparison to the previous way of doing things.

Relating the case to Spelman's concepts of repair (2002) outlined in the previous chapter, there did appear to us to have been a "divide" that might be construed as damage in the way the unit functioned. To recap further, the unit was a base site for technical and sales people to use as administrative and stores support. The people based permanently at the

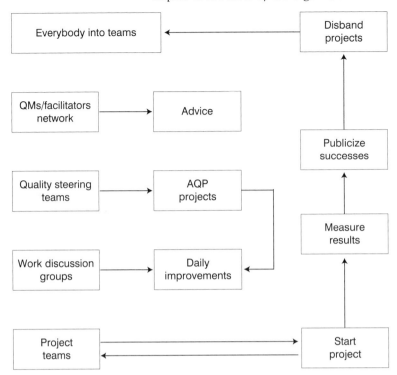

Figure 9.1 Organization and teamwork at Akzo Nobel (Gilbert, 1993, p. 48)

site had an important liaising role with customers and suppliers; however, their role was often subordinated to the itinerant sales and technical staff, who would have the site as their home base but spent most of their time away from it.

The leader of the organization did not apologize for past practice in the way discussed in Spelman (2002), but his relationship with other staff was based on facilitating their work, and he was extremely personable, in the mold of Ross (discussed in chapters 2 and 8). There were frequent opportunities to meet and participate and discuss the work. He used self-deprecating humor (e.g., referring to his car as an ice cream van) and did not stand on ceremony. He backed this up with resourcing training and the well-substantiated proposals for change that the improvement projects generated.

The process analysis and subsequent changes simplified and improved the operations from the customer point of view. The process analysis with its techniques and meetings were perhaps a form of the truth-and-reconciliation process. The measurement system was as comprehensive as the overall approach and backed the view that the changes had improved things greatly.

The framework gave some formerly downtrodden staff who worked permanently on the site the ability to shape their working arrangements and develop their skills, repairing any disaffection with the organization while equipping them better if they should want to leave. It also provided a seeming third-party way of monitoring and justifying changes. In summary, it was holistic in its coverage, did not reflect one particular employee group's interests to the detriment of others, and served to correct a previous fault. The effect of following the process was to foreground formerly background activities, meaning that the distinction was when we visited difficult to maintain, to the universally acknowledged improvement for all concerned.

The next case reexamines an organization that had a choice of frameworks and chose to use the EFQM.

Nortel

The Nortel site was a lot larger than that of Organon Teknika, and the framework they used was a generic, external EFQM-supported excellence model. The framework as previously discussed has nine criteria, some of which are devoted to "enabling" the results. Organizations are intended to develop their own particular approaches, deploy them, and measure the scope of the results before learning from their activities and altering them if they are not successful. After they have built up a performance history, they can enter for a prize, which entails writing a submission for a team of external experts. According to our experience with the Quality Scotland Foundation (backed by research by Soltani et al., 2005), some organizations enter for the prize process before acquiring the necessary performance history to obtain advice as to how best to target their efforts. Nortel illustrates that efforts need to be widespread and intense, not sporadic. The framework provided lots of clues as to how to repair the employment relation with the workforce, used to the damage of repeated layoffs from the plant's history. Considerable investment was made in analyzing the skills and supporting development opportunities, to which much of the workforce responded positively. This could be seen as analogous to an apology being received and accepted.

Again, there was no apology as such, though the company did change where the managers worked and made them visible and accessible, thus reversing the previous arrangements. If the apology serves as a relational bond, the changes that Nortel managers made served to "level" the work relations while communicating the idea that everyone was subject to change, not just the lower paid employees (as was the apparent in our airport case in chapter 7).

The CEO was again not one to stand on ceremony, and we have outlined how often he met with the employees and certainly resourced initiatives, changing the operations and supporting the development of the entire workforce. Again, the framework provided guidance on scope and activities, opportunities for people to convey their views and shape their jobs.

The EFQM model encourages external linkages, and Nortel had more explicit ties to the local "daughter" organization and community, bolstering feedback and reinforcing participation. Scanning outside the organization might be an obvious element of strategy, but the framework encourages this to be as comprehensive as the internal performance criteria. With 30 percent of the people including strategy in their work, there must be a greater sense of security as compared to the days when vast numbers were laid off at short notice. The framework also encourages organizations to consider surveying customers and employees, and externally commissioned employee surveys confirm the high satisfaction levels that the company believes parallel the results from their surveys of customer satisfaction. Perhaps these surveys form a cyclical truth and reconciliation committee?

The Nortel improvement process was successful within the site and certainly so between the site and head office. Goodall and Roberts (2003) discuss how managers who are geographically distant from head offices repair the effects of not seeing people face to face. They found that the performance as such of the sites was not key; rather, the relationships the local management had with the center, and in particular the personal history and closeness of the senior people, had a strong bearing on how the geographically dispersed subunit is perceived.

Nortel Northern Ireland was very well regarded by the head office unit. The performance improvement through the use of the framework had won much favorable publicity within the organization as a whole, and the senior managers used the framework to repair any perception of damage or poor performance. In this sense, the framework acted as an "objective" set of measures to show how well the unit was performing and provided opportunities for contacts between the two units that otherwise would not have existed. By raising the profile in the corporation, the managers were creating hurdles within the organization to closing the site.

In this respect, Nortel was similar to Blue Circle. The senior managers were conscious of the geographical marginality of their sites and were using the initiatives to draw the attention of head-office staff in a positive way. The frameworks could have ended up like the "reifications" in chapter 4; instead, they became virtuous topics of interest to engage senior staff who might otherwise have no reason to think about the site, thus becoming an important tool in the "repairers" kit.

In summary, as we have previously mentioned, the EFQM is very comprehensive, indeed, for some organizations intimidatingly so. A key characteristic in promoting the repair was the more frequent opportunities to meet face to face to discuss strategy and performance, which promoted accountability and a better sense of the interrelatedness of processes. Again, certain processes that were not explored or acknowledged were foregrounded (i.e., the employee relation and layoffs and the attention they received paid dividends and ensured that they did not return to their former obscurity).

It is worth pointing out that the improvement activities that Teknika successfully implemented had been heavily influenced by the MTQ initiative sponsored by Teknika's parent, Akzo Nobel. It is, therefore, surprising that the Teknika unit at Cambridge was one of only a few Akzo Nobel sites to adopt MTQ. The right "chemistry" was in place there but not in other locations. Conversely, Nortel at Monkstown is only one of several units within the Nortel family wherein we understand what are essentially the same improvement activities have been implemented. This suggests to us that there may be several levels within an organization, at each of which a distinctive improvement strategy may be constructively, yet legitimately, developed and which is aimed at attaining objectives that are specific to the subsidiary unit concerned but which does not conflict with those of the parent organization. Both organizations used frameworks to improve the performance in such a way that the local objectives would be developed so that they were consistent with "external" stakeholders, such as other parts of the company.

Analysis

We have found it useful to consider the three case studies used to discuss repair at two levels. At a practical level—Blue Circle and in this chapter Organon Teknika and Nortel—determined that change was essential because (1) their early initiatives aimed at achieving "excellence" by adopting the concept of TQM had not succeeded to the extent expected nor had they produced the tangible benefits envisaged; (2) the levels of customer or employee satisfaction (or both) were unacceptable; (3) employee satisfaction studies had drawn attention to issues of leadership, work content, and how effectively and imaginatively people were being used; (4) the communication skills required to present the organization's perception of the way forward were inadequate; and (5) there was more than a hint of vulnerability that unless their performance was improved, they might not survive either as a company or as a separate entity within a larger organization.

At a somewhat deeper level, more exacting analysis reveals further aspects of the approaches taken by each organization. For example, it is noteworthy that though using different frameworks in different contexts, all three pursued similar improvement activities: They considered and improved the skills of the workforce, they analyzed processes in detail, they discussed objectives and created wider accountability, and the top manager was involved in a highly personal fashion. None of these activities in themselves is particularly innovative; they surface in business texts in, for example, human relations management, operations management, and strategy. They are consistent with Mintzberg (1978), who portrays strategy as a recognizable pattern in a stream of decisions. Developing this concept further (1985), Mintzberg points out that the analysis of a single decision is inadequate to explain the strategy adopted by any given organization. Rather, this should be considered in context, where there are multiple decisions to be taken, they should be consistent with each other.

For Teknika and Nortel, it is evident that the process of learning from the failures of the past played an important part in enabling an approach to "emerge" that was sufficiently persuasive to win over what was likely to have been a skeptical workforce.

Mintzberg et al. (1998) have prescribed how logical incrementalism (1982, small steps to improvement), an approach very similar to kaizen (Imai, 1986), can be applied in practice, examples of which we find realized in our cases:

- *Build credibility by changing symbols.* Nortel managers had their highly visible but separate office tower demolished, relocating those executives who still required individual offices to facilities within the appropriate department.
- *Legitimize new viewpoints.* Teknika developed cross-functional teams to examine "areas for improvement" identified by several different sources, one being the departmental work group. Nortel's production control team has ten members (six shop-floor and four staff). Any member may take the weekly meeting, which has a strong emphasis on performance feedback; problems that cannot be resolved within the team are highlighted for action.
- *Broaden political support.* As pointed out in the case detail, the Nortel CEO developed this in several ways. For example, he regularly reports to the whole workforce, face to face, all relevant business information and answers queries comprehensively and frankly. When he cannot give an immediate answer, he makes sure that the question is responded to promptly. By being highly visible and personally accountable, he does much to combat skepticism.
- *Engage in continuous change.* Nortel argues that it is committed to continuous change interpreted through the medium of "common processes." Improvement is seen as an important outlet to which otherwise frustrated employees can contribute ideas through becoming involved with a "change group."

Finally, we noted that, though in each of the organizations we studied their early initiatives aimed at improving performance had been unsuccessful, some of the quality-associated procedures that had been introduced at the outset were still in place. Their effect might have created damage, but this was not complete.

It is clear that the "excellence" models, which each of the companies developed or used for their subsequent attempt to improve, had not only provided the necessary framework for enhancing performance but enabled this to be brought about. Though the Akzo MTQ and the EFQM models have been designed to evolve as the assessment process matures over time and thus can be applied to most circumstances wherein measurement of organizational performance is required, we think this is unlikely to be the case with Astra Zeneca's YIP process, which we discussed in chapter 4.

The frameworks in use for repair

At no site did the managers officially apologize for past mistakes; however, there are signs of acknowledgement of fault, particularly at Nortel with the demolition of the building and reintegration of management. There is the implication that the status was not deserved and that an equalization process was necessary. The frameworks helped to air problems and allowed for them to be dealt with in a systematic and accountable way.

One point that should not be forgotten is that Nortel and OT had renewed themselves over the years several times, most notably Nortel with its repeated takeovers and its different but similar guises. It is sometimes argued that "brown field sites," such as Nortel, OT, and Blue Circle, are more difficult to change. This ignores Graham and Thrift's point (2007) that forms of social life are constantly renewing themselves.

The frameworks served to bring to the foreground topics that had previously been in the background and, in a permanent fashion, the attention was sustained, enabling it to be very hard to slip back for both organizations. Previously, financial information and products and services for the end customer were foreground, but now they were joined by the repair activities of process and people management. Processes were redesigned with the help of those working on them, and education and training had meant that people felt equipped to participate.

Through this foregrounding, one can see that, whereas some initiatives promise to rectify problems and fix things for the future, the more holistic, complex initiative elaborates knowledge of the process and generates a potentially overwhelming list of things to do. Effort levels have to be higher, and it is, perhaps, not surprising that people give up. There is perhaps a mismatch between expectations and reality that has an effect on failure rates for initiatives. Attempting to improve performance can, by its very enactment, generate a further list of problems that can demoralize some.

After a while, this process can even out, and the types of "self-healing" that Graham and Thrift (2007) point to in computer systems can apply to organizations. Nortel, Blue Circle, and OT experienced faster problem rectification after the initial push was embedded.

What can be said is that after a certain point it is would be very hard, if not impossible, to revert to previous ways of working or eradicate the changes. Blue Circle illustrates this, with the site continuing after the departure of the manager who initiated the process. In chapter 4, we suggest that management credibility and wider confidence, however, are lost if this happens frequently.

Though the texts on performance improvement seem reluctant to acknowledge the past, creating a new recent past—a track record of improvement—can galvanize people and reinforce confidence in the organization and the approach. Again, the repair constitutes a shift; the resulting effect is different from the past, like Willie's patched-up vehicles in chapter 8.

Performance measurement and improvement are often associated with negative policing of operations; the targets can become counter productive and the procedures repressive. The force of the initiatives we saw in Nortel and Organon Teknika was their potential to generate innovations, not as a high-expense additional functional unit but part and parcel of the normal operation of the organization. The capability to build wider views into the strategic decision and accountability process yielded additional opportunities to develop the organization and its product offerings. Connections that were formed were extremely valuable.

Conclusions

In all our studies on performance improvement, we have been struck by the number of organizations seemingly well motivated to change but whose attempts to do so had achieved only limited success. Our study of the literature revealed that this was commonplace and, moreover, that it was de-motivating, undermining, and alienating people from participating in improvement activities. This chapter suggests that the use of frameworks can be of material assistance in rehabilitating improvements despite previous failures, and it describes two cases wherein these fresh initiatives were sustained. We feel confident that we can add the case from the previous chapter, Blue Circle, to support Fountain's assertion (ibid) that the specific framework employed is not critical but rather that the comprehensiveness of the framework and the processes of installing and operating it had the affect of repairing past damage and sustaining improvement.

Summary conclusions

This chapter discussed:

• That the complexity of frameworks actually facilitates the improvement process by helping to sustain activities and interest
• Maintenance and repair as overlooked concepts in management
• The importance of setting up self-repair mechanisms
• That it does not matter which framework is adopted; it is more important to be considered and systematic in implementation.

Discussion questions

• Which framework would you pick: your own or an external framework? Why?
• How would you go about organizing people for improvement?
• What are the self-healing features of your organization? What are the "self-destruct" elements?

Further reading

Graham, S., Thrift, N. 2007. Out of order: Understanding repair and maintenance. *Theory Culture and Society* 24 (3):1–25..
Taylor, W. A., Wright, G. H. 2003. A Longitudinal Study of TQM Implementation: Factors Influencing Success and Failure. *Omega* 31:97–111.

10 Conclusions

Introduction

In this short chapter, we draw together some of our major points from the book. We begin by making some concluding points regarding what we consider to be the meaning of improvement in the organizations. It is very clear that, though we have tried to be constructive and cite examples wherein initiatives have succeeded in improving performance, all too frequently activities did not always achieve what they set out to do or, in some circumstances, even set performance back. An important part of our book has been to address what to do in these circumstances, and considering the concept of repair is one way to start. We also make some suggestions to researchers based on our experience of interacting with companies and give some indicators of things to watch out for so that one is not taken in by a display of "pinkness" (see chapter 5).

We then draw out our main conclusions and discuss the implications for performance improvement, which feeds into our somewhat tongue-in-cheek end to the book—our own version of a guru list of suggestions.

What constitutes performance improvement?

At a glib level, we might say that it is surprisingly difficult to tell! Despite all the effort, there are few examples we have any confidence in and in which we would place a bet for the long term. Most organizations could tell us at a general level that they thought they had improved performance by carrying out activities; however, only a very few could show us in any detail about how and where it was achieved. Even fewer could present a track record of "continuous" improvement lasting several years. The types of initiative they attempted were remarkably similar, with the differentiator being that those organizations that embraced a more inclusive, holistic—dare we say "measured"—approach succeeded when those that focused on a process and specific form of initiative did not achieve the same perceptible degree of change.

By far the worst case was described in chapter 7, wherein an entirely phantom project won a prize in a global organization's contest to encourage positive activity. In our earlier studies, we filtered out those organizations wherein managers described what they intended to do, preferring to spend our time studying projects we could see had already had some effect. Thus, the book is slightly imbalanced in favor of discussion of the few organizations that did succeed rather than the many that did not.

The cases wherein management expected others to change and had specific figures in mind were the initiatives that stalled or failed; indeed, in some instances, they can be argued to have set back the cause for a while. We witnessed this in the airplane engine maintenance sector, the automotive sector, the agro-chemical company, and an airport. The specific reasons for the "stall" or reverse are all slightly different, but a common feature was that they had a restricted number of people designing changes that other people had then to implement. The effects of this are different, too, ranging through apparent compliance, resignation, some minor incidents of sabotage, and a wholesale strike.

Where we have cited some organization as improving its performance, often we have had some form of external verification (e.g., European Foundation for Quality Management assessments) to support this and a spread of indicators showing improvements that several people have described to us in detail and that, in many instances, we have seen for ourselves in operation. We know that improvements can be short-lived and have tried to pinpoint how longer-established activities have managed to sustain momentum, because we think that embedding the improvement ethos within an organization is the only way to realize material outcomes. Just as advocates of quality control suggest that one should focus on the process, not the product (see, for example, Imai, 1986), we believe that particularly in the first years, paying attention to the means is more important than the ends.

We did not see much following of "gurus" but rather that their ideas were embedded in frameworks of which they might even disapprove. What was very evident, and not covered well in other texts, was that the organizations we studied had pasts with which the people working in them had varying relationships. Our organizations were not new starts, and some employees had seen more than thirty years of failed improvement initiatives, knowing the organization still survived. It meant that in some cases, the progressive layering of initiatives belittled the management and certainly had an adverse affect on employee attitude, which only a few organizations succeeded in overturning.

Some comments on our methodology

We thank again the people in the companies we visited, who gave of their time and were so helpful to us. We were forced into adopting a longitudinal approach by circumstances—work and health! It had some benefits in enabling us to see beyond the various brands of initiative and seeing whether some initiatives stand the test of time. We now think it is the only appropriate method to study improvement and would strongly recommend that even those who do not like actually engaging with organizations try "cohort" studies. Lynne's student chose her own length of participant observation to construct the case in chapter 5, and we both would welcome the type of freedom to carry out that kind of study over time.

It was extremely useful having one another to sit in and alternate roles in interviews and discuss perceptions afterward, though this might not be particularly efficient or discussed extensively in the methodology texts. Research is often seen as a singular process, and by far our best fun was on the trips piecing together our impressions of what was going on. Our companies were kind enough to approve our written-up case studies. When we have created another construction of events that we think might cause problems, we have made the company anonymous, as we have with individuals. We now discuss our main conclusions and draw out some implications from them.

Key points for tangible improvement

In this section, we go through each of our chapters and draw out our main points on each topic, beginning with leadership. It is undoubtedly a common feature that successful improvements had leaders who conformed to the ideal types portrayed in the literature. It is not the case that this was by design: The individuals had themselves made the best of the opportunities they had personally to create some momentum. By and large, these individuals had (negative) experience, which had shaped their ideas on how to improve things. Deleuze and Guattari (1997) argue that some concepts are like "rhizomes" or complex root systems, like those found on a hyacinth plant. We think this is a useful idea in highlighting the complexity of relationships necessary to work for an improvement to be substantial and material for any length of time. The paradox for us is encoded in the apparent "egolessness" of some of our leaders, who had sufficient faith not to avail themselves of the perks of office or require others to change their working lives but not their own. The best leaders were most successful at creating other leaders within the organization, and it would be evidence of this that would be part of our "test" for longevity. This is in stark contrast to the more "egotistical" leaders who paid attention to the symbolic rather than to the nitty-gritty of improving the day-to-day operations. It was always someone else's task to effect change, and initiatives were often not followed through. The lack of authenticity had an adverse effect on improvement.

Strategy, derived from its military origins, is in theory about planning how to achieve an objective. Historically, there was always a piece of land to be annexed or state to be taken over. The management literature on the area, for something that is at first glance so potentially exciting, is frequently the dullest we have consulted and the most moribund.

The topic is essentially about taking a more-long-term perspective, and we are struck about how appealing yet nebulous it is. Paradoxically, it is about framing and providing direction, but one of the first areas in which organizations seem to lose impetus is with their implementation of strategies. Our research would seem to suggest that too often it remains at the level of the plan in organizations and, for the wider employee body, it remains almost completely a paper exercise, again carried out by other people and foisted on them. The organizations we chose to highlight for this topic shared a common concern for external stakeholders. The force of their internal improvements was guided by their links with other organizations. This is often articulated in the improvement literature as being customer-sensitive; however, our cases go beyond this to gain much direction from cognate and nearby organizations. The point is the multiple links with diverse sources—thoughtful cultivation as opposed to reacting to process failure. Our organizations deliberately sought a variety of "mirrors" to reflect their performance and give them guidance for further improvement, and it created a "tension," which was constructive for sustaining momentum. If managers were to revisit their external stakeholders, they had to have some tangible evidence that they had addressed ideas and concerns.

Performance measurement in history has been a highly contentious topic, a focal point in cost reduction. What to measure, when, and by whom to have different possible answers, and whereas some see this as a legitimate task for management, others see it as a way of undermining the employee. We would say that any kind of "system" that has multiple criteria that are seen to affect each other is useful. However, it is usually one group of people's views that get encoded in a system; our cases show that broadening out to consider nonfinancial measures enabled employees to participate in the design of the system and fared better than those organizations that did not. Again, the longevity of the initiative depended on wide participation and wide scope of the criteria considered. There are many external models that organizations can use to shape their set of criteria and, again, dropping the boundary of the organization to engage with external opinion generated benefits for the managers who were bold enough to do so; their systems were more aligned with the work processes. If the measurement system encapsulated a range of enabling criteria instead of merely crude value extraction, the outputs materialized. It is more difficult to devise a bespoke internal system that is sufficiently comprehensive but not impossible.

The next chapters, used as they are to highlight the kinds of damage that improvement initiatives can cause, are designed to address how the merely "'symbolic" comes about in performance improvement. We discuss implementation issues, beginning with a chapter devoted to showing how complex some organizations' superficial attempts at improvement can be. To draw an analogy, we think that if performance improvement were a sport, many of the managers we interviewed would be armchair experts. They could discuss the finer points of, for example, tennis until the cows came home but could not actually execute a backhand stroke. They would also have all the gear and might try a few strokes but give up after a couple of attempts because it was too hard. They are up-to-date with the latest players and technology, but they cannot actually apply it themselves.

The managers we respected made a decision to learn the views of their colleagues and stuck at their chosen approach. It depresses us no end that the symbolic improver is rewarded in the same way as the improver who achieves material effects. They often move away from the place wherein they created the impression that they were improving things before they can be accountable for the failure, and the pity for the employees— whose livelihoods depend on them, and indeed the ambitious managers themselves—is that sticking around to develop implementation skills would be more socially useful in the long run. It depresses us still further to speak to long-standing employees who are fully aware they have been managed by the self-serving and are seriously "alienated" from any form of improvement initiative because they have seen it all before and it is a fairy story they will not get taken in by again.

The process at the airport in the next chapter was very textbook and supported by knowledgeable consultants. However, the textbook approach was the "quick fix" of business process reengineering—the improvement equivalent of fat removal by liposuction as opposed to a careful combination of reduced intake and managed exercise. We do not know whether organizations will ever stop being "gluttons" for customers. However, many we visited were attempting to process customers for whom they had no capacity or only limited ability to meet their needs. The self-imposed excess was not a help when trying to improve performance. We recognize that consultants have an important role in facilitating change; however, the type of change envisaged frequently suits the consultant's processes rather than those of the host organization. The organizations, which took a more grounded and less "fanfared" approach, seemed to us to do better and suffered less than those on a "yo-yo diet" cycle of improvement initiatives.

It is common to discuss employee involvement; it is rare to discuss gender and particularly its relation to improvement, though in the organizations that had a balanced proportion of genders it did appear to us to be a feature. It helps us to look at why it is not helpful to have a uniform concept of the employee. Several of the organizations classified the personalities of their employees as part of getting them to "'apply" for new positions. The ones who did not succeed were not made redundant. They were redeployed. Characteristics, that used to be associated with successful management were no longer valued, and people in more senior positions were told that they did not fit the new way of doing things. It was in every case in our experience a man who was displaced. Our chapter argues this was not a "feminization" of the organization, but rather a shift in masculinities. The gendered nature of the organizations remained and served to show that not all employees are equal; the improvement literature will need to come to terms with this, as race, sexuality, and religion are also likely to affect individuals' approaches to improvement. The current writing is too simplistic and hampers potential improvement; moreover, it creates further damage in need of repair.

We find it amazing that despite the fact that commentators repeatedly acknowledge the failure of most initiatives, the failures are seldom labeled as such in organizations; no label is given to the initiative at all, and it is replaced by another. It is very rare for anyone to take responsibility for investigating what went wrong, let alone apologize. Curiously, the phantom project we discuss in chapter 7 was supposed to be about project postmortems, but the organization did not actually carry it out. In most other circumstances, when mistakes are made, they are acknowledged as such, and lessons that are drawn up are implemented. Spelman's book (2002) describes some major human catastrophes wherein this was attempted. It is amazing that it has not been done with improvement initiatives. It is sometimes done when there has been a service failure.

Perhaps we do not fully understand different forms of apologies. Chapter 8 shows apology in the guise of humor. The manager acknowledged that he was not perfect and had a memory of the past, which he used as a way of showing a connection with the other employees. Fostering the connection and investing in employee suggestions was a good way to repair the damage of past failures. Creating a personal link at a human level was key in showing authenticity and the ethical underpinning of his intentions for the site.

It is possible to see an extension of this in the use of frameworks, with their extensive structure for "enabling" performance to be realized. The enablers mean that people have to be invested in, instead of ignored or fired. We have witnessed that this renews their early enthusiasm for the organization and willingness to contribute to improvement. The framework measurement systems enable a "'truth-and-reconciliation" process that, if followed as it is intended to be, means that it is less possible to fake commitment and responsibility; therefore, improvement in performance is more likely to be achieved.

Truisms

In the first chapter, we raised the point that many books and articles on our subject area seem to state broadly similar criteria for people in organizations to follow if they want to improve performance. The gurus in the area generally agree on what is necessary to address to succeed. Despite this, we constantly encounter slight changes of emphases and apparently "new" techniques and methods to improve performance. We think it is not the criteria that need to change but the approaches taken to implementing the necessary changes, and we do not underestimate the amount of effort that this entails.

It is from this standpoint that we make our own short list of suggestions. As we mentioned earlier, they are slightly tongue-in-cheek because we realize that they are again quite obvious, but it is amazing how often they are ignored!

- Do not expect anyone else to do something you would not do yourself! Those people who find themselves leading improvement initiatives should be subject to change, too.
- Submit your plans to a range of people, including those outside the organization, and build in their input. They need to be the sort who remember what you promised and are certain to check up on you!
- Performance measurement systems can be useful if they are balanced and cascading. They should incorporate measures from customers and employees, because this is a way of keeping the system from becoming detached from the improvement process.
- Keeping up appearances for head office or customers when nothing has actually been implemented has the effect of undermining your credibility with employees—with long-term implications.
- Fashions in improvement approaches are attractive, but they undermine the long-term performance of the organization. The complexity and "buy-in" necessary to effect genuine improvement take a long time to secure and consolidate.
- It is odd that many performance improvement initiatives begin by appearing to weaken the organization's commitment to the employee by forcing them to apply for new jobs. If you want people to join in, show your long-term commitment to them as individuals!
- That which many believe to be a sign of weakness—acknowledging failure and admitting gaps in knowledge—can help to repair the damage caused by past failed initiatives.

- Frameworks, with their breadth and attention to "enablers," provide opportunities to repair failed initiatives.

Concluding remarks

We said from the outset that we hope the book provides fresh insights into an important area. We hope that the reader will have found some points of interest, especially some different perspectives on perennial problems. We also hope this has not been an entirely dull process and would love to claim that some improvement has gone better because of our work!

Discussion question hints

These discussion question hints are intended to be a help to assist students and interested parties consider the ramifications of each chapter. Typically, small groups of people can use them to shape discussion. As one of Lynne's students once commented, the answer to everything is "It depends!" and the following subquestions and clues are proposed to assist people to develop their own ideas about on what it depends!

Chapter 2

How can the people in an organization tell whether a good leader will last?

What constitutes a good leader?
How long are leaders typically in position?
What constitutes good leadership from an employee point of view?
How would you characterize the relationship?
What are the long-lasting features of it?
What are the mechanisms in place to support it?

How can an "egoless" leader still maintain momentum?

How is "egolessness" displayed?
How are the other people supposed to behave?
What are the objectives?
How can progress toward the objectives be supported irrespective of any one individual?

Is enabling everyone to be a leader creating chaos?

What would constitute chaos?
How can one manage contradictory views?
Of what should leadership training consist?

How can interrelatedness be communicated?
What are the problems created when only one person's views are taken into consideration?

Chapter 3

Think of an organization with which you are familiar. Who would be the external stakeholders who would keep tabs on progress?

Who has an interest in whether your chosen organization succeeds?
What are the purposes of the organization?
Who has an interest in the community where your organization is based?
Does the organization have links to any sector groups?
Does the organization have any links to other organizations devoted to improvement?

What would you do to manage contradictions in the way strategy is implemented?

How is the strategy to be communicated?
How is the strategy to be rolled out?
Who is involved?
Are you aware of hoisin kanri?
Have you programmed any meeting time and space for people to talk through any contradictions?

Does the strategy formulation process need to be inclusive?

What are the benefits of having a restricted number of people involved in developing the strategy?
What are the problems associated with having a restricted number of people involved in developing the strategy?
Is the strategy being articulated at a general level?
Have the ramifications been thought through, for the rest of the organization and beyond?
What would the customers and suppliers think of the strategy?

Chapter 4

Why might Deming think performance measurement systems and targets are counterproductive?

Are you familiar with basic quality guru thinking?

What are Deming's fourteen points? http://www.ifm.eng.cam.ac.uk/dstools/process/Deming.html
How can targets run counter to process improvement?
How can targets remain realistic?

How can interest be sustained in any system?

Who set it up in the first place?
Who is interested in the results?
When are they interested in the results?
Why are they interested in results?
Can they change the system?

What system of measuring performance would you devise for yourself?

Chapter 5

Of which communities of practice are you a member? Do they help you to participate in improvement?

What is a community of practice?
What separates a community of practice from any particular network?
What are the processes involved in the running of the community of practice?
What either reifications or things involved in the community?
Can procedures hamper improvement?

Can you think of any other forms of symbolic improvements that have had no material effect?

Sources can come from personal experience, business histories, politics, and the wider community.
Pieces of new technology
Dusty folders on shelves
Unaccessed Web pages
Television clips from the past, heralding great promises

Can you think of an example where you were "pink" at work?

Have you a poor piece of work in a flash folder?
Have you pretended to know something when you don't?
Are you prone to exaggerate your qualifications?

Do you pretend to know somebody when you don't?
How are you with deadlines?

Chapter 6

Is there an ideal employee?

Think of a specific example or small range of examples
What would the employees need to do?
How would they need to behave?
How would you like them to get on with employees?
What would they need to know?

How do different genders behave in meetings? Does this affect improvement?

Patricia Martin's article is brilliant on this. One of the points that she makes is that not all activity at meetings is devoted to the purpose of the meeting. Can you think how the genders differ in this respect?
Can you attach both a positive and a negative implication to each difference?
Have you any experience of participating in an improvement team?
How did people behave?

How would you encourage a reticent but competent employee to contribute?

Why are they keeping their mouths shut? (Or other forms of reticence!)
How do you know they are competent?
How do you arrange things so that people can contribute?
Are there opportunities outside of meetings?
Who is hogging the limelight and why?

Chapter 7

How would you go about improving airport processes?
This discussion question is intended to tease out the customer perspective of the airport, which is mainly about flow

How would you go about researching where any problem area lies?
Who would you involve?
What approach would you take?
When would you know whether you are successful?

What other aspects of the organization are like the "'body?"
Have fun with this one! It is possible to be serious; for example,
early work on organization structure by Burns and Stalker
(1961, *The Management of Innovation*, Routledge and Kegan
Paul, London) likened it to the body, as have other authors

Can you think of departments as organs?
Can you see some processes like diseases?

Which improvement shortcuts prove successful?

Describe the improvement
List the activities.
Time the activities
In what way is it a shortcut?
How would you prove it was successful (especially in the long term)?

Chapter 8

With which forms of damage as a consequence of improvement processes are you familiar?

List all the effects of the improvement process.
How do you determine whether which are good or bad?
How do you define damage?
Who perceives them as damaged?
What effect will it have on subsequent initiatives?

Have you ever heard a manager apologize for a failed initiative?

Apologies come in different guises: list them.
How easy is it to tell that an initiative failed?
Choose an initiative and pinpoint where you think it failed.
How did people respond to it?
Is it okay to move on without considering any possible damage?

Do you have any evidence of broken work relationships? How might you repair them?

Are there any people who haven't talked to each other?
Are there are people who don't turn up to meetings?
Are there any people suffering from stress or repeatedly absent?
For any of the above

- Talk to them
- Or find out what they do.
- Try to identify some tangible things to work on.
- Select appropriate materials; remember Spelman.
- What kind of repair would everybody involved see as desirable.
- Is it better left damaged?

Chapter 9

Which framework would you pick (your own or an external framework)? Why?

How would you devise your own framework?
How would it differ from external frameworks?
Why would it be more useful than an external framework?
Where would it support initiatives, and what does it not cover?
What do external frameworks not cover?

How would you go about organizing people for improvement?

Scope the improvement.
Who needs to the involved?
How often might they need to meet?
How would decisions be reached?
Who does not need to be involved and why?

What are the self-healing features of your organization? What are the "self-destruct" elements?

Who helps things go more smoothly?
What processes work well?
What have been the highlights of working for this organization?
Which problems repeat themselves?
Where are the areas of poor communication?
How is process failure monitored?

References

Abdel-Maksoud, A., Dugdale, D., Luther, R. 2005. Non-financial Performance Measurement in Manufacturing Companies. *The British Accounting Review* 37:261–97.

Adair, J. 1990. *Not Bosses but Leaders*. London: Kogan Page.

Akao, I. 1991. *Hoshin Kanri*. Portland: Productivity Press.

Alvesson, M., Sveningsson, S. 2003. Managers Doing Leadership: The extraordinarization of the mundane. *Working Papers*, Lund: University of Lund.

Andrews, R., Boyne, G.A., Walker, R.M. 2006. Strategy Content and Organizational Performance: An Empirical Analysis. *Public Administration Review* 66 (1):52–63

Ansoff, I. 1965. *Corporate Strategy*. New York: McGraw-Hill.

Ashcraft, K.L., Mumby, D.K. 2004. *Reworking Gender: A Feminist Communicology of Organization*. London: Sage.

Bank. J. 1992. *The Essence of Total Quality Management*. Hemel Hempstead: Prentice-Hall.

Baxter, L.F., Hirschhauser, C. 2004. Reification and Representation in the Implementation of Quality Improvement Programmes. *International Journal of Operations and Production Management* 24 (2):207–24.

Beckford, J. 2000. *Quality, A Critical Introduction*. London: Routledge.

Bennis, W., Biederman, P.W. 1997. *Organizing Genius*. London: Brealey Publishing.

Benson, T.E. 1993. TQM: A Child Takes a First Few Faltering Steps. *Industry Week* 242 (7):16–7.

Bessire, D., Baker, C.R. 2005. The French Tableau de Bord and the American Balanced Scorecard: A Critical Analysis. *Critical Perspectives in Accounting* 16 (6):645–64.

Bordo, S. 1993. *Unbearable Weight: Feminism, Western Culture and the Body*. Berkeley and Los Angeles: University of California Press.

Braverman, H. 1974. *Labor and Monopoly Capital: The Degradation of Work in the Twentieth Century*. London: Monthly Review Press.

Brod, H, Kaufman, M. 1994. *Theorizing Masculinities*. Thousand Oaks: Sage.

Buchanan, D.A., Huczynski, A.A. 1985. *Organizational Behavior: An Introductory Text*. London: Prentice Hall International.

Buchanan, D.A. 1997. The Limitations and Operations of BPR in a Politicized Organization Climate. *Human Relations* 50 (1):51–72.

Burkitt, I. 1999. *Bodies of Thought*. London: Sage.

Burns, J.M. 1978. *Leadership*. New York: Harper and Row.

Butler, J. 1990. *Gender Trouble*. London: Routledge.

Butler, J. 2004. *Undoing Gender*. New York: Routledge.

Case, P. 1999. Remember Re-engineering? The Rhetorical Appeal of a Managerial Salvation Device. *Journal of Management Studies* 36 (4):419–41.

Chandler, A.D. 1962. *Strategy and Structure: Chapters in the History of the Industrial Enterprise*. Cambridge, MA: MIT Press.

Christenson, R. 1987. *Business Policy: Text & Cases*. Homewood: Irwin.

Coe, S., Coe, P. 1983. *Running for Fitness*. London: Pavillion.

Collins, J.C., Porras, J.I. 1998. *Built to Last: Successful Habits of Visionary Companies*. London: Random House.

Collinson, D., Hearn, J. 1996. *Men as Managers, Managers as Men*. London: Sage.

Collinson, D., Collinson, M. 1997. Delayering Managers, Time-Space Surveillance and its Gendered Effects. *Organization* 4 (3):373–405.

Connell, R.G. 1995. *Masculinities*. Berkeley: University of California Press.

Corbett, M. 2006. What to Do with the "Temps Perdu," Paper presented the the 24th Standing Conference on Orgaizational Studies, Nijmegen, The Netherlands.

Crosby, P. 1980. *Quality is Free*. New York: Mentor.

Croteau, A-M., Bergeron, F. 2001. An Information Technology Trilogy: Business Strategy, Technology Deployment and Organizational Performance. *Journal of Stragetic Information Systems* 10 (2):77–99.

Currie, R. M. 1977. *Work Study*. London: Pitman.

Davis, K. 1995. *Reshaping the Female Body: The Dilemma of Cosmetic Surgery*. London: Routledge.

———. 1997. *Embodied Practices*. London: Sage.

Dawson, P. 1998. The Rhetoric and Bureaucracy of Quality Management. *Personnel Review* 27 (1):5–22.

De Cock, C., Hipkin, I. 1997. TQM and BPR: Beyond the Beyond Myth. *Journal of Management Studies* 34 (5):659–75.

Deleuze, G., Guattari, F. 1987. *A Thousand Plateau*. Minneapolis: University of Minnesota Press.

Deming, W. Edwards. 1982. *Quality, Productivity and Competitive Position*. Cambridge, MA: MIT Center for Advanced Engineering Study.

Drucker, P.E. 1955. *The Practice of Management*. London: Heinemann.

Drucker, P.E. 1990. *Managing the Non-profit Organization-Practices and Principles*. Oxford: Butterworth and Heinemann.

DTI. 1990. Quality Circles. Broadgate Promotional and Financial Print: Department of Trade and Industry.

Due Billing, Y., Alvesson, M. 2000. Questioning the Notion of Feminine Leadership: A Critical Perspective in the Gender Labelling of Leadership. *Gender Work and Organizations* 7 (3):144–57.

EFQM. 1998. Self-Assessment Guidelines for Companies. Brussels: European Foundation for Quality Management.

Elgin, C.Z. 1997. *Between the Absolute and the Arbitrary*. Ithaca: Cornell University Press.

Evans, J.R., Lindsay, W.M. 1999. *The Management and Control of Quality*. Cincinatti: Southwestern University Press.

Evans, J.R. 2004. An Exploratory Study of Performance Measurement Systems and Relationships with Performance Results. *Journal of Operations Management* 22:219–32.

Farkas, C.M., De Backer, P. 1995. *Maximum Leadership: The World's Top Businessmen Discuss How They Add Value To Their Companies*. London: Orion.

Feigenbaum, A.V. 1991. *Total Quality Control*. New York: McGraw-Hill.

Feinberg, S. 1996. How Managers Defeat TQM. *The TQM Magazine* 8 (2):7–10.

Flannigan-Saint-Aubin, A. 1994. The Male Body and Literary Metaphors for Masculinity. In *Theorizing Masculinities*, edited by H. Brod, Kaufman, M. Thousand Oaks: Sage.

Fountain, M. 1998. The Target Assessment Model As an International Standard for Self-Assessment. *Total Quality Management* 9 (4):595–600.

Francis, G., Humphreys, I., Fry, J. 2005. The Nature and Prevalence of the Use of Performance Measurement Techniques by Airlines. *Journal of Air Transport Management* 11:207–17.

Friedman, A.L. 1977. *Industry and Labor: Class Struggle at Work and Monopoly Capitalism*. London: Macmillan.

Gadd, K., Oakland, J.S., Porter, L.J. 1996. Self-Assessment—an Evaluation of Current European Practice. Paper read at Proceedings of the 1996 Leading Edge Conference at Paris.

George, C.S. 1972. *History of Management Thought*. Englewood Cliffs: Prentice Hall.

Gherardi, S. 1995. *Gender, Symbolism and Organizational Cultures*. London: Sage.

Giddens, A. 1976. *New Rules of Sociological Method: A Positive Critique of Interpretive Sociologies*. London: Hutchinson.

Gilbert, J. 1993. *Managing Total Quality*. Hengelo: Akzo Nobel Chemicals.

Gilbreth, F.B., Carey, E.G. 1949. *Cheaper by the Dozen*. London: Heinemann.

Goodall, K., Roberts, J.D. 2003. Repairing Managerial Knowledge—Ability over Distance. *Organisation Studies* 24 (7):1153–75.

Graham, S., Thrift, N. 2007. Out of Order: Understanding Repair and Maintenance. *Theory Culture and Society* 24 (3):1–25..

Grint, K., Case, P. 1998. The Violent Rhetoric of Re-engineering Management Consultancy on the Offensive. *Journal of Management Studies* 35 (5):557–77.

Guttenman, D. 1994. Postmodernism and the Interrogation of Masculinity. In *Theorizing Masculinities*, edited by H. Brod, Kaufman, M. Thousand Oaks: Sage.

Hackman, R., Wageman, R. 1995. Total Quality Management: Empirical, Conceptual and Practical Issues. *Administrative Science Quarterly* 40 (2):309–42.

Hamel, G., Prahalad, C.K. 1994. *Competing for the Future*. Boston: Harvard Business School.

Hammer, M., Champy, J. 1993. *Reengineering the Corporation: A Manifesto for Business Revolution*. London: Brealey.

Hammer, M. 1996. *Beyond Reengineering*. London: HarperCollins Business.

Hanmer, J. 1990. Men, Power and the Exploitation of Women. In *Men, Masculinities and Social Theory*, edited by J. Hearn, Morgan, D. London: Unwin Hyman.

HBS. 1991. *Business Policy: Text and Cases*. Boston: Harvard University Press.

Hearn, J., Collinson, D. 1994. Theorizing Unities and Differences Between Men and Between Masculinities. In *Theorizing Masculinities*, edited by H. Brod, Kaufman, M. Thousand Oaks: Sage.

Hedley, B. 1977. Strategy and the Business Portfolio. *Long Range Planning* 10:9–15.

Heller, R. 1997. *In Search of European Excellence*. London: HarperCollins Business.

Hersey, P., Blanchard, K. 1993. *Management of Organizational Behavior*. 6th ed. Englewood Cliffs: Prentice Hall.

Hill, S. 1991. How do You Manage a Flexible Firm? *Work Employment and Society* 5 (3):397–415.

Hill, T. 1995. *Manufacturing Strategy*. Basingstoke: Macmillan.

Hirschhorn, L. 1988. *The Workplace Within: Psychodynamics of Organizational Life*. Cambridge: MIT Press.

Hollway, W. 1996. Masters and Men in the Transition from Factory Hands to Sentimental Workers. In *Men as Managers, Managers as Men*, edited by H. J. Collinson D. London: Sage.

Hopper Wruck, K., Jensen, M.C. 1998. The Two Key Principles Behind Effective TQM Programs. *European Financial Management* 4 (3):401–23.

Hoschchild, A. 2003. *The Managed Heart*. 20th anniversary ed. Berkeley: University of California.

Hutchins, D. 1990. *In Pursuit of Quality: Participative Techniques for Quality Improvement*. London: Pitman.

Imai, M. 1986. *Kaizen*. London: McGraw-Hill.

Inkpen, A., Choudhury, N. 1995. The Seeking of Strategy Where It Is Not—Towards a Theory of Strategy Absence. *Strategic Management Journal* 16 (4):313–23.

Ittner, C.D., Larcker, D.F. 1998. Innovations in Performance Measurement: Trends and Research Implications. *Journal of Management Accounting Research* 10:205–38.

Itzin, C. 1995. The Gender Culture in Organizations In *Gender, Culture and Organizational Change*, edited by C. Itzin, Newman, J. London: Routledge.

Jackowski, E.J. 1995. *Hold it! You're Exercising Wrong!* . New York: Simon and Schuster.

Juran, J., Gryna, F. 1988. *Quality Control Handbook*. 4th ed. New York: McGraw-Hill.

Kao, J. 1996. *Jamming: The Art and Discipline of Business Creativity*. New York: Harper Business.

Kaplan, R., Norton, D.P. 1992. The Balanced Scorecard: Measures that Drive Performance. *Harvard Business Review* 70:71–9.

Kay, J. 1993. *Foundations of Corporate Success: How Corporate Strategies Add Value*. Oxford: Oxford University Press.

Kearney, A.T. 1992. *Total Quality: Time to Take off the Rose-Tinted Spectacles*. Kempston: IFS Publicatons.

Kerfoot, D., Knights, D. 1993. Management, Masculinity and Manipulation: From Paternalism to Corporate Strategy in Financial Services in Britain. *Journal of Management Studies* 30 (4):659–77.

———. 1996. "The Best is Yet to Come?": The Quest for Embodiment in Managerial Work. In *Men as Managers, Managers as Men*, edited by H. J. Collinson D. London: Sage.

Khema, A. 1987. *Being Nobody, Going Nowhere*. Boston: Wisdom.

Kiefer, C. 1994. Executive Team Leadership. In *The Fifth Discipline Fieldbook*, edited by P. Senge. London: Brealey.

Kim, W., Mauborgne, R. 2004. Blue Ocean Strategy. *Harvard Business Review* 82 (10):76–84.

Knights, D., McCabe, D. 2000. Bewitched, Bothered and Bewildered: The Meaning and Experience of Teamworking for Employees in an Automobile Company. *Human Relations* 53 (11):1481–1517.

Kondo, D. 1990. *Crafting Selves: Power Gender and Discourses of Identity in a Japanese Workplace*. Chicago: University of Chicago Press.

Kotter, J.P. 1990. *A Force for Change: How Leadership Differs from Management*. New York: Free Press.

Langer, L. 1991. *Holocaust Testimonies: The Ruins of the Memory*. New Haven: Yale University Press.

Lasch, C. 1979. *Haven in a Heartless World: The Family Besieged*. New York: Basic Books.

Lave, J., Wenger, E. 1991. *Situated Learning: Legitimate Peripheral Participation*. Cambridge: Cambridge University Press.

Linstead, S. 2001. Comment: Gender Blindness or Gender Suppression? A Comment on Fiona Wilson's Research Note. *Organization Studies* 21 (1):297–303.

Lipman-Blumen, J. 2005. *The Allure of Toxic Leaders*. Oxford: Oxford University Press.

Llewellyn, S., Tappin, E. 2003. Strategy in the Public Sector: Management in the Wilderness. *Journal of Management Studies* 40 (4):955–82.

Lottringer, S., Virilio, P. 2005. *The Accident of Art*. Boston: Semiotext(e).

Mair, A. 1998. Internationalization at Honda: Transfer and Adoption of Management systems. *Employee Relations* 20 (3):285–302.

Marchington, M. 1995. Fairy Tales and Magic Wands: New Employee Practices in Perspective. *Employee Relations* 17 (1):51–66.

Martin, P.Y. 1996. Gendering and Evaluating Dynamics: Men Masculinities and Managements. In *Men as Managers, Managers as Men* edited by H. J. Collinson D. London: Sage.

Martin, P.Y. 2001. Mobilizing Masculinities: Women's Experiences of Men at Work. *Organization* 8 (4):587–618.

Mayo, E. 1933. *The Human Problems of an Industrial Civilisation*. London: Macmillan.

McDowell, L. 2001. Men, Management and Multiple Masculinities in Organizations. *Geoforum* 32:181–98.

Metcalfe, B., Linstead, A 2003. Gendering Teamwork: Re-writing the Feminine. *Gender Work and Organizations* 10 (1):94–119.

Meyer, M.W. 2005. Can Performance Studies Create Actionable Knowledge If We Can't Measure the Performance of the Firm? *Journal of Management Inquiry* 14 (3):287–91.

Micklethwait, J., Wooldridge, A. 1996. *The Witch Doctors*. London: Heinemann.

Miles, R., Snow, C.C. 1978. *Organizational Strategy and Structure and Process*. New York: McGraw-Hill.

Miller, D. 1992. The Generic Strategy Trap. *The Journal of Business Strategy* 13 (1):37–41.

Mintzberg, H. 1978. Patterns in Strategy Formation. *Management Science* 24:934–48

Mintzberg, H., Waters, J.A. 1985. Of Strategies, Deliberate and Emergent. *Strategic Management Journal* 6:257–71.

Mintzberg, H. 1994. *The Rise and Fall of Strategic Planning: Reconceiving Roles for Planning, Plans, Planners*. New York: The Free Press.

Mintzberg, H., Ahlstrand, B., Lampel, J. 1998. *Strategy Safari*. Hemel Hempstead: Prentice Hall.

New York Times 1993. Back to school for Honda Workers. March 29.

NIST. 2000. *Annual "Baldrige Index."* Gaithersburg: National Institute of Standards and Technology.

NIST. 2005. *Baldrige Award Criteria*. Gaithersburg: National Institute of Standards and Technology.

Nonaka I., Takeuchi, H. 1995. *The Knowledge Creating Company*. Oxford.: Oxford University Press.

Numerof, E.R., Abrams, M.N. 1992. How to Avoid Failure when Implementing a Quality Effort. *Tapping the Network Journal* 3 (4):10–4.

Oakland, J.S. 1995. *Total Quality Management*. Oxford: Butterworth Heinemann.

Oakland, J.S. 1999. *Total Organizational Excellence*. Oxford.: Butterworth Heineman.

Ohno, T. 1988. *Toyota Production System—Beyond Large-scale Production*. Portland: Productivity Press.

Oliver, N. 1990. Employee Commitment and Total Quality Control. *International Journal of Quality and Reliability Management* 7 (1): 21–9.

Otley, D. 1999. Performance Management—A Framework for Management Control System Research. *Management Accounting Research* 16:293–320.

Oxford university Press. 1994. *Concise Dictionary*. Oxford: Oxford University Press.

Park, K., Cassani, B. 2003. *Go: An Airline Adventure*. London: TimeWarner.

Parker, M., Slaughter, J. 1993. Should the Labor Movement Buy TQM? *Journal of Organizational Change Management* 6 (4):43–56.

Pascale, R.T. 1990. *Managing on the Edge: How Successful Companies Use Conflict to Stay Ahead*. London.: Viking.

Pease, B. 2000. *Recreating Men—Post Modern Masculinity Politics*. London: Sage.

Pedler, M., Aspinwall, K. 2004. *Concise Guide to the Learning Organisation*. London: Lemos & Crane.

Peters, T., Austin, N. 1985. *A Passion for Excellence*. Glasgow: Collins.

Peters, T.H., Waterman, R.H. 1982. *In Search of Excellence*. New York: Harper & Row.

Porter, L., Tanner, S. 1996. *Assessing Business Excellence*. Oxford.: Butterworth-Heinemann.

Porter, M.E. 1980. *Competitive Strategy: Techniques for Analysing Industries and Competitors*. New York: Free Press.

———. 1985. *Competitive Advantage: Creating and Sustaining Superior Performance*. New York: Free Press.

Price, T.L. 2003. The Ethics of Authentic Transformational Leadership. *Leadership Quarterly* 14 (1):67–81.

Pun, K.F., White, A.S. 2005. A Performance Measurement Paradigm for Integrating Strategy Formulation: A Review of Systems and Frameworks. *International Journal of Management Reviews* 7 (1):49–71.

Rahman, S., Bullock, P. 2005. Soft TQM, Hard TQM, and Organizational Performance Relationships: An Empirical Investigation. *Omega* 33:73–83.

Ramsay, H. 1996. Engendering Participation: Department of Human Resource Management, Glasgow: Strathclyde University.

Reichers, A.E., Wanous, J.P., Austin, J.T. 1997. Understanding and Managing Cynicism about Organizational Change. *Academy of Management Executive* 11 (1):48–59.

Rosener, J. 1990. Ways Women Lead. *Harvard Business Review* 68 (6):119–25.

Rudberg, M. 1997. The Researching Body: The Epistemophilic Project. In *Embodied Practices: Feminist Perspectives on the Body*, edited by K. Davis. London: Sage.

Runciman, W. 1978. *Max Weber: Selections in Translation*. Cambridge: Cambridge University Press.

Samson, D., Terziovski, M. 1999. The Relationship Between TQM Practices and Operational Performance. *Journal of Operations Management* 17:393–409.

Schaffer, R.H., Thomson, H.A. 1992. Successful Change Programs Begin with Results. *Harvard Business Review* 70 (1):80–93.

Schonberger, R. 1979. *Just in Time Manufacturing*. New York: Free Press.

Schonberger, R.J. 1982. *Japanese Manufacturing Techniques*. New York: Free Press.

Segal, L. 1990. *Slow Motion*. London: Virago.

Seidler, V.J. 1997. *Man Enough: Embodying Masculinities*. London: Sage.

Semler, R. 1995. *Maverick!* London: Warner Books.

———. 2003. *The Seven Day Weekend*. London: Century.

Senge, P.M. 1990. *The Fifth Discipline*. New York: Doubleday.

Shewhart, W. 1931. *The Economic Control of Quality of Manufacturers' Product*. New York: Van Nostrand.

Shildrick, M. 2002. *Embodying the Monster*. London.: Sage

Sinclair, D., Zairi, M. 2000. Performance Measurement: A Critical Analysis of the Literature with Respect to Total Quality Management. *International Journal of Management Reviews* 2 (2):145–68.

Skinner, W. 1969. Manufacturing—The Missing Link to Corporate Strategy. *Harvard Business Review* 47 (3):136–44.

Smith, A. 1990. Profit and the Human Face of TQM. *Total Quality Management* 2 (?):233–6.

Smith, T.M., Reece, J.S. 1999. The Relationship of Strategy, Fit, Productivity and Business Performance in Services Settings. *Journal of Operations Management* 17:145–61

Soltani, E., van der Meer, R., Williams T.M. 2005. A Contrast of HRM and TQM Approaches to Performance Management: Some Evidence. *British Journal of Management* 16:211–30.

Spelman. 2002. *Repair: The Impulse to Restore in a Fragile World*. Boston: Beacon Press.

Stogdill, R.M. 1948. Personal Factors Associated with Leadership: A Survey of the Literature. *Journal of Psychology* 25:35–71.

———. 1950. Leadership, Membership and Organization. *Psychological Bulletin* 47 (1–14).

Stone, C.L., Banks, J.M. 1996. Improving Business Performance through Customers and Employees: The EFQM as a Driver of New Measurement Practice. Paper read at Learning Edge Conference. European Foundation for Quality Management, at Paris.

Tampoe, M. 1998. *Liberating Leadership—Releasing Leadership Potential Throughout the Organization*. London: Spiro Press.

Tannenbaum, R., Schmidt, W.H. 1973. How to Choose a Leadership Pattern. *Harvard Business Review* 53:162–80.

Taylor, W.A., Wright, G.H. 2003. A Longitudinal Study of TQM Implementation: Factors Influencing Success and Failure. *Omega* 31:97–111.

Tuomela, T. 2005. The Interplay of Different Levers of Control: A Case Study of Introducing a New Performance Measurement System. *Management Accounting Research* 16:293–320.

Upton, D.M., Macadam, S. 1997. Why (and How) to Take a Plant Tour. *Harvard Business Review* 75 (3):97–106.

Van der Plas, R. 1990. *The Bicycle Fitness Book*. San Francisco: Bicycle Books.

van der Wiele, T. 1995. How Companies Rate Self-assessment. *European Quality* 2:36–40

Waggoner, D.B., Neely, A.D., Kennerley, M.P. 1999. The Forces that Shape Organizational Performance Measurement Systems: An Interdisciplinary Review. *International Journal of Production Economics* 60–61:53–60.

Wajcman, J. 1998. *Managing like a Man, Women and Men in Corporate Management*. Cambridge: Polity.

Walsh, M. 1995. Overcoming Chronic TQM Fatigue. *The TQM Magazine* 17 (5):58–64.

Welch, J. 2003. *Jack: Straight from the Gut*. London: Headline.

Wenger, E. 1998. *Communities of Practice, Learning, Meaning and Identity*. Cambridge: Cambridge University Press.

Whitehead, S. 2001. Man: The Invisible Gendered Subject. In *The Masculinities Reader*, edited by S. Whitehead, Barrett, F. Cambridge: Polity Press.

Wilkinson, A., Marchington, M., Goodman, J., Ackers P. 1992. Total Quality Management and Employee Involvement. *Human Resource Management Journal* 2 (4):1–20.

Wilkinson, A., Redman, T., Snape, E., Marchington, M. 1998. *Managing with Total Quality Management: Theory and Practice*. Basingstoke: Macmillan.

Wilson, F.M. 1996. Organization Theory: Blind and Deaf to Gender? *Organization Studies* 17 (5):825–42.

Wolff Olins. 2007. *Go Case Study* 2002 [cited January 2007]. Available from http://www.wolff-olins.com/files/GoCaseStudyWeb.pdf.

Young, I.M. 1990. *Throwing it Like a Girl*. Bloomington:University of Indiana Press.

Zbaracki, M.J. 1998. The Rhetoric and Reality of Total Quality Management. *Administrative Science Quarterly* 43 (3):602–36.

Index

TQSG (total quality steering group):
  Blue Circle case study 27–8
training 89–91
trait theory 18, 100
transactional leadership 20–3
transforming leadership 20–3
truisms 173–4
Tuomela, T. 60, 62, 63

Upton, D. M. and Macadam, S. 94

Van der Plas, R. 116, 117
van der Wiele, T. 152
Virilio, P. and Lotringer, S. 156

Waggoner, D. B. *et al.* 55
Wajcman, J. 98, 99, 100, 102
Walsh, M. 89
Waterman, R. H. and Peters, T. H. 20,
  40

Weber, Max 16, 32
Welch, J. 3, 115
Wenger, E. 77, 80, 82, 83, 84, 91, 94.
  See also Lave, J. and Wenger, E.
White, A. S. and Pun, K. F. 56, 60
Whitehead, S. 98
Wilkinson, A. *et al.* 79, 85, 115
Wilson, F. M. 99
window dressing 86
Wolff Olins 19
Wooldridge, A. and Micklethwait, J.
  21, 31
work study 59

YIP (Yalding Improvement Plan): Astra
  Zeneca 67–9, 73

Zbaracki, M. J. 80, 92, 93, 94